"In *Irreversible Damage*, Abigail Shrier provides a thought-provoking examination of a new clinical phenomenon mainly affecting adolescent females—what some have termed rapid-onset gender dysphoria—that has, at lightning speed, swept across North America and parts of Western Europe and Scandinavia. In so doing, Shrier does not shy away from the politics that pervade the field of gender dysphoria. It is a book that will be of great interest to parents, the general public, and mental health clinicians."

> **—KENNETH J. ZUCKER, PH.D.**, adolescent and child psychologist and chair of the DSM-5 Work Group on Sexual and Gender Identity Disorders

"Thoroughly researched and beautifully written."

> **—RAY BLANCHARD, PH.D.**, head of Clinical Sexology Services at the Centre for Addiction and Mental Health from 1995–2010

"For no other topic have science and conventional wisdom changed—been thrown away—more rapidly than for gender dysphoria. For a small but rapidly growing number of adolescent girls and their families, consequences have been tragic. This urgently needed book is fascinating, wrenching, and wise. Unlike so many of the currently woke, Abigail Shrier sees clearly what is in front of our faces and is brave enough to name it. *Irreversible Damage* will be a rallying point to reversing the damage being done."

> **—J. MICHAEL BAILEY**, author of *The Man Who Would Be Queen* and professor of psychology at Northwestern University

"Abigail Shrier has shed light on the profound discontent of an entire generation of women and girls and exposed how transgender extremists have brainwashed not just these young women, but large portions of the country."

> **—BETHANY MANDEL**, editor at Ricochet.com, columnist at the *Jewish Daily Forward*, and homeschooling mother of four

"Every parent needs to read this gripping travelogue through Gender Land, a perilous place where large numbers of teenage girls come to grief despite their loving parents' efforts to rescue them."

—HELEN JOYCE, senior staff writer at the *Economist*

"Shrier's timely and wise exploration is simultaneously deeply compassionate and hard-hitting. First carefully laying out many of the physical, psychological, and societal effects of the 'transgender craze,' she then points to the inconsistencies within the ideology itself. This book deftly arms the reader with tools for both recognizing and resisting, and will prove important for parents, health care professionals, and policy makers alike."

—HEATHER HEYING, evolutionary biologist and visiting professor at Princeton University

"Writing honestly about a difficult and vital topic, Shrier compassionately analyzes the evidence regarding rapid-onset gender dysphoria (ROGD), a phenomenon declared off-limits by many in the media and the scientific establishment. Shrier simply isn't willing to abandon the future of a child's mental health to propagandistic political efforts. Shrier has actual courage."

—BEN SHAPIRO, editor in chief of The Daily Wire and host of *The Ben Shapiro Show*

IRREVERSIBLE DAMAGE

IRREVERSIBLE DAMAGE

The Transgender Craze Seducing Our Daughters

ABIGAIL SHRIER

REGNERY PUBLISHING
A Division of Salem Media Group

Regnery® is a registered trademark of Salem Communications Holding Corporation

ISBN 978-1-68451-031-3
ebook ISBN 978-1-68451-046-7
LCCN 2020932265

Published in the United States by
Regnery Publishing
A Division of Salem Media Group
300 New Jersey Ave NW
Washington, DC 20001
www.Regnery.com

Manufactured in the United States of America

10 9 8 7 6 5 4 3 2

Books are available in quantity for promotional or premium use. For information on discounts and terms, please visit our website: www.Regnery.com

For Zach,

whose love is my secret weapon

She hides like a child

But she's always a woman to me.

—Billy Joel

CONTENTS

AUTHOR'S NOTE

I take it for granted that teenagers are not quite adults. For the sake of clarity and honesty, I refer to biologically female teens caught up in this transgender craze as "she" and "her."

Transgender adults are a different matter. I refer to them by the names and pronouns they prefer wherever I can do so without causing confusion.

Finally, I have changed the names and certain minor details of transgender-identifying adolescents (and their parents) to ensure that none is able to recognize herself and accuse her battle-worn parents of treachery. Because the stories of those vulnerable to this contagion are strikingly similar, some readers may believe they have recognized themselves—only to be wrong.

THE CONTAGION

Lucy had always been a "girly girl," her mother swore. As a child, she would climb into high heels and frilly dresses to do her chores, retiring to a bedroom packed with Beanie Babies and an expansive array of pets she tended—rabbits, gerbils, parakeets. Dress-up was a favorite game, and she had a trunk full of gowns and wigs she would dip into, inhabiting an assortment of characters—every one of them female. She embraced the girlhood of the late 1990s, adoring the Disney princess movies, especially *The Little Mermaid,* and later, *Twilight* and its sequels.

Lucy was precocious. At five, she read at a fourth grade level and showed early artistic promise, for which she would later win a district-wide prize. But as she reached middle school, her anxiety spiked. The waters of depression rushed in. Her affluent parents—mom was a prominent Southern attorney—took her to psychiatrists and therapists for treatment and medication, but no amount of talk therapy or drugs leveled her social obstacles: the cliques that didn't want her, her nervous tendency to flub social tests casually administered by other girls.

Boys gave her less trouble, and she had male friends and boyfriends throughout high school. Home life wasn't easy; her older sister fell into a drug addiction that tore through the family like a hurricane, consuming both parents' attention. Lucy's ups and downs eventually resolved in a bipolar II diagnosis. But making and keeping female friends proved a trial that never concluded in her favor nor ever really let up.

Liberal arts college in the Northeast began, as it so often does these days, with an invitation to state her name, sexual orientation, and gender pronouns. Lucy registered the new chance at social acceptance, a first whiff of belonging. When her anxiety flared later that autumn, she decided, with several of her friends, that their angst had a fashionable cause: "gender dysphoria." Within a year, Lucy had begun a course of testosterone. But her real drug—the one that hooked her—was the promise of a new identity. A shaved head, boys' clothes, and a new name formed the baptismal waters of a female-to-male rebirth.

The next step—if she took it—would be "top surgery," a euphemism for a voluntary double mastectomy.

"How do you know this wasn't gender dysphoria?" I asked her mother.

"Because she'd never shown anything like that. I never heard her ever express any discomfort over her body. She got her period when she was in the fourth grade, and that was super embarrassing for her because it was so early, but I never heard her complain about her body."

Her mother paused as she searched for an apt memory. "I made her get a pixie haircut when she was five and she just cried buckets over it because she thought she looked like a boy. She hated it." And then, "She'd dated boys. She'd always dated boys."

This book is not about transgender adults, though in the course of writing it I interviewed many—those who present as women and those who present as men. They are kind, thoughtful, and decent. They describe the relentless chafe of a body that feels all wrong, that seems somehow a lie. It is a feeling that has dogged them for as long as they can remember.

Their dysphoria certainly never made them popular; more often than not, it was a source of unease and embarrassment. Growing up, none of them knew a single other trans person, and the internet did not yet exist to supply mentors. But they didn't want or need mentors: they knew how they felt. Presenting as the opposite sex simply makes them more comfortable. They do not seek to be celebrated for the life they have chosen. They want to "pass"—and, in many cases, to be left alone.

I spoke with some on the record and others off. For their honesty and courage, they easily won my admiration. One became a friend. That so much trans activism claims to speak in their name is neither their fault nor their intention. They have very little to do with the current trans epidemic plaguing teenage girls.

The Salem witch trials of the seventeenth century are closer to the mark. So are the nervous disorders of the eighteenth century and the neurasthenia epidemic of the nineteenth century.[1] Anorexia nervosa,[2] repressed memory,[3] bulimia, and the cutting contagion in the twentieth.[4] One protagonist has led them all, notorious for magnifying and spreading her own psychic pain: the adolescent girl.[5]

Her distress is real. But her self-diagnosis, in each case, is flawed—more the result of encouragement and suggestion than psychological necessity.

Three decades ago, these girls might have hankered for liposuction while their physical forms wasted away. Two decades ago, today's trans-identified teens might have "discovered" a repressed memory of childhood trauma. Today's diagnostic craze isn't demonic possession—it's "gender dysphoria." And its "cure" is not exorcism, laxatives, or purging. It's testosterone and "top surgery."

○ ○ ○

You're not supposed to pick favorites among the amendments, because it's silly, but I have one, and it's the First. My commitment to free speech led me into the world of transgender politics, through a back door.

In October 2017, my own state, California, enacted a law that threatened jail time for healthcare workers who refuse to use patients' requested
gender pronouns.[6] New York had adopted a similar law, which applied to
employers, landlords, and business owners.[7] Both laws are facially and
thoroughly unconstitutional. The First Amendment has long protected the
right to say unpopular things without government interference. It also
guarantees our right to refuse to say things the government wants said.

This isn't a matter of constitutional nuance; it's remarkably straightforward. In *West Virginia State Board of Education v. Barnette* (1943),
the Supreme Court upheld students' right not to salute an American flag.
Writing for the majority, Justice Robert H. Jackson declared, "If there is
any fixed star in our constitutional constellation, it is that no official,
high or petty, can prescribe what shall be orthodox in politics, national-
ism, religion or other matters of opinion or force citizens to confess by
word or act their faith therein."

If the government can't force students to salute a flag, the government can't force a healthcare worker to utter a particular pronoun. In
America, the government can't make people say things—not even for the
sake of politeness. Not for any reason at all.

I wrote about this in the *Wall Street Journal*, under the headline "The
Transgender Language War," and a reader—a prominent Southern lawyer,
Lucy's mother—saw my piece and found something in it: hope. She contacted me under a pseudonym and asked me to write about her daughter,
who had announced during adolescence that she was "transgender"—
despite never having shown any signs of gender dysphoria in her youth.
She said Lucy had discovered this identity with the help of the internet,
which provides an endless array of transgender mentors who coach adolescents in the art of slipping into a new gender identity—what to wear,
how to walk, what to say. Which internet companies sell the best breast
binders (a breast-compression garment, worn under clothes); which organizations send them for free and guarantee discreet packaging so that
parents never find out. How to persuade doctors to supply the hormones
you want. How to deceive parents—or, if they resist your new identity,
how to break away entirely.

Under the influence of testosterone and the spell of transgression—the mother said—Lucy became churlish and aggressive, refusing to explain this new identity or answer any questions about it. She accused her mother of being a "gatekeeper" and "transphobe." Lucy's manufactured story of having "always known she was different" and having "always been trans," her mother later discovered, had been lifted verbatim from the internet.

In her new, highly combustible state, Lucy would fly into rage if her parents used her legal name—the one they had given her—or failed to use her new pronouns. In short order, her parents hardly recognized her. They became alarmed by Lucy's sudden thrall to a gender ideology that seemed, well, a lot of mumbo jumbo, biologically speaking. Her mother said it seemed as though Lucy had joined a cult; she feared it might never release her daughter.

○ ○ ○

Gender dysphoria—formerly known as "gender identity disorder"—is characterized by a severe and persistent discomfort in one's biological sex.[8] It typically begins in early childhood—ages two to four—though it may grow more severe in adolescence. But in most cases—nearly 70 percent—childhood gender dysphoria resolves.[9] Historically, it afflicted a tiny sliver of the population (roughly .01 percent) and almost exclusively boys. Before 2012, in fact, there was no scientific literature on girls ages eleven to twenty-one ever having developed gender dysphoria at all.

In the last decade that has changed, and dramatically. The Western world has seen a sudden surge of adolescents claiming to have gender dysphoria and self-identifying as "transgender." For the first time in medical history, natal girls are not only present among those so identifying—they constitute the majority.[10]

Why? What happened? How did an age group that had always been the minority of those afflicted (adolescents) come to form the majority? Perhaps more significantly—why did the sex ratio flip: from overwhelmingly boys, to majority adolescent girls?

I liked Lucy's mother, the Southern lawyer, and fell readily into the story she told, but I was an opinion writer, not an investigative reporter. I passed her story on to another journalist and assured Lucy's mother she was in good hands. Long after I had moved on to other topics for the *Wall Street Journal* and the lawyer was swept from my inbox, her story remained stubbornly lodged in my brain.

Three months later, I got back in touch with Lucy's mother and all the contacts she had initially sent. I spoke with physicians—endocrinologists, psychiatrists, world-renowned psychologists specializing in gender dysphoria. I spoke with psychotherapists. I spoke with transgender adolescents and transgender adults to gain a glimpse of the interiority of their experience, the liberating tug of cross-sex identification. I also spoke with "desisters," those who once identified as transgender and later stopped, and with "detransitioners," those who had undergone medical procedures to alter their appearances, only to arrive at regret and scramble to reverse course. The more I learned about the adolescents who suddenly identify as transgender, the more haunted I became by one question: *what's ailing these girls?*

In January 2019, the *Wall Street Journal* ran my piece, "When Your Daughter Defies Biology." It provoked nearly a thousand comments, and hundreds of responses to those comments. A transgender writer, Jennifer Finney Boylan, quickly wrote a rebuttal in an op-ed that appeared two days later in the *New York Times*. Her op-ed garnered hundreds of comments and hundreds more reactions to those comments. All of a sudden, I was flooded with emails from readers who had experienced with their own children the phenomenon I had described or had witnessed its occurrence at their kids' schools—clusters of adolescents in a single grade, suddenly discovering transgender identities together, begging for hormones, desperate for surgery.

When transgender activists attacked me online, I offered them the opportunity to tell me their stories as well. Several took me up on this, and we spoke. Detransitioners got in touch too. I opened a Tumblr account and invited transgender individuals and detransitioners to speak with me; many did. I sent the same invitations on Instagram, where hashtags like #testosterone, #transboy, and #ftm link hundreds of thousands of followers. Again and again, I reiterated my desire to listen to anyone who had something to offer on this issue. The responses I received formed the basis of this book.

This is a story Americans need to hear. Whether or not you have an adolescent daughter, whether or not your child has fallen for this transgender craze, America has become fertile ground for this mass enthusiasm for reasons that have everything to do with our cultural frailty: parents are undermined; experts are over–relied upon; dissenters in science and medicine are intimidated; free speech truckles under renewed attack; government healthcare laws harbor hidden consequences; and an intersectional era has arisen in which the desire to escape a dominant identity encourages individuals to take cover in victim groups.

To tell the story of these adolescent girls, I conducted nearly two hundred interviews and spoke to over four dozen families of adolescents. I have relied in part on parent accounts. Since traditional dysphoria begins in early childhood and has long been marked by a "persistent, insistent and consistent"[11] sense of a child's discomfort in his body (not something a young child can easily hide) parents are often in the best position to know whether the passionate dysphoria of adolescence began in early childhood. They are in the best position to know, in other words, whether the distress afflicting so many teenage girls represents traditional gender dysphoria or a different phenomenon altogether.

Parents cannot entirely be trusted to know how their adolescents feel about their transgender identities or the new lives forged in its name. But parents can report the facts of their kids' academic or professional standing, their financial stability and family formation or lack thereof, and even, sometimes, their social successes and failures. Are these transgender-identified adolescents still in school, or did they drop out? Do they maintain contact with old friends? Do they speak to any family members at all? Are they building toward a future with a romantic partner? Are they engaged in subsistence living on wages from the local coffee shop?

I do not pretend to capture these adolescents' whole stories, much less the fullness of the transgender experience. Transgender success stories are everywhere told and celebrated. They march under the banner of civil rights. They promise to breach the next cultural frontier, to shatter one more basis of human division.

But the phenomenon sweeping teenage girls is different. It originates not in traditional gender dysphoria but in videos found on the internet. It represents mimicry inspired by internet gurus, a pledge taken with girlfriends—hands and breath held, eyes squeezed shut. For these girls, trans identification offers freedom from anxiety's relentless pursuit; it satisfies the deepest need for acceptance, the thrill of transgression, the seductive lilt of belonging.

As one transgender adolescent, "Kyle," put it to me: "Arguably, the internet is half the reason I had the courage to come out. Chase Ross—a YouTuber. I was twelve. I followed him religiously." Chase Ross was kind enough to speak to me, to help me understand what's in the sauce. I present his story in Chapter Three.

This is the story of the American family—decent, loving, hardworking and kind. It wants to do the right thing. But it finds itself set in a society that increasingly regards parents as obstacles, bigots, and dupes. We cheer as teenage girls with no history of dysphoria steep themselves in a radical gender ideology taught in school or found on the internet. Peers and therapists and teachers and internet heroes egg these girls on. But here, the cost of so much youthful indiscretion is not a piercing or tattoo. It's closer to a pound of flesh.

Some small proportion of the population will always be transgender. But perhaps the current craze will not always lure troubled young girls with no history of gender dysphoria, enlisting them in a lifetime of hormone dependency and disfiguring surgeries. If this is a social contagion, society—perhaps—can arrest it.

No adolescent should pay this high a price for having been, briefly, a follower.

CHAPTER ONE

THE GIRLS

If you're an American born before 1990, the words "teenage girls" likely invoke a clutch of young women giggling at the mall. Backs against the pile carpet of a bedroom floor, hair splayed, listening to a song on repeat while conversation runs a similar circuit, chasing some ambiguous interaction with a boy or a girl. Untold hours poorly spent that somehow add up to the truest friendship. Recounting a first kiss or heartache or longing for both and neither, nail polish remover spoiling the air like turpentine.

To understand the contemporary trans epidemic among teenage girls, we'll need to explore just how far girlhood has departed from this picture. It isn't merely that the image requires a gadget update—Spotify for CDs, text messages swapped in for telephone talk. It's that adolescence today contains far fewer of the in-person comforts and torments and consolations that once filled the everyday life of teenage girls. Being asked out or rejected or kissed or fondled—crying and celebrating and laughing about it with your best friend, her voice and expression, not just her words, promising you weren't alone.

I remember my first kiss, with Joel, at lunchtime, behind the Jewish day school we attended. His eyes were a liquid brown. His breath smelled like cinnamon gum. A shock of tongue and panting breath, the dizzying cloy of his Drakkar Noir knocked me punch-drunk, left me dumb.

When it was over, I willed myself to walk casually back indoors. Did I look different? I felt sure I must. Every molecule of the world seemed subtly rearranged. I had the urge to run and scream and laugh and also, strangely, to take it all back—gripped as I was with the worry I had done something wrong. But by the logic of 1990s middle school, submitting to the orchestrated kiss was the least I could do. I was Joel's girlfriend, after all.

Until two weeks later, when I wasn't anymore. He told one of my friends I wasn't a "good kisser." Fair enough. Then again, I was twelve. He had wanted to dump me sooner, but he'd had to wait until he had the chance to catch me alone, in person.

My friend Yael filled me in on the details she had gathered from his friends—a litany of my demerits as girlfriend material. I went back to my other friends: Aaron, who had missed me during my brief withdrawal; Jill, who'd never thought Joel was that great anyway; Ariel, who took the opportunity to punish me for my brief romantic success, pointing out that everyone knew Joel preferred Jennifer. Even the best of friends didn't always excel at comforting.

But however imperfect their support, there it was: Joel, delivering the news; Yael, providing context and commentary; Aaron, helpfully oblivious to the trauma of it all; Jill, rolling her eyes, begging me to kick around a soccer ball; Ariel, chiding me before taking me back. The fibrous humanity of the average dumping. Each bit of hurt or comfort delivered by someone who looked me straight in the eye; someone I could reach out and hug, if I'd wanted to.

The communal nature of in-person adolescent embarrassments more or less held true for young women born in 1990, and 1980, and 1970, perhaps going all the way back to the 1920s. For those women born in 1978, as I was—those who came of age when American teenagers were like charged particles, always crashing into each other—it's hard to imagine the isolation of today's adolescents.[1]

Teens of my era who came of age in the early 1990s set the high watermark in the U.S. for teenage pregnancy.[2] It's been plummeting ever since—as have rates of teenage sex—recently reaching multi-decade lows.[3] This is at least partly the result of lack of opportunity: Today's adolescents spend far less time in person with friends—up to an hour less *per day*—than did members of Gen X.[4] And dear God, they are lonely. They report greater loneliness than any generation on record.[5]

But let's resist nostalgia's trap. Teenagers are more broadly tolerant today, according to academic psychologist Jean Twenge, an expert on the generation born beginning in 2000 ("Gen Z" or "iGen"). Rates of teenage abortion have plummeted.[6] It has been decades since a rash of middle school bathroom blowjobs was cause for widespread societal alarm.

To understand how some of the brightest, most capable young women of this era could fall victim to a transgender craze, we should begin by noting that adolescent girls today are in a lot of pain. In America, Britain, and Canada, teenagers are in the midst of what academic psychologist Jonathan Haidt has called a "mental health crisis"—evincing record levels of anxiety and depression.[7]

Between 2009 and 2017, the number of high schoolers who contemplated suicide increased 25 percent.[8] The number of teens diagnosed with clinical depression grew 37 percent between 2005 and 2014. And the worst hit—experiencing depression at a rate three times that of boys—were teenage girls.[9]

Lest one assume that these girls are merely *reporting* their depression in greater numbers (and not necessarily experiencing more of it), Haidt points out that the average rates of self-harm reflect the same spike: an increase of 62 percent since 2009—all among teenage girls.[10] Among preteen girls aged ten to fourteen, rates of self-harm are up 189 percent since 2010, nearly triple what they were only six years before.

What happened? podcast host Joe Rogan asked Haidt. Why the sudden spike in anxiety, depression, self-harm? "Social media," was Haidt's immediate reply.[11]

As Twenge wrote for *The Atlantic*, "It's not an exaggeration to describe iGen as being on the brink of the worst mental-health crisis in decades. Much of this deterioration can be traced to their phones."[12]

The iPhone was released in 2007. By 2018—a decade later—95 percent of teens had access to a smartphone and 45 percent reported being online "almost constantly."[13] Tumblr, Instagram, TikTok, and YouTube—all very popular with teens—host a wide array of visual tutorials and pictorial inspiration to self-harm: anorexia ("thinspiration" or "thinspo"), cutting, and suicide. Posting one's experiences with any of these afflictions offers the chance to win hundreds—even thousands— of followers.[14] Anorexia, cutting, and suicide have all spiked dramatically since the arrival of the smartphone.[15]

Teenage girlhood in America is practically synonymous with the worry that one's body does not measure up. In eras prior, ideal beauty may have taken the form of a few girls in your class: the ones who could not help being beautiful, leaning into their lockers, tossing their hair, and—most inexplicable to me—knowing when to smile and keep their mouths shut. But only a few members of my class were traditionally beautiful, something the rest of us grudgingly accepted. And even *they* weren't perfect—not really. They were human, as so many of our (always in-person) interactions confirmed—messy and vulnerable, inclined to mortification and misstep, same as the rest of us. They wore too much perfume. Their smiles shone with braces. Puberty struck decisively and without warning: they bled through their jeans and sweated through their gym clothes.

Social media personas—that is to say, the "friends" most relevant to today's teens and with whom they spend the most time—admit no such imperfection. Carefully curated and "facetuned,"[16] their photographs set a beauty standard no real girl can meet. And they sit constantly in a girl's pocket, feeding fears of inadequacy, fueling obsession over her perceived flaws—all the while vastly exaggerating them.[17]

Even under the best of circumstances, teenage girls have been cruelly unforgiving critics of their own bodies—and each others'. But today, social media supplies the microscope and performs the math.

How much less beautiful are you than your friend? Today's teen needn't venture a guess. A simple subtraction of "likes" renders that calculation easy enough. Failure is predetermined, public, and deeply personal.

We know that social media makes people anxious and sad. We know that, as a group, adolescent girls are the hardest hit by its negative effects. But there is something else too: adolescent girls, who historically faced life's challenges in pairs and groups, are now more likely to face them alone.

Members of Gen Z are less likely to go to parties, hang out with friends, date, go for a car ride, head to shopping malls, or even go to a movie than were those of previous generations.[18] By 2015, high school seniors were going out with friends less often than eighth graders did just six years earlier.[19] When they do meet up in person, they are much more likely to bring along a parent.

With mom always hanging around, they are also far less likely to take risks—less likely to smoke or drink or drive recklessly. That would seem to be a good thing. Only 71 percent of eligible high school students have a driver's license—the lowest percentage in decades.

But coddling has its costs. Risk-taking provides an indispensable bridge on the bumpy route to adulthood.[20] Eighteen-year-olds today have the emotional maturity of Gen X's fifteen-year-olds; thirteen-year-olds today, of Gen X's ten-year-olds, according to Twenge. "Teens are physically safer than ever, yet they are more mentally vulnerable," she writes.[21]

They are far less likely to suffer the wounds brought on by adolescent heedlessness—but they've also failed to be toughened by the scars. Plunge into the furnace of adolescent experimentation, and you may suffer harm. Survive, and you are likely to emerge steelier, so much fragility having been banged out.

In researching this transgender craze, I spoke with over four dozen parents. Again and again, I heard a variant on, "My daughter is seventeen, but if you met her, you'd think she was fourteen."

Many of the adolescent girls who fall for the transgender craze lead upper-middle-class, Gen Z lives. Carefully tended by those for whom "parent" is an active verb, even a life's work, they are often stellar students. Until the transgender craze strikes, these adolescents are notable for their agreeableness, companionability, and utter lack of rebellion. They've never smoked a cigarette; they don't ever drink.

They've also never been sexually active. Many have never had a kiss—with boy or girl. According to Sasha Ayad, a therapist whose practice is largely devoted to trans-identifying adolescents, many have never masturbated. Their bodies are a mystery to them, their deepest desires under-explored and largely unknown.

But they are in pain—lots of it. They are anxious and depressed. They are awkward and afraid. Like the infant that learns to avoid the edge of a bed,[22] they sense a dangerous chasm lies between the unsteady girls they are and the glamorous women social media tells them they should be. Bridging that gap feels hopeless.

The internet never gives them a day—or even an hour—of reprieve. They want to feel the highs and lows of teenage romance, but most of their life occurs on the iPhone. They try cutting. They dabble in anorexia. Parents rush them to psychiatrists who supply medications to pad their moods like so much cotton batting, which helps—unless feeling something is the point.

Where is all the raucous fun that should, by right, be theirs? They've heard their parents' stories; they've seen the movies. That epic road trip is hard to recreate when few of your friends drive and parents prefer it that way. They could go to the mall, if it hadn't closed down, and if teenagers still went to the mall (they don't). Local environs can't begin to compare with the labyrinthine corridors, ingeniously customized, supplied by their phones.

○ ○ ○

A decade ago, if it ever occurred to you that female-to-male transsexuals existed, you might have thought of Hilary Swank's portrayal of Teena Brandon in the 1999 biopic *Boys Don't Cry*. Swank's characterization is captivating. Teena Brandon renames herself "Brandon Teena," chases girls, swigs beer, and joyrides through rural Nebraska dressed as a boy, and mostly passing as one. Brandon chases a strikingly conservative vision of happiness. What Brandon wants is to find the right girl, win her, marry her, make her happy.

You spend the entire movie hoping like hell she'll succeed. The abuse Brandon heroically endures, the knowledge that no one in her place and time is likely to offer the kindness or acceptance Brandon craves, the devastating certainty that this story can only end in tragedy—all of it registers in the viewer's clenched gut.

The adolescent girls currently identifying as transgender have almost nothing in common with this picture. They don't want to "pass"—not really. They typically reject the boy–girl dichotomy that Brandon Teena took for granted. They make little effort to adopt the stereotypical habits of men: They rarely buy a weight set, watch football, or ogle girls. If they cover themselves with tattoos, they prefer feminine ones—flowers or cartoon animals, the kind that mark them as something besides stereotypically male; they want to be seen as "queer," definitely not as "cis men." They flee womanhood like a house on fire, their minds fixed on escape, not on any particular destination.

Only 12 percent of natal females who identify as transgender have undergone or even desire phalloplasty.[23] They have no plans to obtain the male appendage that most people would consider a defining feature of manhood. As Sasha Ayad put it to me, "A common response that I get from female clients is something along these lines: 'I don't know exactly that I want to be a guy. I just know I don't want to be a girl.'"

"JULIE"

For most girls, the prospect of becoming a professional ballet dancer is a pipe dream, but by Julie's middle school years it was a proximate possibility. She was distinguishing herself *en pointe*, nabbing top roles in her dance company and dancing, well, all the time. Summer meant more dance, not less, and she qualified for an exclusive summer intensive, which she attended each July.

Her mothers are gay Midwesterners—an estate lawyer and a school counselor—neither of them ideological or activist. "None of our friends are gay or lesbian, just because our friends are who our friends are. So our friends are normal," Shirley, one of Julie's moms, told me, before bursting into sudden laughter: "There's that word, 'normal'!" Based on Julie's crushes, they always believed Julie was straight, and that was more than fine with them.

They homeschooled Julie through the third grade. In fourth grade, her moms enrolled her in all-girls' private school, where she immediately excelled academically and struggled socially. Julie had some friends, but not many. "She has always been a very physical kid. Part of the reason she took to dance, she had a lot of physical energy." In middle school, she shoved a girl and was suspended. "The kids were all being rowdy at the bus stop and it turned out that the girl had recently had abdominal surgery, although of course [Julie] didn't know that."

In the ninth grade, all the girls were encouraged to join a school activity, and Julie joined the Gay–Straight Alliance (GSA), a popular student club. Her mothers regarded this as a welcome showing of solidarity with a community that included her mothers. Julie's participation in the club was not attended by a coming-out announcement. "As far as I knew, she identified as straight. She was pretty girly and feminine. She seemed normal," Shirley said, again bursting into embarrassed laughter.

Julie had no history of gender dysphoria—neither as a child nor even through puberty. "She was a developing body, wearing a bikini at the pool. You know, normal fifteen-, sixteen-year-old."

More than once her mother encouraged her to skip the early-morning GSA meeting and sleep in. Julie refused. There was an older girl at the GSA, Lauren—a sophomore—and Julie seemed in thrall to Lauren's good opinion. "Everything was all about Lauren," Shirley told me.

Her mothers were a little unnerved by the extent to which Julie seemed to revere her new friend. After school, Julie would often meet up with Lauren, who introduced her to anime, computer-animated images of anthropomorphized creatures. "I had no idea it was tied into this whole trans culture," Shirley said to me. Online, Julie began to visit DeviantArt, an art-sharing website with a large transgender following and a lot of gender ideology in its comments section.[24]

Her sophomore year, Julie landed the part of Cinderella in the eponymous ballet. She invited all her friends and two of her teachers to the performance. "She was thrilled and did a really good job of it." But when Julie came out on stage to take her bows, Shirley noticed her catch Lauren's eye. She "sort of looked like she was ashamed of herself and faded. All of her joy sucked out of her body." By then, Lauren had come out as "transgender," although Julie's mothers didn't know it yet. Nor did they know Julie was toying with adopting that identity as well.

Gendered performances, such as occur in ballet, fly in the face of trans identification. To transgender adolescents, gendered behavior that accords with one's sex is the ultimate blunder—it unmasks as frauds those who lack commitment, who are really just "cis" after all.

But Julie was still feeling her way around gender ideology. One of Julie's friends gave an oral presentation that year on gender and sexual identity for class. The friend introduced the "Genderbread Person," a classic tool of gender identity instruction, in which a gingerbread cookie outline of a person is diagrammed. Arrows locate the seat of gender "identity" as the brain; the seat of "attraction" as the heart; "gender expression" as the whole body; and for biological "sex," an arrow points to where genitals would be.

Julie was captivated. Shirley was disturbed. "I thought, 'Does this really make sense, to chop a person up like this? Why would you cut yourself up into all these little compartments?'"

Sophomore year, the pressures of Julie's ballet company—the cattiness and fierce competition with the other performers—intensified. "She was anxious and depressed. She told us she had been cutting." Her mothers quickly found Julie a therapist. During their first meeting, the therapist raised the possibility with Julie that she had gender dysphoria and referred Julie to an endocrinologist for hormone therapy. "It was the first and last meeting, put it that way."

Her mothers found another therapist, who met with Julie two to three times a month. "It was everything we could possibly afford." Her mothers were also paying for expensive private school and ballet.

The therapist began the session by asking Julie her preferred name and pronouns. Julie supplied a male name and pronouns, which is how the therapist referred to her from then on. But rather than satisfying Julie, all this affirmation seemed to make her more anxious and unhappy. "Every time our daughter came out of that session, when that therapist was affirming her . . . she was angry, and detached and cocky."

By junior year, Julie had grown disenchanted with ballet and excited by a different dream: becoming a boy. She cut off her hair and demanded that her mothers use her new name and pronouns. "We resisted that for a period of time. And then we thought, 'Well, maybe we could try this out and see how it goes.' Same thing: when we started calling her by her chosen name she became angrier, more distant, emotionally detached. After a couple of days or a week, we're seeing a pattern, it's like, 'Well this isn't getting us anywhere.' We ditched that."

Shirley met with the school administrators, who assured her that as long as Julie was at their all-girls' school, they would treat her as a girl and use her given name and female pronouns. "Well, that's not what happened."

Without her mothers' knowledge or permission, Julie's teachers, administrators, and friends all acceded to Julie's request and began referring to her as a male student and by her new male name. Julie began to lead a kind of double life. "When she was too much at school, too much at her computer, she became morose, withdrawn, angry. We had no idea she was indoctrinating herself with these YouTube videos."

Julie's mothers didn't yet know about the trans influencers on YouTube that she had started watching intensively. But they sensed their daughter was slipping away. "One time I do remember quite clearly," Shirley said, "I sat her down, and I said, 'You know, if I really believed that this was the right fit for you, I would be helping you do whatever it was going to be to help you be comfortable in your skin. But there is nothing that matches your history that leads me to believe this is somehow right for you.'" Julie went upstairs to her room to think about it. When she came back down, she seemed to have regained her calm.

There was another point, over dinner, when Julie was talking about various gender identities, and her mother, a little exasperated, said, "That seems like a small box to put yourself in. So a woman is someone who identifies as a Barbie doll and wears bikinis and is really catty? Biology—not hyper-feminized stereotypes—is what makes someone a woman."

Julie's mental health began to deteriorate. One evening, when one of her mothers came home from a second job, she found Julie in a full-blown panic attack. They took Julie to the hospital, where the doctors confirmed that she was physically fine. The next morning, while their daughter slept in, one of her mothers checked Julie's phone. She found a series of texts between Julie and another girl, referring to Julie as "the best boyfriend" she ever had. Her mother became distraught—both that this other girl was addressing Julie as a boy, and that none of this seemed to be doing her daughter very much good.

Senior year, Julie was accepted on a partial scholarship to a collegiate fine arts program. But having witnessed Julie's transformation into a surly adolescent with faltering mental health, her mothers were nervous to let her go. They asked her to take a year off.

At eighteen, Julie moved out of the house, signed up for Medicaid—although she was still on her mothers' insurance—and began a course of testosterone. Julie found a local dance company that would permit her to train as a male. But she wasn't strong enough, Shirley told me. "From what I understand, the choreographer had to rechoreograph it three times because she couldn't keep up [as a man]. . . . She dropped a couple of dancers." Her mother was frightened that Julie's apparent fixation was going to hurt her or someone else. She reprimanded her, "It's not just *your* body and *your* career. You're talking about someone else's body and their career. You're going to hurt them."

But by then, Julie was done taking advice from her mothers. She abruptly cut off contact with them. She has hundreds of followers on Instagram; her mothers are blocked from viewing her account.

"We have someone who's been able to snoop in on her [Instagram] . . . I saw the picture of her, right after her mastectomy, lying in the hospital bed, talking about how this is the best day of her life, tears of joy, this kind of thing, and four hundred of her cheerleaders saying, 'Yay,' 'Awesome job,' 'We're so proud of you,' 'You can do this.' You know—the usual."

CARVING UP GIRLHOOD

When I think back to my own high school years in the 1990s, no one came out as "trans." And until the last five years, that is precisely what the statistics for gender dysphoria would have predicted. Somewhere around .01 percent of the population means that you probably didn't go to high school with anyone who was "trans" either.[25] But that doesn't mean that girls were a monolith, or that we all expressed girlishness in the same way.

I had been a "tomboy," which basically meant I excelled at sports and preferred the comparatively straightforward company of boys. Friendship with girls so often seemed unnervingly like breaking into a bank vault, all those invisible lasers shooting every which way, triggering alarms of sudden offense.

But there is no such thing as a "tomboy" anymore, as any teenage girl will tell you. In its place is an endless litany of sexual and gender identities—public, rigid, and confining. As sixteen-year-old Riley, a young woman who began identifying as a boy at thirteen, put it to me: "I think being a masculine girl today is hard because they don't exist. They transition." Transition, that is—to boys.

Years after my high school graduation, some of us who had dated the cutest boys would come out as gay. Others we might have silently suspected of being gay turned out not to be. None of us then felt pressured to make any identity decisions we couldn't easily take back.

Teens and tweens today are everywhere pressed to locate themselves on a gender spectrum and within a sexuality taxonomy—long before they have finished the sexual development that would otherwise guide discovery of who they are or what they desire. Long before they may have had any romantic or sexual experience at all. Young women judged insufficiently feminine by their peers are today asked outright, "Are you trans?"

Many of the girls now being cornered into a trans identity might, in an earlier era, have come out as gay. "You've got a situation where young lesbians are being pressured if they don't give into this new idea of what it is to be a lesbian," prominent gay writer Julia D. Robertson told me. That "new idea" is that lesbians do not exist: girls with more masculine presentations are "really" boys.

Some adolescents today do identify as lesbian, but it's hard to miss that this identity has considerably less cachet than being trans. Riley told me that fifteen students in her British all-girls' school of five hundred have come out as transgender. "How many girls are lesbian?" I asked her. She thought about it for a moment, and I watched her be surprised by the answer: "None," she said.

"SALLY"

Had she been born to a prior generation, Sally would have been called a "tomboy"—prodigiously athletic and physically daring. "She was always the first one off the high dive," her mother told me. "She had a lot of physical confidence, I think." The youngest of three kids, she spent her early years fighting to keep up with her two older brothers.

"She went through a very short period, when she was four or five, of wanting to be a boy. And we thought that was very much of a piece with having these older brothers. And you know, she cut her own hair with scissors."

Her parents didn't think much of it. Her two older brothers were her whole world, and her desire to be a boy was neither pronounced, severe, nor persistent, just a "little phase" that "kind of came and went." Academic literature supports the idea that it is not uncommon for young children periodically to express the desire to be the opposite sex.[26]

"The only thing we did say to each other," her mother, Mary, said in a Midwestern accent thick as buttermilk, "was 'Gee, I wonder if she's going to be a lesbian.'"

In her mother's telling, Sally was a dream child: happy, obedient, the sort who drew friends toward her, who ran on her own steam. "Oh, gosh, she was my easiest kid," her mother told me. "She has two older brothers, so I had my three in five years. It was a zoo. It was always a zoo. But she just always went and did her own thing. It was before the whole computer thing was really a big deal. They'd make a club or a newspaper."

Sally's prodigious athletic ability continued to assert itself. At eleven, Sally taught herself to ride the unicycle her parents gave her for her birthday. Practicing in the driveway, she would hold on to the family sedan. "Oh my God, she fell a million times," her mother told me. "But then she used to ride the unicycle around town and people would be like, 'Wow, look at that kid!'" By middle school, Sally was distinguishing herself as a swimmer.

Freshman year of high school, Sally swam varsity. Three years in a row, she was all-state, shattering her high school's records in freestyle and butterfly and winning the state title. But it was the character of the girl interviewed in local newspapers for the records she broke that made

Mary proudest: smile white as caster sugar, careful to thank her coaches and praise her teammates. Never admitting—and perhaps never believing—she could possibly have achieved so much without them. "I was just so proud of her," her mother told me. "She was really just a very happy and normal and well-adjusted person."

Her junior year of high school, Sally dated a boy in her class, Jordan. "And we really liked this kid. I think she gave it a try. I think she thought maybe she could make a go of it with him and then she finally said, 'I'm just not feeling this. He's a nice guy, he's a great guy, never done anything wrong to me, but I'm just not feeling it.'" Mary and her husband Dave quietly accepted what they had suspected for years: Sally was likely gay.

Mary and Dave tried to give Sally space to come out to them if she wanted to. Mary had always been a political liberal, a PFLAG leader, and a supporter of gay marriage long before it was legal. Mary watched from afar as her daughter fell headlong into crushes on other girls. It pained Mary to notice that these often went unrequited.

Still, high school was a time of glorious achievement for Sally. By senior year, she had added National Merit finalist to her resume. Sally was admitted to her top-choice Ivy League school, where she had been recruited to the swim team. Mary was overjoyed. "In a lot of ways it even felt like wish fulfillment for me, to see the beautiful dorms and the campus and the historic buildings and to know my daughter" would be "able to experience all that."

Ivy League college was expensive for Mary and Dave; they took on $100,000 in debt to pay for it. "I was very proud. I paid that happily," Mary said. "We went in, we took out that second mortgage happily."

Sally's freshman year, she came out as a lesbian at college and to her parents; Mary and Dave were relieved. "You know, we thought it was nice. We were very receptive. We liked her girlfriends. You know, they would come and stay at the house."

But by then, Mary was also more than a little distracted. Her eldest son Henry, once a scholar athlete, had been a passenger in a car crash a few years out of college. In the course of rehabilitation he was prescribed heavy doses of opioids. Addiction followed. Sally's junior year, Henry's doctors abruptly cut off the opioids, but by then he'd been riding their cloud for years. Jonesing for relief, he turned eventually to heroin.

Sally's long-term girlfriend, with whom she was desperately in love, dumped her and broke her heart. "One thing that was very hard was this other girl was very popular. And it seemed like most of the girls just gravitated toward the other person. Here was my daughter, senior year of college, no friends." Girls wrote catty and mean things about Sally on the most popular campus online forum. They ridiculed Sally's appearance, detailing the precise anatomy of her physical flaws. They intimated she had deserved to be dumped.

Sally emotionally collapsed. She went on crying jags that lasted into the night. For the first time in a long time, Mary was really worried about Sally. Not knowing what else to do, Sally sought out a campus mental health counselor. "It was then that we felt the whole idea of being transgender first was suggested," Mary said. Sally "was having a crew cut and was wearing a suit and tie. I guess it was a natural thing for them to suggest that this might be her issue."

Except that until it was suggested to her by her therapist, Sally had never thought that she *was* transgender. Sally had always just seen herself as a lesbian. She liked wearing masculine clothes which, for her, were simply part and parcel of being a gay woman. She was never bothered by her breasts or her body; she had never claimed she was in any way "really" a boy. Now Sally began to talk in these terms for the first time.

When she came home for spring break, Sally left her Facebook page open, and Mary, desperate for insight, read her daughter's correspondence. "She was in touch with a girl . . . who had had a mastectomy and she was kind of coaching my daughter on how you come out to your parents, and how do you let 'em know you're trans."

Sally did "come out" to her parents, this time as "trans," and indicated that she wanted to start hormones so that her body would reflect this identity. For Mary, this was a bridge too far. She told Sally, "I just don't think you ought to do any medical things. I think that would be a huge mistake because I don't think that you are a guy, and I don't think you can ever become a guy."

For a while, that message seemed to sink in; Sally stopped bringing up transitioning, and Mary was relieved. Sally graduated and moved to New York to begin an unpaid internship in the non-profit sector. Mary and Dave covered her security deposit and her first year's rent while Sally endeavored to turn an unpaid internship into a full-time job. Sally didn't mention any plans for gender medical treatments to her parents, but the friends she made in New York all seemed to be transgender. Sally began seeing a gender therapist. "And she really went full bore into the trans thing."

When Sally came home for a visit, Mary noticed she was binding her breasts and smoking cigarettes. Mary also noticed that Sally's Instagram page had become increasingly devoted to her transgender identity and to marijuana. "We had gone on a little trip together, and [Sally] had been having some breathing problems. She had wound up in the ER twice, not able to breathe. . . . And I said between the smoking and the binding, I'm not surprised you're having trouble breathing." That comment, Sally later informed her, not only hurt Sally's feelings; it made Sally "feel unsafe."

But the final straw was laid by Dave. Sally was looking for a job in legal services and struggling to find one. One day Sally met her father in the city for lunch. Dave offered her what he considered just good sense: "You might want to try appearing a little less unusual when you go for these jobs," he said. "If you want to get a job, you should probably tone it down a little bit."

Sally eventually obtained the job she was looking for, high-paying enough to cover her rent. A week later, Sally sent her parents an email informing them that she considered them "toxic," did not feel "safe" with them, and would no longer be in touch. Mary scrambled to explain herself to her daughter, worried that Sally was headed down a bad road, but Sally no longer wanted to hear it.

"We paid for her tuition 100 percent the whole way through. We paid for her to get settled in New York City. We paid for her first six months when she had her unpaid internship so she could get her first job. The week before she cut off all contact with us, she borrowed two thousand dollars." Mary and Dave continued paying for Sally's cell phone and health insurance long after she wouldn't return their calls or emails. "We're toxic, but our money isn't."

PUBERTY IS HELL

Puberty is a trial for anyone, perhaps girls especially. Cramping and bloating and acne all conspire to confirm: your body really does hate you. Why else would it set off fireworks so obviously designed to confuse and alarm—the crushing pain and the sudden rush of blood? They are never more severe than for the newly inducted.

The girls weathering these changes have never been so young. The average age of menarche among American girls is now twelve, according to *Scientific American*,[27] down from age fourteen a century ago. The average age of breast development is now nine to ten years old.

All of which would be bad enough if puberty were a private matter; it isn't. No debut so immediately captures the interest of boys and men as the arrival of breasts. The alteration thrusts a young girl under the klieg lights of uncomfortable attention from men her father's age. Girls may not *feel* sexual when their breasts arrive (very often, they don't). They are almost certainly psychologically unprepared for sexual advances—but attention from men they will receive, and they have never received it so young.

Puberty is also when today's transgender craze among girls typically takes hold. Girls feel alienated from a body pummeling them from the inside. The stress brought on by puberty is age-old. What is new is today's adolescents' relative inability to bear it—and the constant presence of apparent alternatives.

And then there is the mise-en-scène of our "quick fix" era—marked by the conviction that no one should ever endure any manner of discomfort. Ritalin for inattention; opioids for pain; Xanax for nerves; Lexapro for the blues; testosterone for female puberty.

Adolescence is a long haul, and today's screen-loving teens are an impatient crew. They might be forgiven, then, for adopting the contemporary creed: *There must be a pill for that.*

"GAYATRI"

Gayatri had always been "pretty girlish," her father, an Indian immigrant and physician, told me. As a child she loved Dora the Explorer and Disney princesses. She loved to dress up in fancy clothes and played happily with other girls. She showed no signs of gender dysphoria at all.

Which isn't to say her body always made things easy. Gayatri was born with a minor neurological disorder that made fine motor control a struggle and gross motor control an occasional embarrassment. Her hands shook when she held a glass of water. Running typically occasioned a fall.

She was bright, but never an academic star on level with her older brother. Her handwriting was often illegible. As a kid, running around, it was easier to overlook her physical awkwardness, but when she hit puberty it became more obvious that she couldn't bring her body into alignment with the sleeker expectations of adolescence. Her loping walk, her irregular stance.

During her last year of middle school, one of her elementary school friends "transitioned"—began binding her breasts, announced that she had a new name, and asked others to use masculine pronouns when addressing her. Gayatri's parents were fairly progressive. At the time, neither thought much of the change, and it seemed to make little impression on their daughter.

But the next year, ninth grade, her parents bought Gayatri a laptop and—after much pleading—a smartphone. She began spending a great deal of time on Tumblr and DeviantArt, the art-sharing website with a large transgender following. She began talking to her mother about gender identity. The conversations had a loose, hypothetical feel, and her parents had no idea her thoughts had anything to do with her time on the internet. Summer came, long days stretched before her like an open hand. Every free moment she had—and she had a lot of them—she seemed to spend online.

Maybe her parents should have been concerned, but her mother was a software engineer. They were comfortable with technology and fully accepted the internet as an important fixture of modern life. Gayatri was a very good girl; they trusted her.

In the fall she cut her hair short and joined her high school's GSA. She informed her mother of her new name and pronouns. But her mother, relieved that at last she had friends, chalked up the gender thing to a phase. After years of social insecurity, Gayatri had discovered a cause that gave her common language with her peers. A little puzzled, her parents went along with this eccentric hobby, though they never acceded to her new name or pronouns.

They lived in a liberal coastal city; when in Rome, well, it wasn't surprising she'd want a toga. "Especially because, at her school, we know of four kids, including my daughter, who are going through this, it looked exactly like a contagion to me," her father said. "Especially because she never exhibited any discomfort with being a girl throughout her childhood."

In the second half of her freshman year, one of her teachers nominated her for a leadership retreat, and her parents were thrilled, eagerly paying the fee. "I always had great appreciation and respect for all the institutions in the United States, starting with the government, and the federal nature of everything, the school districts being independent and all that," her father said. He examined the flyer for the retreat, believing his daughter had been recognized for a special honor. The flyer contained "all positive things" about leadership and social justice, which sounded like a good thing. "I trusted the school completely."

At the end of the weekend-long retreat, the students performed a play for the parents. "The whole play focused on sexuality and gender," Gayatri's mother told me. "It was all about these depressed kids with no motivation."

Each kid stood up and introduced themselves with some alleged hardship identity—"I'm depressed," "I'm gay." Then, Gayatri stood up. "'I'm transgender, and I go by they/them.' We were like in tears, we didn't know what to do," her mother said. After the camp, Gayatri discarded all of her girls' clothes and set up an Instagram account announcing her new name.

One day, while she was walking the dog with her parents, Gayatri floated the idea of starting testosterone and getting top surgery. Her parents became alarmed.

By then, they had learned that Gayatri's school had been using her "new name" and pronouns (though never on any documentation sent home) entirely without their knowledge. No longer merely the class bungler, Gayatri had reinvented herself as the edgy trans kid. The "likes" and emojis showered on her Instagram profile spoke for themselves: this new identity was an upgrade. As a "trans boy," Gayatri had friends—lots of them.

TEENAGERS LOOKING FOR GUIDANCE

Let me be the first to admit that Amanda—the high priestess of sexual advice at my middle school—fell short of the ideal sexual mentor. None of us knew any of the boys with whom she claimed to have gained her experience. (They conveniently attended public school in a neighboring city.) She generously offered us all manner of instruction, which we solemnly received, ranging from how to French-kiss (she had practiced with another girl in our class) and how to administer a hand job. (Her description made it sound disturbingly similar to peeling a banana.)

She glorified frivolous sexual encounters. She encouraged many of us to experiment before we were ready. She discouraged condom use

("Boys don't like them"), insisted sex was "no big deal," and never mentioned the emotional toll that a girl so often pays for a casual sexual encounter—the sinking feeling that a protective amulet has slipped through her grasp, lost for good.

Teenage girls today are in some ways more worldly, less likely to rely on a single peer for their sex education. From the earliest days of seventh grade, they can name for you every shade of sexual identity—from "pansexual" (formerly known as "bi") to "queer" and "demisexual." They know every variant on gender identity, from "non-binary" and "gender fluid," to "two spirit" and "transgender"—they may have even learned these at school, from a teacher. What they lack is in-person contact with each other.

"Kids feel very anxious about in-person interactions," Sasha Ayad told me. Even something as humdrum as flirting is "incredibly challenging for these kids," Ayad said. "If there's a safe way to connect with someone that doesn't require face-to-face contact," they'll opt for it every time. But the questions and wonder and panic that attend adolescence do not ease up merely because they have no friend to ask. And so they take their questions somewhere else.

For up to nine hours a day, today's teens slip down a customized internet oubliette, alone. They browse glamorous pages that offer airbrushed takes on the lives of friends and celebrities and internet influencers. They tunnel into YouTube, TikTok, Instagram, Reddit, and Tumblr, imbibing life advice from the denizens that await them.

"If they're questioning their sexuality, for example," Ayad told me, "rather than giving it some time and seeing, okay, 'Who do I develop a crush on? Do I want to hold this girl's hand?'" members of Gen Z head for the internet. Uncountable strangers happily furnish sexual identity guidance. "That's not necessarily the most helpful way to try and understand your own experiences of things."

Extensive daily internet use provides casual conversance with every sort of sexual fetish. They know what a "furry" is and have seen bondage porn. They're au fait with the "lesbian" videos so popular on PornHub. The average age at which they first viewed pornography is eleven.[28]

Adolescents are far less likely to have *had* actual sex than the women of my generation were at their age—or even to have proceeded along the traditional bases. As Kate Julian observed in *The Atlantic*, we are in the midst of a "sex recession" especially severe among members of Gen Z. In 1994, 74 percent of seventeen-year-old women had had a "special romantic relationship" in the past eighteen months. "In 2014, when the Pew Research Center asked seventeen-year-olds whether they had 'ever dated, hooked up with or otherwise had a romantic relationship with another person'—seemingly a broader category than the earlier one—only 46 percent said yes."[29]

Many of the adolescent girls who adopt a transgender identity have never had a single sexual or romantic experience. They have never been kissed by a boy or a girl. What they lack in life experience, they make up for with a sex-studded vocabulary and avant-garde gender theory. Deep in the caverns of the internet, a squadron of healers waits to advise them. Gurus far worse than Amanda.

○ ○ ○

For nearly a decade, while this trans epidemic worked its grip, none of the gender dysphoria experts seemed to notice. Or perhaps—like so many physicians who contacted me off the record, leading lives of quiet desperation—they merely kept their observations to themselves. A steady drip turned to a torrent. Adolescent girls flooded gender clinics eager for testosterone. Providers happily served up puberty blockers and courses of testosterone. Nothing to see here.

Social media saturation, anxiety, and depression fell together like so much dry tinder and kindling. Smoke curled. Flames followed. It took a woman from outside the psychological community to yank the fire pull and sound the alarm.

CHAPTER TWO

THE PUZZLE

In 2016, Lisa Littman, ob-gyn turned public health researcher and mother of two, was scrolling through social media when she noticed a statistical peculiarity: several adolescents, most of them girls, from her small town in Rhode Island had come out as transgender—all from within the same friend group. "With the first two announcements, I thought, 'Wow, that's great,'" Dr. Littman said, a light New Jersey accent tweaking her vowels. Then came announcements three, four, five, and six.

Dr. Littman knew almost nothing about gender dysphoria—her research interests had been confined to reproductive health: abortion stigma and contraception. But she knew enough to recognize that the numbers were much higher than extant prevalence data would have predicted. "I studied epidemiology . . . and when you see numbers that greatly exceed your expectations, it's worth it to look at what might be causing it. Maybe it's a difference of how you're counting. It could be a lot of things. But you know, those were high numbers."

In fact, they turned out to be unprecedented. In America and across the Western world, adolescents were reporting a sudden spike in gender dysphoria—the medical condition associated with the social designation "transgender." Between 2016 and 2017 the number of gender surgeries for natal females in the U.S. quadrupled, with biological women suddenly accounting for—as we have seen—70 percent of all gender surgeries.[1] In 2018, the UK reported a 4,400 percent rise over the previous decade in teenage girls seeking gender treatments.[2] In Canada, Sweden, Finland, and the UK, clinicians and gender therapists began reporting a sudden and dramatic shift in the demographics of those presenting with gender dysphoria—from predominately preschool-aged boys to predominately adolescent girls.[3]

Dr. Littman's curiosity snagged on the social media posts she'd seen. Why would a psychological ailment that had been almost exclusively the province of boys suddenly befall teenage girls? And why would the incidence of gender dysphoria be so much higher in friend clusters?

Maybe she had missed something. She immersed herself in the scientific literature on gender dysphoria. She needed to understand the nature, presentation, and common treatment of this disorder.

Dr. Littman began preparing a study of her own, gathering data from parents of trans-identifying adolescents who had had no childhood history of gender dysphoria. The lack of childhood history was critical; as we have seen, traditional gender dysphoria typically begins in early childhood. That was true especially for the small number of natal girls who presented with it.[4] Dr. Littman wanted to know whether what she was seeing was a new variant on an old affliction or something else entirely. She assembled 256 detailed parent reports and analyzed the data. Her results astonished her.

Two patterns stood out: First, the clear majority (65 percent) of the adolescent girls who had discovered transgender identity in adolescence—"out of the blue"[5]—had done so after a period of prolonged social media immersion. Second, the prevalence of transgender identification within some of the girls' friend groups was more than seventy times the expected rate.[6] Why?

Dr. Littman knew that a spike in transgender identification among adolescent girls might be explained by one of several causes. Increased societal acceptance of LGBTQ members might have allowed teenagers who would have been reluctant to "come out" in earlier eras to do so today, for example. But this did not explain why transgender identification was sharply clustered in friend groups. Perhaps people with gender dysphoria naturally gravitated toward one another?

Then again, the rates were so high, the age of onset had increased from preschool-aged to adolescence, and the sex ratio had flipped. The atypical nature of this dysphoria—occurring in adolescents with no childhood history of it—nudged Dr. Littman toward a hypothesis everyone else had overlooked: peer contagion. Dr. Littman gave this atypical expression of gender dysphoria a name: "rapid-onset gender dysphoria" ("ROGD").

○ ○ ○

Many of the adolescent girls suddenly identifying as transgender seemed to be caught in a "craze"—a cultural enthusiasm that spreads like a virus. "Craze" is a technical term in sociology, not a pejorative, and that is how I use it here. (Dr. Littman never does.) It applies to Hula-Hoops and Pokémon and all sorts of cultural fads.

Early twentieth-century psychiatrist Lionel Penrose, who introduced the term, explained that an idea that quickly spreads through a community "is not necessarily harmful or unreasonable because it is infectious."[7] What distinguishes a craze—what makes it a "crowd mental illness"—is that during its reign "an abnormal amount of energy is discharged in one direction and that, as a result, matters more vital to the welfare of the group may be neglected."[8]

If this sudden spike in transgender identification among adolescent girls is a peer contagion, as Dr. Littman hypothesized, then the girls rushing toward "transition" are not getting the treatment they most need. Instead of immediately accommodating every adolescent's demands for hormones and surgeries, doctors ought to be working to understand what else might be wrong. At best, doctors' treatments are ineffective; at worst, doctors are administering needless hormonal treatments and irreversible surgeries on patients likely to regret them. Dr. Littman's theory was more than enough to touch a nerve.

Activists stormed the Twitter page of *PLoS One*, the peer-reviewed scientific journal of the Public Library of Science that had published Dr. Littman's paper, accusing her of anti-trans bigotry. They claimed that Dr. Littman had deliberately solicited parent reports from conservative, anti-trans parent groups. (In fact, over 85 percent of the parents self-identified as supporting LGBT rights.)

Journalists saw smoke and rushed over, flagons of gasoline in hand. A graduate student and self-described "transgender advocate" in Dr. Littman's own Brown University department disparaged Dr. Littman in the press, calling her work shoddy—"below scientific standards"—and published an article accusing Dr. Littman of having been motivated by bias.[9] Other transgender activists accused Dr. Littman of having hurt people with the paper.[10] They called her work "dangerous" and insisted it could lead to "worse mental health outcomes" for trans-identifying adolescents.[11]

Brown University stripped its own press release on her paper from its website and replaced it with an apology from the dean of public health, who lamented that "the conclusions of the study could be used to discredit efforts to support transgender youth."[12] *PLoS One*'s editor in chief took the rare step of issuing an apology for not having provided better "context" for the research and promised additional review into possible "methodological errors" the paper might have contained.[13]

Dr. Littman's paper had already been peer-reviewed by two independent academics and one academic editor. But Brown and *PLoS One* knew a woke mob when they saw one. They decided it was best not to make any fast moves, to slowly hand over their wallets.

Diane Ehrensaft, a prominent child gender psychologist, told *The Economist* that Dr. Littman's use of parent reports was akin to "recruiting from Klan or alt-right sites to demonstrate that blacks really were an infe-rior race."[14] (The "Klan," in this case, was the parents, who had simply been asked questions about their own children.) Few cared that the sur-veyed parents had not expressed anti-transgender attitudes generally, but rather had expressed disbelief and upset that their daughters had adopted this identity "out of the blue" without any childhood history of gender dysphoria—and that following this identification, their adolescents' mental health seemed to get worse.

None of the attacks acknowledged that parent report is a standard method for assessing child and adolescent mental health.[15] (How else would you obtain the psychological history of a child, if not from parent report?) Nor did any of these critics mention that the primary academic research used to promote "social transition" (changing an adolescent's name and pronouns with school and friends) for gender dysphoric chil-dren similarly relies on parent surveys.[16] *PLoS One* issued a correction that suggested Dr. Littman's methods had not been made sufficiently clear, despite the fact that the words "parent reports" had appeared in the paper's title.

Dr. Littman's paper became one of the most widely discussed aca-demic articles of 2018.[17] Her analysis and conclusions drew praise from some of the most distinguished world experts on gender dysphoria.[18] Dozens of parents wrote to her to thank her for giving name to the phe-nomenon they were observing in their adolescents.

But she was also widely tarred as a bigot and a bully. This, despite the fact that she had neither the security of tenure nor a faculty coauthor for cover.[19] She wasn't right-wing or anti-trans. She had spent several years working part-time for Planned Parenthood and, with her husband, contributed several pieces to HuffPost on such topics as the rotten GOP approach to healthcare,[20] but the truth no longer seemed to matter much.

Psychology Today published an open letter from "transgender-identified [and] cisgender allies . . . with vast expertise in gender and sexuality" purporting to refute Dr. Littman's paper. The letter called her work "methodologically flawed" (for having relied on parental report) and "unethical" (for having reached its conclusions) and accused Dr. Littman of harboring "overt ideological bias" (for having dared examine the causes of trans identification at all).[21]

Activist clinicians hunted Dr. Littman to the Rhode Island Department of Health, where she worked part-time as a physician consultant on projects related to the health of pregnant women and preterm infants. Her work there had nothing to do with transgender youth; it had nothing to do with young children or adolescents per se at all. Her interest in preemies stemmed from her years of training in obstetrics. Caring for preemies had been a passion of hers ever since she had given birth to a preemie of her own, just over one pound at birth.

The activists denounced Littman to her employer, the DOH, claiming that she had written a paper "harmful" to transgender youth. They demanded that the DOH "terminate its relationship with Dr. Littman immediately." Adding a dash of threat, the authors airily suggested that the DOH might add "a gender-neutral restroom" to its facilities to send a message to the community "that trans and gender diverse lives are valued by DOH."

The activists wanted a head on a pike. The DOH gave them Dr. Littman's. Her paid consultancy was over.

○ ○ ○

I met Lisa Littman in a family style Italian chain restaurant along Route 1 just outside of Boston. Her shoulder-length dark brown hair was lightly mussed from a busy workday and the stress of the traffic that had delayed her. Clutching her purse strap as she rushed toward our table, she looked every bit the suburban mom: eager to fill the unforgiving minute, hoping I hadn't been waiting there too long.

She has large brown eyes, tortoiseshell glasses, a broad reassuring smile, and a nervous laugh. As she told me several times, she hates being interviewed. Based on her many follow-up questions about how I would ensure the accuracy of everything I wrote, it was clear she was telling the truth.

She refuses my prodding to theorize beyond the limits of her data, declining invitations to speculate about what in the culture has encouraged American teenagers to go down this road. I invite Dr. Littman to wonder about the increased popularity of Pride events, the shock of once–Bruce Jenner, now "Caitlyn," America's beloved Olympian, strapped into a bustier on the cover of *Vanity Fair*, eyeing the camera hungrily. I wonder aloud whether inflated collegiate sexual assault statistics haven't scared adolescent girls off of womanhood entirely, whether transgender identification hasn't received a boost from our hapless tendency to self-diagnose based on things we read on the internet.

I wonder things I don't say aloud, too: Whether this transgender craze isn't partially the result of over-parented, coddled kids desperate to stake out territory for rebellion. Whether it is no coincidence that so many of these kids come from upper-middle-class white families, seeking cover in a minority identity? Or is it the fact that they overwhelmingly come from progressive families—raised with few walls, they hunt for barriers to knock down? And then there's our modern-day obsession with mental health, medicating every-one toward the optimal level of happiness, as if we are all just tires in need of topping up. With the help of battalions of therapists, the upper-middle class has made a habit of extirpating anxiety, depression, and even the occasional disappointment wherever they find them. Perhaps we've trained adolescents to regard happiness as a natural and constantly accessible state. Perhaps they've come to believe momentary sadness amounts to a crisis—teenage doldrums a catastrophe to rectify rather than a phase to ignore.

Dr. Littman doesn't want to offend, but she seems genuinely mystified that anyone would be so reckless with speculation, so thoroughly comfort-able diagnosing without data.

"Yeah, I don't know," she says.

○ ○ ○

In March 1985, during her sophomore year at Rutgers, tragedy pierced Dr. Littman's family like a stray bullet. Her younger brother,

Mark, a high school senior, was visiting a prestigious Southern university where he had just been admitted. "He was not a troublemaker," she told me. "He was an honor student, he wrote poetry and he did sports." He called home during his visit and told his parents he needed to switch the room assignment he'd been given. Later that evening, he called a family friend at the university and asked if he could sleep on her floor; she turned him down. Her family realized only later that Mark had been trying to avoid an informal hazing event. He died of alcohol poisoning that night.

"Teenagers are social creatures," Dr. Littman told me thirty-four years after the incident. "They are influenced by peers and that's part of how they develop." But it's also why teenagers lead each other to harm.

Dr. Littman wrote academic papers about contraception, reproductive health knowledge, beliefs about abortion risk, and abortion stigma. She studied women of childbearing age—what choices they were making about their bodies and why. Then, when her own kids had reached adolescence, she became more intrigued by how their generation was faring.

The most recent *Diagnostic and Statistical Manual (DSM-5)* reports an expected incidence of gender dysphoria at .005–.014 percent for natal males, and a much lower .002–.003 percent for natal females, based on the numbers of those who, a decade ago, sought medical intervention.[22] This is an incidence of fewer than 1 in 10,000 people.

In the last decade, as Dr. Littman began to discover, adolescent gender dysphoria has surged across the West. In the United States, the prevalence has increased by over 1,000 percent.[23] Two percent of high school students now identify as "transgender," according to a 2017 survey of teens issued by the Centers for Disease Control and and Prevention (CDC).[24] In Britain, the increase is 4,000 percent,[25] and three-quarters of those referred for gender treatment are girls.[26]

Given the sudden surge, and the abrupt shift in demographics—from majority boys with history of childhood gender dysphoria to majority adolescent girls with no such history—this was the sort of thing that should have been on many scientists' radar. It wasn't. When Dr. Littman looked for academic research or popular reporting to explain why adolescent girls might be experiencing a spike in gender dysphoria, she couldn't find anything.

Over the next year, as Dr. Littman prepared her study, analyzed the data, and wrote her paper, clinicians across the Western world began reporting seeing more female adolescents presenting with gender dysphoria.[27] Clinics in Sweden,[28] Toronto, and Amsterdam reported that their ratios of gender dysphoria had flipped, from predominately natal males prior to 2006, to predominately natal females from 2006 to 2013.[29] By 2018, academics in Europe were reporting a dramatic increase from the prior decade among adolescents presenting with gender dysphoria—most of the increase "due to an influx of birth-assigned females coming forward."[30]

In 2016, natal females accounted for 46 percent of all sex reassignment surgeries in the United States. A year later, it was 70 percent.[31]

Eventually, Dr. Littman discovered websites where parents were describing what would become, to her, a familiar pattern: A daughter with social struggles and anxiety, but no manifestations of gender identity issues in childhood, enters high school. She falls in with a group of friends in which many of the kids come out as "transgender." The daughter makes a similar announcement about herself; then her mental health worsens. "They didn't find their 'true selves' and flourish," Dr. Littman recalled from the parent reports she read. The daughters "became more angry and sullen and hostile to the parents." The more they suffered dysphoria, the more they pulled away from the people who might help.

Struck by the salient social aspect of their gender dysphoria—the evidence she noted from the prevalence of trans-identification within friend clusters—Dr. Littman began reading everything she could about another peer contagion: anorexia nervosa. Like the new crop of transgender teens, anorexic girls suffered from an obsessive focus on the perceived flaws of their bodies and valorized the willingness to self-harm. Dr. Littman searched out the "pro-mia" (pro-bulimia) and "pro-ana" (pro-anorexia) sites, where adolescents coach each other in how to lose the most weight and how to deceive parents about their eating.

"The pro–eating disorder sites, they basically declare anorexia as this lifestyle of striving for perfection. They turn it around and make it very positive like it's a lifestyle of discipline and they share tips and tricks about how to lose weight," she said.

The sort of "advice" they offer? *If you take an apple and cut it into eight pieces, and eat one piece every couple of hours, you'll feel full even though you've only eaten one apple.*

"They'll give this advice," Dr. Littman said: "Your parents are out of the house, you should put things in a bowl that you would normally eat, like cereal. Put the milk in, take out the spoon and dump it down the garbage disposal and then leave the bowl and the spoon there and then you can tell them that you had cereal."

The pro-anorexia sites resembled a set of videos that had begun colonizing the internet: social media sites of trans influencers, in which natal girls calling themselves "transgender boys" or "trans men" boast of how their lives have improved since they started a course of testosterone. The rush it gives them, the thrill at the "happy trail" of dark hair appearing on their bellies, the dissipation—they insist—of all social anxiety.

Transgender influencers coach other adolescents on how to wheedle a testosterone prescription from a skeptical clinician.[32] They advise teens to study the *DSM* diagnostic criteria for gender dysphoria and prepare a pat story about how they "always knew" they were trans. They tell you to claim that you've felt this dysphoria for a very long time. They convey the urgency of transition—if you don't do it now, you never will. You're already at high risk for suicide.[33]

Dr. Littman noticed that both the anorexia and transgender sites had a strong in-group-versus-out-group flavor. The trans sites ridicule "cis" people and depict gender dysphoria as a valorous condition—and those without it as ignorant or benighted. It reminded her of the culture of eating disorder patients in inpatient and outpatient settings—translating thinness into virtue, extremism into integrity. "There's often a sub-culture where the thinnest patients and the ones that have the most illnesses related to their thinness and their eating disorder are admired and revered as the 'real deal.' And the ones who want to follow doctors' orders or maybe aren't as underweight, they're called 'outside anorexics,' like they're not good enough to be on the inside [of hospitals]." The pro-anorexia sites effectively turned mental illness into a heroic social identity, to which you show your commitment by ever greater self-harm.

○ ○ ○

Dr. Littman is often accused by her attackers of being "right-wing"[34] or assumed to be a religious Christian. Both characterizations are wrong to the point of being absurd: Dr. Littman has never voted Republican. For years, she and her husband Michael were members of a progressive Humanistic Jewish Congregation. But her truest religion, the one in which she has perfect faith—is Family.

"Was it fun raising kids?" I ask her.

"Oh my God, yes. It was everything," she says.

The thread of family alienation that ran through the transgender sites and the parent reports troubled Dr. Littman and spurred her interest in the topic. Even after all the hate she has received, the attacks on her reputation, the loss of a job she loved, it's this worry over families splitting apart that sustains her research interest in this topic. "To see kids turning on their parents . . . I found that very heartbreaking," she said. "It's kind of my worst nightmare."

Psychologists who study peer influence ask what it is about teenage girls that makes them so susceptible to peer contagion and so good at spreading it. Many believe it has something to do with the way girls tend to socialize.[35] "When we listen to girls versus boys talk to each other, girls are much more likely to reply with statements that are validating and supportive than questioning," Amanda Rose, professor of psychology at the University of Missouri, told me. "They're willing to suspend reality to get into their friends' worlds more. For this reason, adolescent girls are more likely to take on, for instance, the depression their friends are going through and become depressed themselves."

This female tendency to meet our friends where they are and share in their pain can be a productive and valuable social skill. Co-rumination (excessive discussion of a hardship) "does make the relationship between girls stronger," Professor Rose told me.

But it also leads friends to take on each other's ailments. Teenage girls spread psychic illness because of features natural to their modes of friendship: co-rumination; excessive reassurance seeking; and negative-feedback seeking, in which someone maintains a feeling of control by angling for confirmation of her low self-concept from others.[36] It isn't hard to see why the 24/7 forum of social media intensifies and increases the incidence of each. Dr. Littman developed a survey to explore her hunch that gender dysphoria might be one more peer contagion to have hit adolescent girls.

According to the *DSM-5*, gender dysphoria in children is a condition defined by the presence of at least six of the following symptoms:

1. *A strong desire to be of the other gender or an insistence that one is the other gender*
2. *A strong preference for cross-dressing or simulating [other gender] attire*
3. *A strong preference for cross-gender roles in make-believe play or fantasy play*
4. *A strong preference for the toys, games, or activities stereotypically used or engaged in by the other gender*
5. *A strong preference for playmates of the other gender*
6. *A strong rejection of toys, games and activities typically associated with birth sex*
7. *A strong dislike of one's sexual anatomy*
8. *A strong desire for the primary and/or secondary sex characteristics that match one's experienced gender*

These are not the sorts of things a small child can easily conceal from parents; five are readily observable behaviors and preferences.

Dr. Littman created a ninety-question survey consisting of multiple-choice Likert-type (scale-of-agreement based) and open-ended questions. Data were collected anonymously from 256 parents whose kids had not met the criteria for gender dysphoria in childhood, but had suddenly identified as transgender in adolescence. Among Dr. Littman's findings (in her own words, lightly edited):

- Over 80 percent of the adolescents were natal females, with a mean age of 16.4 years.
- Most were living at home with parents at the time of their transgender announcement.
- The vast majority had had *zero* indicators of childhood gender dysphoria (in addition to universally failing to meet the six-criteria requirement for child-onset gender dysphoria).
- Almost a third of the adolescents did not seem at all gender dysphoric, according to parents, prior to the adolescents' announcement of being trans.
- A majority had had one or more psychiatric diagnosis and almost half were engaging in self-harm prior to the onset of the gender dysphoria.
- Forty-one percent had expressed a non-heterosexual sexual orientation before identifying as transgender.
- Nearly half (47.4 percent) had been formally assessed as academically gifted.
- Nearly 70 percent of the teenagers belonged to a peer group in which at least one friend had also come out as transgender. In some groups, the majority of the friends had done so.

- Over 65 percent of teens had increased their social media use and time spent online immediately prior to their announcement of transgender identity.
- Among parents who knew their children's social status, over 60 percent said the announcement brought a popularity boost.
- Over 90 percent of the parents surveyed were white.
- More than 70 percent of the parents had earned bachelor's or graduate degrees.
- Over 85 percent of parents reported supporting the right of gay couples to marry.
- Over 88 percent of parents surveyed reported being supportive of transgender rights.
- Nearly 64 percent of parents had been called "transphobic" or "bigoted" by their children for such reasons as: disagreeing with the child about the child's self-assessment of being transgender, recommending that the child take more time to figure out if the child's feelings of gender dysphoria persisted, calling their child by the wrong pronouns, telling their child that hormones or surgeries were unlikely to help, calling their child by his or her birth name, or recommending that the child work on other underlying mental health issues before undergoing medical transition.
- Fewer than 13 percent of the parents believed that their adolescents' mental health had improved after transgender identification. Over 47 percent reported that mental health had worsened.

Dr. Littman never suggested that gender dysphoria doesn't exist or that these girls didn't have it. What she hypothesized was that these adolescents' gender dysphoria had an atypical etiology, that is, a set of causes that differed from the classic diagnosis. Unlike traditional gender dysphoria, this one seemed encouraged and intensified by friends and social media.

But what part of this, exactly, was contagious? Dr. Littman hypothesized three things (again, I have lightly edited her words):

1. *the belief that non-specific symptoms should be perceived as gender dysphoria and that their presence is proof of being transgender*
2. *the belief that the only path to happiness is transition*
3. *the belief that anyone who disagrees with the self-assessment of being transgender or opposes the plan for transition is transphobic, abusive, and should be cut off*

She theorized that the drive to transition might represent a "maladaptive coping mechanism" for dealing with legitimate stressors and strong emotions. She considered the possibility that this atypical strain of gender dysphoria might itself constitute a form of intentional self-harm. She stated expressly that her analysis did not imply that no adolescents would benefit from transition. Instead, she concluded merely that "*not all* [adolescents] presenting at these vulnerable ages are correct in their self-assessment of the cause of their symptoms."

Never before had gender dysphoria sufferers "come out" as trans based on the encouragement of friends or following self-saturation in social media. Never before had identification as "transgender" *preceded* the experience of gender dysphoria itself.

Two weeks after Dr. Littman's study was published, in response to activist outcry, *PLoS One* announced it would conduct a post-publication review of her paper and that a "correction" would be forthcoming. Dr. Littman was subjected to a battery of revision. "A lot of Ben and Jerry's ice cream happened along the way," she told me. "It was pretty stressful." In March 2019, seven months after the initial publication, *PLoS One* issued Littman's "correction."

None of her results had changed.

CHAPTER THREE

THE INFLUENCERS

Before he was a YouTube sensation, Chase Ross had a job selling running shoes, and it isn't hard to believe he was great at it. He flashes genuine charisma with his big blue eyes. He's full of information and happy to share. Like many a world-class salesman, he has mastered the art of the light touch.

His show begins with a jaunty four-chord progression and a synthesized drum set, which had me bopping along like a parakeet. "Hello everybody, it is Chaseypoo!" he crows, mugging for the camera in mock-hysterical fashion.[1] His color-war-team-captain enthusiasm for all things transgender is infectious. It's the sort of act that might have prompted an earlier generation to cry "Go team!" But it is more likely to rouse this generation to "This sucks less than everything else!"

Since 2006, the twenty-eight-year-old Canadian female-to-male's wildly successful YouTube channel, "UppercaseChase1," has garnered more than 10 million views. (He maintains a regular audience of more than 166,000 subscribers.) Chase offers self-deprecating humor, advice, encouragement, and deeply personal confessions for the benefit of gender-confused (and otherwise confused) adolescents.

Chase is joyous, he's cool. He's got a septum ring, a lip ring, and several cat tattoos. With the help of nearly a decade on testosterone, he has an impressively thick beard, broad shoulders, and apparently no fear of embarrassment. He has (mostly) banished his period. If you were an anxious teenage girl, plagued by menstrual cramps and social anxiety, you might just look at him and say: "I'll have what he's having."

○ ○ ○

Discovering online trans gurus is equal parts thrilling and disconcerting to curious tweens—like the pornography they're curious about but not quite ready to see. One young woman I interviewed told me that in high school, she fell for the boy-band looks of social media influencer Wes Tucker, only to be thrown into a tailspin when she learned Wes was biologically female. (The young woman decided her crush was evidence that she herself was also "trans.")

Which brings me back to Chase Ross, one of the more measured and obviously mature internet gurus. I approached Chase for an interview after another female-to-male adolescent told me that Chase's videos had been the source of her transgender epiphany. Glad to hear he had inspired another, he responded to my email and invited me to call.

But first, I watched all of his videos. Hours and hours and hours of them. His physical transformation is compelling. He has abundant facial and body hair, a widened nose, a squared jaw, a deepened voice—all the results of testosterone, and each convincingly masculine. He even shows you, with his thumb, the size of his "peen"—that is, his testosterone-enlarged clitoris. While he could pass as a small man if he wanted to, he seems to have something else in mind. His earrings, cat tattoos, flop of hair dyed every vivid shade of parrot, and nail polish all slyly nod toward the sex of his birth. Keeping others off balance seems part of the fun and very much the point.

Chase believes he is helping trans-identified adolescents and seems sincerely motivated by that calling. (Unlike other influencers I interviewed, for instance, he didn't ask that I encourage everyone to visit his GoFundMe page for his gender surgeries.) He hosts giveaways of breast binders and reviews female-to-male transgender sex toys, a service presumably helpful to part of his target audience. He also offers reflections on his own medical transition for those audience members untroubled by his lack of medical training.

If Chase comes across as one of the Lost Boys, he has been through a lot. Chase's mother abandoned the family when Chase was a year old. He grew up as a girl in the Montreal suburbs, raised by a father whom he describes as his "best friend." Chase's father sells things at local flea markets but has never had a steady job.

Like a lot of caring fathers who have trouble making ends meet, his dad urged him to aspire to a stable profession—but Chase decided he wanted to be just like his dad. He began making YouTube videos in 2006, just a year after YouTube's founding. The self-starter, hung-shingle aspect of the forum appealed to him. "Once I realized I was trans, I was like, I kind of want to talk about this, and I don't have access to therapy because I can't afford it, so I might as well talk to myself and upload it."

In fact, YouTube facilitated Chase's own trans epiphany. "I always knew that there was kind of something 'off' about me," he says. "Not like being trans is something off, but I just felt different from other people. I didn't feel like I fit in. And one time I was watching probably cat videos on YouTube when I was fifteen and I stumbled across a trans person."

Chase found the trans videos mesmerizing. "I was like, 'What is this? I don't understand. What is this person?' And after watching a couple of these videos, I was like 'Omigod, everything in my life makes sense.'" At age fifteen, after binging on these videos, Chase decided he was transgender.

But then, he had doubts. In fact, his trajectory to trans identification was less a linear function than a polynomial. "I went through a couple of years of 'Yes-I-am, no-I'm-not, Omigod, that's gross.' To the point where when I was eighteen, I really sat down with myself and said, 'I can't really ignore this anymore. This is really who I am.'"

This back-and-forth is a common experience of trans influencers. The way many gurus like Chase explain it, the trans identity is more the handsome stranger they learn to love than the stalker they're desperate to escape.

Instagram female-to-male trans guru Emre Kaya told me he saw his first trans video when he was in the ninth grade and still identifying as a lesbian: "I showed my teacher, and I wanted her to show the class. She played it for my class, but everyone in the class made me feel bad. They were grossed out." That was 2012; Emre was merely ahead of his time.[2]

There are more than a dozen social media sites and online forums that facilitate the discovery of a trans identity. YouTube, Instagram, Tumblr, Reddit, Twitter, Facebook, DeviantArt, and TikTok are all popular hubs for sharing and documenting a physical transformation, seething over transphobia, celebrating the superpowers conferred by testosterone, offering tips for procuring a prescription, and commiserating about how hard it is to be trans today.

Trans influencers have a few classic mantras. Here's some of the advice you're likely to receive from them:

1. IF YOU THINK YOU MIGHT BE TRANS, YOU ARE

"Trans" is a state of mind. It's innate, permanent, and perfectly knowable. *Cogito ergo sum transgender.*

As female-to-male trans guru Ty Turner reassures his audience through two lip rings: "So if you're asking the question, 'Am I trans?' the answer is probably yes."[3]

Online gurus like Ty Turner take it for granted that "trans" is an important social identity, over and above (and even without) the psychiatric condition once thought to undergird it. Trans influencers typically promote trans as a lifestyle to celebrate, not the result of a malady they hope to cure. No longer the engine of transgender identity, gender dysphoria becomes the caboose, dragged along like so much useless iron or detached and set free. The important thing is the social identity, not any diagnosis. Understood this way, trans is something you might want to become even if you aren't suffering gender dysphoria. Then again, many influencers define "dysphoria" so broadly that nearly every teen would seem to have it.

Chucking the *DSM-5* aside, or perhaps blissfully unaware of it, trans YouTuber Jake Edwards advises that even if you don't have traditional gender dysphoria, you might still have one of the "other types." "For example there is a social dysphoria" which includes "anything in a social situation that makes you feel negative about yourself."[4]

Those of us plagued with social anxiety are officially on notice: we're probably "trans."

Having cast gender dysphoria aside, trans influencers describe symptoms that are vague and ubiquitous: *feeling different, not really fitting in,* and *not feeling feminine* or *masculine enough.* And this one: *ever feeling uncomfortable in your body.* (Spoiler alert: for every woman lolloping about the Western Hemisphere, the answer is "affirmative.")

"So now maybe you're thinking, 'Okay, that sounds like me,'" Ty Turner helpfully prompts his at-home audience. "'I don't identify with my birth-given sex, but how can I figure out where on the spectrum I am or whether I want to go through the process of transitioning completely or if I just want to be smack-dab in the middle?'"[5]

Chase Ross told me he currently identifies as "60 percent male" and the rest, "squiggle."[6] Confused? That may be the point.

Influencers typically claim that "being trans" is like being gay— innate, biologically determined, and immutable. But is this right? Psychologists who study sexuality measure the observable physiological response of the male and female sex organs to visual stimuli. Show a man the right kind of images and—long before he opens his mouth—his body will let you know exactly what he thinks of it.

Not so with "being trans," which has no scientific markers and, like recovered memories, depends entirely on a person's say-so. And even once arrived at, a person's new gender identity can change, again and again.[7] This presents a metaphysical and biological challenge to the very concept of "being trans."

Many influencers will tell you, as "queer" influencer Ashley Wylde puts it, "Having doubts while you question your gender is one hundred percent normal."[8] One might think that they'd advise exercising caution about transitioning given the capriciousness of one's gender feelings, but the reverse is true. Doubts *should never stop* your transition. (As far as I can tell, nothing should.)

In June 2011, at the age of nineteen—less than a year after starting a course of testosterone—Chase Ross seems briefly to have changed his mind.[9] He stopped taking testosterone. A soft-faced, bare-cheeked, and mostly female-looking Chase explained that even though he considered himself trans, he wasn't ready to be known as a "trans guy"—he still wanted to thought of as a lesbian. "I didn't want to lose my . . . gay visibility and look straight to the straight world," he said.

"I was really confused for a very long time," he told me. "I literally went back and forth for so long. 'Yes, I'm trans.' 'No, I'm not.'" He bought a binder, then threw it out. His gender dysphoria was so unconvincing that when he applied to a gender clinic in Canada for testosterone, he was turned down.

Male-to-female Instagram influencer Kaylee Korol admits she too wasn't sure she was trans for a while. "I know for myself, my certainty really ebbed and flowed before hormones, where one day I'd be super certain and the next day, I'd be wondering why I even considered it. And it wasn't only until a little while on hormones that things started to align and I was like 'Aha, this is great, I'm never going back.'"[10]

2. TRYING OUT TRANS? BINDERS ARE A GREAT WAY TO START

Nearly every female-to-male guru started her transformation with a binder—a spandex and polyester compression garment that, worn under clothing, effectively flattens breasts. Trans influencers show off the various styles, compare different brands' effectiveness at creating the impression of a male physique, and sometimes complain about "having" to wear them.

"This is by far one of the most exciting moments in my life okay, look at that," gushes a still obviously female but trans-identifying You-Tuber Elliott James.[11] Elliott tears apart the gray polyethylene envelope, pulls out the cellophane-wrapped binder, dances, tongue-wagging and lightly shrieking. (Breasts may be painful reminders of one's birth sex, but apparently shrieking is not.)

Elliott removes the garment from the plastic wrap, holds it up, inhales through it, and dances again—all from inside what appears to be a dormitory bathroom. "Oh man oh man I'm so excited. I gotta put it on!"

And because the internet knows no shame, Elliot tries it on for our benefit—baring rose-tattooed arms, struggling a little against the punishing elastic, emitting a string of expletives. "Whoo this hurts," Elliott says, smiling proudly. Turning sideways, Elliott shows off her flattened physique, a bulldozed version of a woman's profile. "Oh, my God! Oh, oh! I'm a boy! Wow!" Elliot buries her face in her hands, apparently on the verge of happy tears.

What trans videos like Elliott's rarely mention are the dangerous medical side effects. It turns out that breasts—glandular tissue, fatty tissue, blood vessels, lymph vessels and lymph nodes, lobes, ducts, connective tissue, and ligaments—are not really meant to be squashed flat all day long.[12] Fractured or bruised ribs, punctured or collapsed lungs, shortness of breath, back pain, and deformation of the breast tissue are side effects.

But try convincing a teenager that something she wants to do carries risks. Imagine telling her that she might not want to damage her breast tissue; that she might one day want to have children and, having birthed those children, to nurse them. It's a little like informing her the sun will burn out five billion years in the future.

3. TESTOSTERONE, OR "T," IS *AMAZING*. IT MAY JUST SOLVE ALL OF YOUR PROBLEMS.

Alex Bertie, a British female-to-male YouTuber, and perhaps the most popular (he has over three hundred thousand subscribers), vlogged about his first year on testosterone: "This is the day I never thought would come," enthused boyishly adorable, scruffy-jawed Alex. "I'm officially one year on testosterone. Before hormones, I was struggling with severe self-hate, jealousy, and just the urge to isolate myself from everybody. . . . Now, a year after starting hormones, I couldn't be happier. The changes from testosterone really have improved my quality of life and just made such a difference in shaping my future."

His voice has deepened. He's sprouted body hair and a beard. His shoulders are broader, his arms are bigger, his jaw squarer. His fat is redistributed (less in the thighs and hips). And perhaps most thrilling of all: his period—gone. "Luckily, after two months on T, mine completely stopped, thank God. Within the last year, I also had top surgery. Now this is its own thing. I can make a million videos about how much top surgery has helped me. But hand-in-hand with hormones, this seriously just wiped away my dysphoria. So all in all, testosterone has been pretty amazing."[13]

Because of the mercurial and subjective nature of the trans identity, tension naturally arises about who is *really* trans—or trans enough. For that reason, testosterone can be an important means of establishing one's bona fides. As Chase Ross puts it in his "Trans 101" video series, testosterone "brings more legitimacy to your transition."[14] But then, Chase rushes to reassure: "the legitimacy of your transition is how *you* define your transition."

Not every trans vlogger shares Chase's moderation. Male-to-female Instagram guru Kaylee Korol, a blue-eyed and blue-haired waif who seems like an average teenage girl, offers this "trans tip": "[Y]ou don't need to be a hundred percent sure you're trans to try hormones, you don't," Kaylee assures viewers. "You can try hormones for three months. After three months there starts to be permanent effects, but until around then you can just try hormones and see how you feel. It's great, it's that easy. Hormones aren't as scary as everyone makes them out to be."[15]

You don't have to be certain you're transgender in order to go on hormones. In fact, Kaylee adds, going on hormones is "probably the best way to actually tell if you're trans anyways."[16]

You might have heard that testosterone comes with bad side effects—but you'll rarely hear them mentioned here. YouTube and Insta gurus are about fun, and increased risks of various cancers and prophylactic hysterectomy are certainly not that. The most common side effect of testosterone that gurus talk about is the one that burnishes their trans bona fides: pain. The pain is acknowledged—even conveyed with relish. Like a barefoot dash across fiery coals, braving the agony of an intra-muscular injection proves you've moved beyond playing dress-up. You really are "trans." And you're not messing around.

"So basically I lay down on this little chair thing, with my butt hanging out,"[17] an obviously female Alex Bertie vlogged at age seventeen, documenting her first injection of testosterone. A nurse "shoves a needle in, and I'm kind of like, 'Uh, uh, that hurts a little bit more than I thought it would.' There was like a spike of pain. And then as she injects it, the pain kind of like goes up a little bit, just slowly increasing."[18] Alex Bertie was more than up to the test: "I'm not going to lie, it hurt. It f*ing hurt."[19]

But you can't join a church without a baptism—can't claim to be blood brothers unless you spill a little blood. This is the trans bar mitzvah, and it is joyously undertaken. Pain is proof of commitment to the cause. "Obviously it's a bearable pain and completely worth it," Alex Bertie reassures his viewers, before exclaiming, "Yeah, I'm on testosterone! . . . I'm not pre-T anymore!" You can almost hear him address his YouTube congregation: *Today, I am a man.*

4. IF YOUR PARENTS LOVED YOU, THEY WOULD SUPPORT YOUR TRANS IDENTITY

Jett Taylor is—like his name—hot. Jett has the boy-band looks of a young Justin Bieber: full lips, soft beard hair, big brown eyes, and nice, even features. His face bears a smattering of acne, another side effect of the testosterone—the trans equivalent of battle scars.

But he's not just a pretty face. Jett Taylor has a message: "True love is unconditional love. Love without restrictions. For you not to accept someone as they truly are—is you not truly loving them."[20]

Parents of suddenly trans-identifying teens beware: he's talking about you. If you question your daughter's sudden insistence that she is "transgender," you do not really love your daughter. What is more, you are imminently replaceable. "Those who are meant to stay in your life, those who love you unconditionally, are always going to stay," Jett Taylor tells his audience. "I have an awesome group of friends, right now, and that's all that really matters. Those who love me unconditionally are there for me every step of the way."

There is nothing crueler, more "toxic" to trans gurus than parents who fail to jump on board with each step of gender transition and every tenet of gender ideology. "If you're dealing with family members like this," Jett says, sympathetically, "I just want to say, I'm really sorry. I love you unconditionally. I love you just as you are. I love you as you. If you're feeling sad right now, I'm giving you the biggest hug, the biggest hug in the whole wide world." Just don't expect him to pay your tuition.

But Jett is not the only one making promises. For Mother's Day in May 2017, male-to-female cycling world champion (competing against biological women, that is) Rachel McKinnon was moved to encourage trans-identifying adolescents to cut off their own mothers. "Kids whose parents maybe don't support them as much as we would hope—unfortunately this is too common. I want to give you some hope, though. I want you to know that it's okay to walk away from unsupportive or disrespectful or even abusive parents."[21]

That's a heck of a Mother's Day gift to mom. But McKinnon offers something else—she calls it "hope": "I want to give you hope that you can find what we call your 'glitter family,' your 'queer family.' We are out there, and the relationships that we make in our glitter families are just as real, just as meaningful as our blood families."

Sick with the flu? Find yourself in a car crash? Dumped by the love of your life? Not to worry. McKinnon will be right over.

5. IF YOU'RE NOT SUPPORTED IN YOUR TRANS IDENTITY, YOU'LL PROBABLY KILL YOURSELF

Female-to-male Skylar Kergil recalls that cute boy in your freshman dorm with the tousled auburn hair, lightly rumpled shirts, and chin sandpapered with stubble. "I think in the wake of Leelah Alcorn's suicide," Kergil warns, "it's important to see the role that parents play in the happiness, safety and health of transgender youth."[22]

Leelah Alcorn was the deeply depressed seventeen-year-old male-to-female in Ohio who threw himself in front of traffic after his parents made him undergo Christian conversion therapy. Leelah left a suicide note on his Tumblr blog—explicitly blaming his suicide on his parents' refusal to accept his transgender identity.

Suicide rates among the transgender-identified are, indeed, alarmingly high.[23] Nearly every trans influencer believes, therefore, that anything parents do to make their trans-identified adolescent's life harder—insist on employing the name they gave her, take away her iPhone—is unforgivably cruel. You wouldn't do that to someone on the verge of a nervous breakdown, would you? Don't you know how hard it is just getting through the day?

There is no doubt some truth here: these girls are unquestionably in pain. Their mental anguish would seem to merit adult compassion. Parents ought to offer it. But extending compassion is not the same as giving in to demands, particularly to demands that a parent believes are not in the child's best interests.

But what do parents know? By Skylar's estimation: not much. When your child announces she's trans, Skylar patiently explains, your job as a parent is not to question an adolescent but to *follow her lead*. "Saying

'No you're not, you're wrong, or this is just a phase' just leaves your child feeling unsupported because really, they're not going to change because there's nothing to 'fix.'"[24]

This message is ostensibly directed at parents. But what parents troll YouTube looking for advice from teens on how to raise their children? Of course, the advice isn't for parents, not really. It's a method of coaching their children, helping them to fend off adults who might otherwise convince them to desist.

6. DECEIVING PARENTS AND DOCTORS IS JUSTIFIED IF IT HELPS TRANSITION

Trans influencers typically take a by-any-means-necessary approach to procuring cross-sex hormones. Whatever you have to do, whatever you have to say—do it. Your life is on the line. "Find out what they want to hear if they're gonna give you T and then tell them just that," offers one trans advisor on social media. "It's about getting treatment, not about being true to those around you. It's not their business and a lot of time, doctors will screw stuff up for you."[25]

Another suggests: "Get a story ready in your head, and as suggested keep the lie to a minimum. And only for stuff that can't be verified. Like how you were feeling but was too afraid to tell anyone including your family."[26]

Binders are typically sold in discreet packaging so as not to tip off unsupportive parents. Even Chase Ross is willing to send binders to underage kids at a friend's address if the parents do not approve. "And then there was a time where a kid messaged me and said 'My dad found my binder and he cut it up in front of me.' And that just broke my heart," he told me. "So I sent them another one to their friend's address because that's heartbreaking. You wearing a binder and your dad rips it in front of you? That's heartbreaking."

7. YOU DON'T HAVE TO IDENTIFY AS THE OPPOSITE SEX TO BE "TRANS"

If Chase Ross is among the most likable of influencers, then Ash Hardell left me most confused. Ash is a natal female with a squeaky voice and a strong Midwestern accent, cute as a Kewpie doll. Her elfin adorableness makes her look all of twelve (she's in her late twenties), and she identifies as "non-binary" or "genderqueer"—meaning neither male nor female. (Her pronouns are "they/them.")

Her videos are some of the best produced—they have fun sound effects and are tightly edited, and because she's so articulate they're among the most enjoyable to watch. She has over 650,000 YouTube subscribers to prove it. She's relentlessly upbeat, bright, even Pollyannaish, a remarkable feat for someone wearing a septum ring. And she's willing to share everything.

We watch her tell her mother—for the first time—that she's "trans," and join her on her journey to top surgery, from her first medical consults to the final results. But unlike more traditional transgender adolescents, she does not take testosterone. What Ash wants to be—or thinks she is—is "something in between." She is perhaps the personification of that most desired of attributes among today's adolescents: "quirky."

Perhaps because she's so chatty and adorable and looks like a very young girl, Ash manages to make trans look wholesome. She shows you her torso after top surgery, which, apparently without testosterone's enhancement, looks something like the body of an eight-year-old boy. (Her spouse, Grayson,[27] also had top surgery, and Ash tells us in grisly detail of the joy and chagrin of the post-op results.)

Some non-binary and agender influencers do go on testosterone—but the effect they're shooting for is the in-between state. As Ash's agender friend Chandler explains, "There are two different things that a lot of non-binary people on testosterone will do. Either they will take [T] for a short amount of time at a regular dosage, which is what I plan to do, or they will take it at a lower dosage for a more constant amount of time.

And so I might change my mind and do that." An adult might wonder—as I did—what doctor oversees this witchcraft? This trial-and-error administration of hormones with indeterminate and shifting goals? What would possibly be the Hippocratic justification for removing a natal female's breasts to give her the appearance of a "neither"?

What bothers Chandler—and the reason she started a course of testosterone—was that everyone "read" her consistently as a girl. She wants to get to "a more in-between feeling"—of being identified as a woman only *some* of the time.[28] "They/them" are the pronouns she claims—but sexless, epicene is how she wants to be seen. Very often non-binary teens seem to resist playing your game or speaking your language. They want to topple the board, send the pieces flying, rewrite all the rules, eliminate rules altogether. They don't want to "pass," and they don't want your categories. They are "genderfluid"—and reserve the right to change their minds.

It is worth noting that non-binary identity "affirmation" and surgeries threaten to dismantle the rationale for transgender body alterations in the first place. The underlying rationale for gender surgeries has always been that this is dysphoria—discomfort in a particular "wrongly sexed" body—not discomfort with both sexes or hatred of one's body altogether.

But if what you want from your body is "non-binary"—something that does not, or has not, ever existed—how will you know if you've reached it? Doesn't it seem more likely that you'll never arrive? Like Michael Jackson's "perfect" nose, it may always lie one surgery away, just out of reach.

o o o

Before I watched the videos and interviewed some of their makers, I didn't expect to like trans influencers. Many of the parents I've interviewed regard them as cult leaders or drug dealers. But I didn't dislike them. Riven with piercings and stamped with tattoos, battling the bouts of depression that strike like a summer storm, furiously and without warning, obsessing endlessly over their changing bodies: If these influencers are relentless evangelists for a dangerous cause, they also need all the love and care they can get.

Ecstatic about being "on T," pitying those who can't yet "get access" because their "gatekeeping" parents won't allow it, they are the undeniable drug and surgery boosters of the trans world. Many of them peddle misinformation, outright medical falsehoods, and just bad advice. They extol the glories of testosterone as if it were a protein shake, not a Schedule III controlled substance. They enthuse over double mastectomies as if they were of no more significance than a haircut. They refer to skeptical parents as "toxic"—and encourage their audience to upgrade to a trans "glitter family."[29]

They coach you to lie to doctors by inventing a history of childhood dysphoria or omitting your own mental health history.[30] They suggest that suicidality looms large—but can be banished quickly with transition. Better to transition *right now*, before your dysphoria demons overtake you.

But they're all so young, and so hard-bitten. They're giving the camera everything they've got and more, things they may come one day to regret. Their battles may be internal, but the scars are real—shiny pink rivulets that slash their chests in half-moons, just below where breasts used to be.

They come across as the Artful Dodger, the swaggering street-smart pickpocket of *Oliver Twist*. Dodger's no model citizen; then again, that isn't entirely his fault.

Trans influencers claim to be having the times of their lives and exude genuine enthusiasm for the transgender identity, but they also seem to spend more time focused on their bodies than the average runway model. Their expenses are not inconsiderable—testosterone can cost hundreds of dollars a month. Top surgery typically runs around ten thousand dollars. They remain constantly vulnerable to reminders of their birth sex—to the injury of being "deadnamed" (someone using their birth names to refer to them) or misgendered (the wrong pronouns). They are beset by uncomfortable physical events that are, for them, a kind of crisis: even after nearly a decade on testosterone, Chase Ross occasionally gets his period.

They don't exactly "pass," which makes it hard to imagine their fitting in in a mostly not-transgender world. They're much smaller than the average man: they have more petite hands, and slenderer faces. They seem doomed to snag double takes from passersby when they want to— and just as often, when they don't. Since they almost never undergo the phalloplasty necessary to achieve one of the defining features of manhood, it's hard not to see their male identities as fragile; a quick trip to a urinal, and the jig is up.

Then there's the audience the influencers entertain—teenagers, a famously fickle and faddish bunch. It grants them rapt attention now, but it might just as easily lose interest. The gurus want you to believe their lives are full, that they have a lot more going on than just being trans, but that rarely seems to be the case.

They will occasionally apologize, as transgender heartthrob female-to-male Wes Tucker has, for failing to upload videos on account of depression.[31] They share every private crisis with hundreds of thousands of viewers. The internet shelters they've fashioned seem precariously close to the shoreline, vulnerable to the waves of public opinion or their next mental health crisis.

There does seem to be genuine companionability among them. They give each other encouragement. They profess love and offer acceptance. Like glitter, they add fun adornment without the weight or encumbrance of an actual relationship.

Their confessional videos are shown in schools, ostensibly to broaden LGBTQ understanding, and they cue up automatically on YouTube if Google wants them to.

If you've ever felt different, anxious, or afraid—if you've ever felt like you don't really fit in, why . . . "Consider yourself at home / Consider yourself one of the family / We've taken to you, so strong / It's clear, we're going to get along."

CHAPTER FOUR

THE SCHOOLS

In June 2019, the policy-making arm of the California Teachers Association (CTA) met in Los Angeles at the Westin Bonaventure Hotel.[1] On the agenda for the public school teacher's union's quarterly meeting were a number of routine items: the recent election of new officers, the union's continuing efforts to monitor new charter-school activity. And the delegates voted on New Business Item, #6/19-12, requiring "immediate action." This was a proposal to allow trans-identified minor students to leave campus during school hours to obtain gender hormone treatments without parental permission.[2]

The rationale for the new policy was simple: California state law already allowed "cis minors" to leave school to "receive hormones (that is, birth control) without the barrier of parental permission."[3] Trans kids should also be entitled to leave school to obtain *their* hormones. The delegates voted, and the new item was approved. The CTA would begin to pursue a policy of allowing students age twelve and up to walk out the door during the school day to obtain cross-sex hormones.

As if that weren't enough, in January 2020 the CTA's Civil Rights in Education Subcommittee kicked things up a notch. The committee moved to create "school-based health care clinics" that would provide "cisgender, transgender and non-binary youth equal *and confidential* access to a broad range of physical, mental and behavioral services" (emphasis added).[4] Additional votes are needed before this policy can go into effect. But with any luck, in short order California's minor students who want cross-sex hormones will not only be able to obtain them without parents' knowledge or permission—they may be able to do so without leaving school grounds.

Perhaps you're thinking: *That must be the work of one rogue teacher's union.* Or maybe you figure: *Only in California.* Blotto with sunshine and too much Chablis, California teachers will do anything to avoid doing their actual jobs. I thought the same, believe me.

But when I delved into the gender ideology that pervades the schools, the radicalization of the teacher's unions, and the unions' intimate relationship with activists, I came to understand this new proposal as inevitable. It's the logical extension of all the laws and policies and radical curricula already adopted in California and cropping up across the country.

Educators, activists, and legislators are studying California's blueprints. New York, New Jersey, Colorado, Illinois, Northern Virginia, and Oregon public schools have already adopted a radical approach to gender in their curricula and policies. To say nothing of tony private schools. Why, avant-garde educational philosophy is their métier.

THE EDUCATORS

California boasts the most comprehensive state-wide gender identity and sexual orientation instruction, statutorily mandatory for all students enrolled in grades K–12 and explicitly barring parental opt-out.[5] A clever legerdemain enabled this feat. California law explicitly allows parental opt-out from sexual health education.[6] But the California legislature exempted all materials related to "gender identity, gender expression" and "sexual orientation" from that opt-out. Such instruction—educators contend—is essential to prevent discrimination, harassment, and bully-ing.[7] In order to protect gay and trans kids from harassment, in other words, it was necessary for *all children* to receive gender identity and sexual orientation instruction.

Judy Chiasson knows all about cutting-edge gender identity educa-tion. As program coordinator for human relations, diversity and equity for the Los Angeles Unified School District—the second-largest school district in the U.S., with more than 600,000 students attending more than 1,200 schools—Judy Chiasson oversees all policy with regard to sexual orientation and gender identity education in her district.

I knew gender ideology was a big part of her life the moment I received her email: "Dear Mx. Shrier," she wrote.

I blinked. The "x" remained stubbornly in place. It wasn't a typo. According to her email signature, her pronouns are "she/her."

"The role of schools has changed," she told me, over the phone. "Technically, we are an educational institution, right? Reading, writing, and arithmetic. Technically, that's what we are." That seemed reassuring. "But schools have expanded to be the hub for a lot more social services and looking more holistically, emotionally, at what's going on with chil-dren," she informed me. "Looking at schools as a source of social justice. Our role continues to expand. The outreach now is profound."

The array of services and support California public schools offer students is indeed astonishing: three meals a day; backpacks full of cloth-ing; free medical and dental services on campus. Public schools that provide these services might have good reason to assume they act in loco parentis, even with regard to matters that directly contravene the wishes and values of the actual parents.

"I think that society looks to schools—because we have access to children—to be able to address a lot of social issues." School violence and school shootings are two examples she gave me. "Not that we're replacing family. But things that used to be the exclusive domain of fam-ily or society, we're now asking schools to look at those a little more intentionally."

Many of today's educators regard the gender and sexual identity education kids receive from their parents as hopelessly inadequate. They are stepping up to correct the omission, to drag America's families into the twenty-first century. LGBTQ students "need to have teachers and parents who are very comfortable—just go ahead, say the word 'gay.' Say it out loud! You know, in a very positive way," Dr. Chiasson said. "Talk about transgender. Talk about gender diversity. Talk about your transgender uncle. This needs to just be part of our daily conversation. That's what they need. And they need, when that happens, they need their parents to call the school and say 'Thank you.'"

Too often, Dr. Chiasson says, teachers are reluctant to teach kids about sexual orientation and gender identity because they're afraid of parental objections. This, in Dr. Chiasson's view, is a problem. "The reasons that a lot of teachers are hesitant to address LGBTQ issues in the schools, is because they're worried about what the parents might say. And the parents do call up and they complain and they're upset," she said. "Yes, we serve the community, but in some places, we have to lead the community."

THE INSTRUCTION

There have always been women who broke barriers and inhabited male roles, behavior that would today be sufficient to deem them "gender nonconforming": Joan of Arc, Catherine the Great, George Eliot, George Sand, Sally Ride. But none of these women thought she was less of a woman for having taken on traditionally male roles. None insisted that she was *really* a man.

They might then be surprised to learn that that is precisely how schoolchildren across America are increasingly being taught to see them: on the female side of the spectrum, perhaps, but not *entirely* female.[8] A little more to the male side. Or somewhere in between.

California, New Jersey, Colorado, and Illinois all have laws mandating LGBTQ history be taught in schools. As a practical matter, this has meant rewriting social studies textbooks and curricula to "out" the likes of Sally Ride, who kept her lesbianism a secret—perhaps because that wasn't how she wanted to be remembered. She seems to have considered being the first woman in space a little more important. Other giants of history are similarly vulnerable to a "baptism of the dead"—the chance to reemerge as non-binary, genderqueer, or trans.

While all this sexual identity politics marches through the front door, a large-scale robbery is taking place: the theft of women's achievement. The more incredible a woman is, the more barriers she busts through, the more "gender nonconforming" she is deemed to be. In this perverse schema, by definition, the more amazing a woman is, the less she counts as a woman.

○ ○ ○

In schools across America, kindergarteners are taught that biological sex and gender very often come apart; one has no essential connection to the other. There are some people for whom gender identity aligns perfectly with the sex they were assigned at birth: "cisgender" they are called—meaning "on this side of gender," coined to be the definitional opposite of "transgender," meaning "across from gender."[9] As it is presented in schools, "cisgender" often seems to be a null set. Faced with a heaping buffet of gender identities to choose from, it's hard to imagine everyone isn't at least a little bit something.

Girls who like math, or sports, or are logical; boys who sing, or act, or like to draw are all "gender nonconforming." They may have turned up to school as a "girl who excels at math" or "boy with vocal talent," but they leave rebranded as "a person whose behaviors or gender expression falls outside what is generally considered typical for their assigned sex at birth."[10]

And anyone who "broaden[s] their own culture's commonly held definitions of gender, including expectations for its expression, identities, roles and/or other perceived gender norms," is not a feminist or a path-breaker; she is "gender expansive."[11] By excelling at math or wrestling or physics, she is necessarily challenging the gender binary.[12] She may even be "gender questioning." But she is certainly not merely "female."

The ACLU, Planned Parenthood, and GLSEN (formerly the "Gay and Lesbian Independent School Teachers Network") supply curriculum materials. Their members are routinely brought into schools to lecture students on sexual orientation and gender. They provide teacher training and videos and even coach the Gay–Straight Alliance (GSA), a popular after-school club.[13]

This is how gender ideology is taught in schools: with the materials, curricula, speakers, and teacher training supplied by gender activists.[14] Kindergarteners are introduced to the "Genderbread Person"[15] and "Gender Unicorn."[16] Kindergarten teachers read from *I Am Jazz*, and the little ones are taught that they might have a "girl brain in a boy body" or vice versa.[17]

Schools that administer this instruction never acknowledge that, as a scientific matter, it's gibberish. It is biologically nonsensical to suggest that a girl's brain—every cell of it stamped with XX chromosomes— might inhabit a boy's body. No mention is made of the fact that there are no diagnostic or empirical criteria for deciding that a biological girl is in fact "really a boy." Nonetheless, this drivel is taught with the same sobriety and apparent thoroughness as facts about human reproduction and sexually transmitted disease.

Imagine if anti-vaxxer groups—also representing a position miles outside the scientific mainstream—were brought in to speak to students, asked to provide materials for health class, allowed to present their own versions of science and offered a lectern from which to argue for the connection between autism and vaccination. It does not seem far-fetched to imagine that more students who had been vaccinated would begin to notice themselves fixating, struggling with empathy, misreading social cues, engaging in repetitive movements, tending to self-harm, and diagnose mild cases of autism in each other. It would not at all be surprising if such students began to adopt anti-vaxxer "science" and became more hostile to the perceived conspiracy by mainstream medicine to deny it.

The gender literature is vast. I include here a few samples of each level of instruction. They are full of dogmatic insistence and gentle prodding: Where do *you* fit on the gender spectrum? How do you know? Are you *sure*?

K-6

What to teach kindergarteners about gender identity? Begin by introducing preschoolers to gender stereotypes. "Discuss gender with kindergarteners," suggests the California Board of Education, "by exploring gender stereotypes and asking open-ended questions, such as what are preferred colors, toys, and activities for boys/girls."[18]

It isn't hard to imagine that this might be the first time a young girl even hears of these stereotypes. Her Gen X parents may never have found it necessary to tell her that sports were once allegedly the exclusive province of boys or that art, after being male-dominated for most of history, later came to be associated with girls. But gender ideologues make sure she learns that things like sports and math are for boys. It's essential that she learns gender stereotypes because, without them, "gender identity" makes no sense at all. And when a boy realizes that he enjoys some of the "girl" activities, like painting or dancing, the revelation that he is not entirely a "boy" readily tees up.

The California Board of Education provides, through its virtual libraries, a book intended for kindergarten teachers to read to their students: *Who Are You? The Kid's Guide to Gender Identity* by Brook Pessin-Whedbee.[19] The author begins with a familiar origin story: "Babies can't talk, so grown-ups make a guess by looking at their bodies. This is the sex assigned to you at birth, male or female."[20]

This author runs the gamut of typical kindergarten gender identity instruction. *Who Are You?* offers kids a smorgasbord of gender options. ("These are just a few words people use: trans, genderqueer, non-binary, gender fluid, transgender, gender neutral, agender, neutrois, bigender, third gender, two-spirit. . . .") The way baby boomers once learned to rattle off state capitals, elementary school kids are now taught today's gender taxonomy often enough to have committed it to memory. And while gender ideologues insist they are merely presenting an objective ontology, it is hard to miss that they seem to hope kids will pick a fun, "gender-creative"[21] option for themselves.

Lindsay Amer is an educator who identifies as "queer"—that is, outside the binary of traditional genders. Amer regularly visits schools to play her ukulele and sing a song Amer wrote for preschoolers (think of it as the gender ideologue's answer to "Free to Be You and Me"): "It's OK to be gay. We are different in many ways. Doesn't matter if you're a boy, girl or somewhere in between, we all are part of one big family. Gay means 'happy.'"

In her view, preschool kids must be taught about gender because "[t]his is when children are developing their sense of self. They're observing the world around them, absorbing that information and internalizing it."[22] What kids require, then, is the gender vocabulary to enable them to pick out their own point on the spectrum.

According to *Schools in Transition*, perhaps the most widely used policy guide for dealing with transgender kids in public school: "[I]t is critical to recognize that transgender students are not the only youth affected by gender at school. Stereotypes about gender are reinforced in many ways in the school environment, which prevents all youth from reaching their full potential."[23] No one seems to notice that at least one of the reasons gender stereotypes are reinforced in school is because educators are actively teaching them.

The last tenet of gender ideology that *Who Are You?* presents is a child's feelings as an infallible indicator of gender: "You are who you say you are, because YOU know best," the book coos. A hell of a thing, really, telling small children *they* know best. Parents must *listen* to their children, the book insists; but what it really seems to mean is that parents must *agree* with them.

In a TED Talk Amer explains: "I make queer media for kids because I wish I had this when I was their age. I make it so others don't have to struggle through what I did, not understanding my identity because I didn't have any exposure to who I could be."

MIDDLE SCHOOL

Positive Prevention PLUS is among the most highly respected health curricula in use in schools that employ gender-identity instruction. This curriculum, designed for middle school students, instructs teachers to engage students in an "Imagining a Different Gender Activity."[24] Teachers are directed: "Ask students to stand up, turn around twice, and sit down again. Then say, 'I want each of you to imagine that you are a different gender.'" If the students fail to engage, the teacher should press them: "Ask 'What would be different in your life if you were a different gender?' List student responses on the board. . . . Then ask, 'How would you feel to be another gender? What would be fun about being another gender? What things in your life would not change if you are another gender?'"[25]

This is the drumbeat: place yourself in the shoes of a gender-questioning person. Are you *entirely* female? Are you *sure*?

As "Trans 102," one video shown in schools, puts it: "Being a teen can suck. You're not wrong. It's even harder if you're not a girly girl. Or a jock. Or pretty much anything that anyone else considers weird. So imagine knowing you're a boy when everyone else tells you that you're a girl. Or knowing you're neither. Or, a bit of both."

The only rule is that sexual dimorphism must be rejected outright. Teachers present an array of gender and sexual identity options and appear pleasantly surprised when a child chooses wisely (that is, anything but cisgender). The kid is certainly not encouraged to share the big news with her folks.

As fifth grade public school teacher and Equality California (LGBTQ activist group) liaison to the California Teachers Association, C. Scott

Miller, explained to me: "As much as parents want to have rights, what they need to do is be involved in the process. And the more they're involved with their kids anyway, the more they're going to know what's going on. It's not the school's obligation to call up and 'out' a kid to a parent because you're not sending that kid home to the gay pride parade. You're sending them home to somewhere that's going to be very unsafe and a lot of misinformation, a lot of anger and it's just not going to be a safe place for that kid."

HIGH SCHOOL

The high school versions of three of the most highly respected health curricula[26] that include gender identity and sexual orientation instruction are so raunchy, explicit, and radical that I couldn't decide whether they were trying to excite adolescents to the point of orgasm or turn them off of sex entirely. Anal sex is promoted so often that one would assume the writers believed they had invented it. Fisting and anal stimulation by mouth are discussed in supplementary materials, leaving nothing to the imagination. No orifice is left behind.

What is the cumulative effect of all of this LGBTQ education? "I think what it does is it normalizes us," Dr. Chiasson offers, including herself in LGBTQ. And presumably it does. Gay students can no longer be easily marginalized or openly ridiculed for their sexuality.

But it does something else, too. All this purported education encourages adolescents to focus relentlessly on their own gender identities and sexual orientations. It encourages students to look constantly for landmark feelings or impulses, anything that might point toward "gender-fluid," "genderqueer," "asexual," or "non-binary." And it encourages the subtle formation of two camps: *us* and *them*. The imaginary divide between those who fit perfectly into cartoonish gender stereotypes and those who don't. The dauntless young, who welcome different gender identities and sexual orientations, versus their phobic elders, who don't.

Indeed, the school calendars at so many schools insist that LGBTQ students be not merely treated equally and fairly, but revered for their bravery. The year-long Pride Parade often begins in October with "Coming Out Day," "International Pronouns Day," and LGBTQ History Month; November brings "Transgender Awareness Week," capped off by "Transgender Day of Remembrance," a vigil for transgender individuals killed for this identity. March is "Transgender Visibility Month." April contributes "Day of Silence / Day of Action" to spread awareness of bullying and harassment of LGBTQ students. May offers "Harvey Milk Day," dedicated to mourning the prominent gay rights activist; and June, of course, is Pride Month—thirty days dedicated to celebrating LGBTQ identities and decrying anti-LGBTQ oppression.

I spoke to one mother, Faith, whose very bright adolescent daughter had had trouble fitting in in seventh grade. Pride Month was an intense and confusing time for her daughter. "She goes to middle school, and there's a fantastic celebration for Gay Pride month. For the entirety of June. And it's fun and it's great . . . and then it turned a little odd when they started ostracizing the teachers who weren't wearing the rainbow stickers."

Faith initially thought the Pride celebrations were nice; she had been to many Pride parades herself. But she noticed her daughter seemed to be taking to the rainbow fervor at school with an intensity and gusto. "They had a festival. They had a booth where they were painting rainbow flags on everybody." Her daughter spent a day in seventh grade wearing a rainbow flag.

By the end of seventh grade, Faith's daughter decided she was "asexual," and then "trans." She had never even kissed a boy, had not yet gotten her period. But the new identity gave her both a cause and a team.

"All her friends are bisexual," her mother told me, a year after her daughter's announcement. "There's only one heterosexual girl in her little crew. Everybody else is lesbian, bisexual. My daughter had to one-up them and be 'trans.'"

Another mom, Angela, who sends her daughter to public school in Northern Virginia, told me the same: all of her daughter's friends at school identify as transgender, or lesbian, or gay, or bi. "I feel like it's very important to my daughter and to a lot of these kids who are caught up in this to be part of the LGBT umbrella. I don't think it really matters to them, as much, what they are in that umbrella, but they've got to be in that umbrella because it has become such a tribe of which they are proud of being members."

They want to be part of the team, invited to the party. They want to be the teenage dancers in *Footloose*, not the finger-wagging minister. They want to be the assortment of misfits in *The Breakfast Club*, not the square principal who just doesn't understand. They want to be an ally, not an enemy.

THE EFFECT OF ALL THIS GENDER IDENTITY EDUCATION ON ADOLESCENTS

Let me say, for clarity, that I do not believe that gender identity instruction at schools is the primary, causal driver of adolescent transgender identification. But to those of my generation and older who might be inclined to think: "No adolescents would choose a transgender life unless they were truly, painfully gender dysphoric," I would suggest a caveat—nobody in *your* generation.

You grew up differently. You didn't suffer the acute isolation of today's teenagers. You didn't soak your retinas in the internet's transgender propaganda during a confusing time in your life. And you didn't attend today's public schools, many of which provide K–12 indoctrination in gender ideology that is both so radical and so pervasive that it is hardly surprising so many kids might want to take cover under an LGBTQ umbrella.

The schools are not forcing adolescents to identify as transgender, but they are greasing the skids. The LGBTQ safe house they've fashioned is avant-garde and enticing, framed with moral superiority, insulated with civil rights. Those who teach gender ideology do not *make* adolescents transgender. They simply fill kids' heads with gender options and ideology. Then, when the adolescents do experience a crisis, the heroic solution readily bobs to mind.

THE RATIONALE: ANTI-BULLYING

How did educators and activists manage to mainstream a radical view of gender through the schools? Like so many successful sales, this one was facilitated by irresistible packaging: anti-bullying. Appealing to both a moral imperative and Gen X parents' extreme preoccupation with their children's physical safety, the pitch was hard to resist. All of this sexual orientation and gender identity education was necessary—educators claimed—to prevent the battery, harassment, and acute psychological distress of LGBTQ children.

"Dispelling myths about gender expectations in kindergarten can lay the groundwork for acceptance, inclusiveness, and an anti-bullying environment in schools,"[27] according to the California Board of Education. "Gender non-conformity and physical characteristics are often at the root of many forms of bullying. As students learn to accept differences and unique characteristics of others, they also learn about the characteristics of bullying and how to avoid being a bully."[28]

Educators today are aware of the well-known instances of bullying LGBTQ students have suffered and the appalling ways in which schools have failed to remedy it. Among the most egregious was the 1996 case in Ashland, Wisconsin, involving a middle school student named Jamie Nabozny.[29]

Throughout his public middle school and high school years, Nabozny was relentlessly tormented, picked on, called every anti-gay slur from "faggot" to "fudge packer," assaulted, humiliated, and urinated upon, all for the sin of being openly gay. His treatment by the other students was horrifying, tragic, and unrelenting—in aggregate, his peers seem to have formed one flexed muscle that existed only to pummel him.

But even worse than the cruelty shown to him by other students was the callous indifference shown by the various school administrators he appealed to for protection. Each year, it seemed, his torment resumed, and a new set of counselors or administrators failed to do anything to stop it. At one point, Nabozny was pushed to the ground by male students in his class, who enacted a mock rape of him while the other students laughed. Nabozny reported the incident to his principal, who told him that if he was "going to be so openly gay," he should "expect" this type of treatment from the other students. At the end of his eighth grade year, Nabozny attempted suicide.

When he reached adulthood, Jamie Nabozny sued his school district for failing to protect him. On appeal, the Seventh Circuit declared that the district's having turned a deaf ear to Nabozny's predicament, even after repeated requests for help, amounted to a violation of his Fourteenth Amendment right to equal protection under the law.

But one need not appeal to the case of Jamie Nabozny to believe that—absent a vigilant school environment—LGBTQ students might be picked on more than most. As a group, transgender-identified students are no doubt a uniquely vulnerable population, saddled with higher rates of depression and suicide and likely more abused than non-trans-identified students. A 2019 report by the CDC examining school districts from nineteen states validates our commonsense intuition about the higher rates of violence against and self-harm by transgender high schoolers.[30] Reports by activist groups like GLSEN suggest the same.[31]

I have no doubt that legislators who pass anti-bullying laws and educators and school boards who implement gender identity and sexual orientation education are sincerely concerned about the welfare of LGBTQ-identified students—as all decent human beings ought to be. But where a measure taken to fix a problem goes so far in excess of remedy, it becomes clear that simple remedy was not primarily what the fixer had in mind.

This is the sense in which so much gender identity and sexual orientation education, delivered with the tireless passion of priests, is pretext for an ulterior aim. There is simply no good reason for insisting that students be made to imagine themselves as gay or transgender or pansexual. There is no very good reason to imagine they might be a boy in a girl's body or a girl in a boy's. There is no reason to teach students, in the words of one of the most highly regarded school manuals, that the "expression of transgender identity, or any other form of gender-expansive behavior, is a healthy, appropriate and typical aspect of human development."[32]

All that's required is the insistence that students display decency, civility, and kindness to their classmates. Follow the Golden Rule. Stand up to bullies. Any singling out of others for their differences—physical, religious, sexual, or otherwise—should be met with neither indulgence nor toleration. Bad behavior should be met with swift punishment.

The proof is simply how bullying would be handled in any other context. If a Thai kid were being picked on because she arrived to school wearing a panung sash across her torso and those traditional blousy pants, it's inconceivable that the school board would mandate that every student learn the wai pressed-palms greeting. Or insist students learn the history of King Rama IX. Or offer lessons about desire being the source of human suffering, merely because Buddhist belief holds this to be true. The teacher would simply say: "Knock it off. We don't treat people that way. Go to detention, go see the principal." If the deplorable behavior rose to the level of aggravated assault, as it seems to have in the case of Jamie Nabozny, they might expel the student or involve the police.

But instead "bullying" is used as an excuse for a thorough indoctrination in gender ideology and the insistence that transgender students must be "affirmed" or suffer a steep psychological toll. "The consequences of not affirming a child's gender identity can be severe, and it can interfere with their ability to develop and maintain healthy interpersonal relationships," the National Education Association (NEA) warns. "The longer a transgender youth is not affirmed, the more significant and long-lasting the negative consequences can become, including loss of interest in school, heightened risk for alcohol and drug use, poor mental health and suicide."[33]

The affirmation of trans-identified students is so essential to their welfare and safety, according to educators, that it is the policy of the National Education Association and many public schools, including those in California, New York, and New Jersey, that when a trans-identified student "comes out" at school, the parents *not* be informed. In cases where the student claims to have unsupportive parents, as we have seen, school administrators and staff even go so far as to conceal the student's newly announced identity from the parents, while surreptitiously changing the child's name and pronouns on all school forms.

"Privacy and confidentiality are critically important for transgender students who do not have supportive families. In those situations, even inadvertent disclosures could put the student in a potentially dangerous situation at home, so it is important to have a plan in place to help avoid any mistakes or slip-ups,"[34] according to the NEA.

The NEA even recommends that schools use a confidential "Gender Support Plan," created by the activist group Gender Spectrum. This form explicitly asks, "Are guardian(s) of this student aware and supportive of their child's gender transition? Yes/No." And, "If not, what considerations must be accounted for in implementing this plan?"

I asked Dr. Chiasson why schools wouldn't notify the parents of students who decided they wanted to change their names and pronouns at school. She said it was a violation of the students' privacy under FERPA, the Family Educational Rights and Privacy Act, which shields student educational records. But then she said something else. "Just think about it," she said. "If I wanted to be called Judy instead of Judith, you don't need my parents' permission." It is, quite simply, none of their business.

There are reasons parents might think otherwise. Asserting a child's "new" gender identify may tend to harden it in the child's mind. Children who have been referred to by an opposite-sex name and pronouns for a year—afforded access to opposite-sex bathrooms and assigned to rooms in opposite-sex bunks on overnight school trips—might become more confused about who they are and find it harder to change their minds.[35] One might consider these to be aspects of a child's life a parent retains the right to know.

But as fifth grade public school teacher C. Scott Miller explained to me, parents can't always get what they want. "Even parents that come in and say, 'I don't want my kid to be called that.' That's nice, but their parental right ended when those children were enrolled in public school."

Actually, parents at even the toniest private schools fare little better. I spoke to several Manhattan parents who send their children to some of the most exclusive and expensive private schools in the country. One told me that four transgender speakers had been invited to speak to her daughter's class in the space of a year. When her daughter and her daughter's friends decided they, too, were transgender, this parent had little recourse. She made an appointment to speak to the principal. Administrators greeted her with the glazed look of low-level bureaucrats who can only report on decisions that are out of their hands. Our first obligation is to protect the student, they informed her—not the parent.

WHO ARE THE BULLIES?

Which brings me to my final reason for believing that the anti-bullying effort is only a pretext for gender identity education: the ever expanding notions of what constitutes "bullying" and student "safety." Bullying rarely seems to be a question of physical abuse or even verbal badgering. Even acts as minor as using a student's "wrong" pronouns—which a child's own parents may do—are enough to compromise the child's safety in the minds of these educators: "Not having their gender identity respected and affirmed in their daily lives will likely cause [trans-identified students] significant psychological distress," according to the NEA.[36]

At the end of our interview, Dr. Chiasson invited me to the two-day public school principals' training she was running on transgender student policy. Then she thought better of it and disinvited me. "You're a reporter, and I really want this to be a safe space," she said. A safe space for the principals? My presence as an observer at their conference might be sufficient to menace a room full of adults, apparently.

There are endless forms of abuse, it seems, invented by the gender ideologues. According to the California Board of Education, there is even "spiritual abuse"; that is, "using spiritual beliefs to justify abuse [by] forcing others to adhere to rigid gender roles."[37] Perhaps there are students who might venture, *I'm a Christian, so I believe you're a boy, not a girl as you say you are.* Such a devoutly orthodox student wouldn't last very long, one imagines, in the sort of school environment where gender ideology reigns.

Actually, Dr. Chiasson told me, most school kids today think LGBTQ identities are no big deal. "I would suggest that you interview some straight middle school and high school kids because what I hear from them is it's kind of a non-issue," she said. "I know some high school kids and they're like 'Oh, yeah, that's so and so. They've transitioned.' And it's like no big deal for them."

And that's when it dawned on me what all this "safety" is about. Why schools must declare themselves "safe zones" for LGBTQ students. Why the schools have special forms on which to record new names and pronouns for transgender-identified students, which they keep to themselves. Why so much vigilance is needed to ward off anti-LGBTQ bullying. Why schools sacrifice so much instructional time to the year-round celebration of outré sexual orientations and gender identities. It is because of a belief, held to be self-evident by gender activists and their lackeys in the school system: Bullies are forever circling trans-identified students. They torment these kids whenever they fail to affirm them. They cruelly refuse to use these kids' new names and even sometimes reject the kids' transgender identities altogether.

These bullies must be beaten back with every new LGBTQ policy and so much febrile instruction. They are the barbarians outside the schoolyard gates that teachers are working so hard to fend off. Children's welfare—as defined by activists—is not their priority. These bullies, who know next to nothing about gender theory or queer theory, are officious intermeddlers in school policy and teacher instruction.

They aren't even embarrassed by their own ignorance. They really shouldn't be considered at all, except that America's backward laws insist on allowing the intrusion.

They go by "Mom" and "Dad."

CHAPTER FIVE

THE MOMS AND DADS

Katherine Cave is often accused of being a "transphobe." In truth, had she been less indulgent of her daughter's gender exploration, the last seven years of her life might have been easier. In 2013, when her twelve-year-old daughter Maddie announced she was transgender, Katherine could have told Maddie that that was ridiculous. She might have refused to entertain Maddie's new pronouns or masculine name. Maybe Katherine Cave should have had her opposition ready from the start. Had Katherine not been open to listening to what Maddie had to say—casting aside so many of her own doubts in the process—she might not now feel so betrayed.

But Katherine was on the political Left, a lawyer and a lobbyist for a progressive cause. She enthusiastically supported gay marriage long before it was legal anywhere in America and served as matron of honor in the same-sex wedding of a cousin. And she approached her daughter's announcement with a strikingly open mind. Katherine didn't quite know what to make of her daughter's self-assessment. The description of "gender dysphoria" didn't seem to fit her daughter, who had never been anything like a tomboy—she disliked the sweating associated with sports and had never expressed a preference for any stereotypically masculine activity.

What Maddie had had was a school assembly. And like the transgender fifteen-year-old who had regaled the student body with her gender journey, Maddie informed her mother, she too had always "felt different." She, too, didn't quite fit in with the other girls. For all her verbal precocity and academic success, Maddie was socially awkward and had a tendency towards the fairly rigid—what her mother called being "black-and-white in her thinking." Katherine suspected that her daughter might be on the autism spectrum. In fact, Maddie was later diagnosed with "high-functioning" autism.[1]

It's hard now to cast your mind back, but in 2013, when Maddie was beginning to spend a lot of time on social media, few were yet wise to the dangers of the internet. Katherine did not think much of it at the time. She did notice that her daughter seemed to be fixating on this new identity and becoming increasingly enraged that her mother had not immediately embraced Maddie's self-diagnosis.

But Katherine didn't dismiss it, either. She called ten different therapists and explained the situation to each one: Her daughter had no history of gender dysphoria. She had come upon this idea after a presentation at school. All of the therapists "said the same thing to me. They said: 'At this age, *kids know who they are.*'" If Maddie thought she might be transgender, then—by definition—she was.

That explanation didn't feel right to Katherine. Her daughter just didn't seem like "a boy trapped in a girl's body." She seemed like a girl who had had a lot of trouble fitting in with peers, who had been introduced to an explanation and latched onto it. But when her daughter's fixation on this identity intensified, Katherine began to consider the possibility that Maddie was right.

Katherine searched the internet for an explanation for her daughter's sudden trans-identification—anything that might offer an alternative to the chorus of therapists encouraging her to treat Maddie as a boy. "I couldn't find anything that would support my thoughts. . . . The only thing I could find online was anti-gay sort of hateful criticism. I didn't find anything that supported my own ideas."

Katherine found these websites a turnoff. She decided she needed to consult an expert and took her daughter to a gender therapist. "I tried to put all my doubts aside."

At the gender clinic, Katherine joined a group of parents whose adolescent children had come forward with similar epiphanies. The gender therapist assured Katherine that using Maddie's new male name and male pronouns was entirely reversible. There seemed no good reason not to affirm. And his verdict was resolute: "He said that my daughter was at high risk of suicide if I didn't 'affirm.' He said that parental affirmation is the key—that's the most powerful way to prevent her possible suicide. So that of course brought chills to me."

Alarmed by the therapist's warning, Katherine acquiesced to his expertise and followed his advice. "We ended up going through with the pronoun changes, with the name changes. I ended up buying her a binder," she recalls, a note of unmistakable regret in her voice. "He told me that it was much safer to buy the binder online because she would duct-tape if I didn't do this."

Katherine began taking her daughter to the gender clinic regularly, feeling her way around the idea that her daughter was—somehow—actually her son. With regular therapy, she hoped her daughter's dysphoria might fade. She hoped that affirmation would soothe her daughter's anxiety and maybe, having won the battle, Maddie might be persuaded to call off the war. Instead, her daughter's dysphoria seemed to intensify.

"What I found was that this so-called therapy was really about putting her to the next step. And I actually finally eavesdropped on a conversation [between Maddie and the therapist] because I didn't see that there was any exploration of feelings or how this came to be. Rather it was, okay, what is your next plan? And my daughter would be pushing even harder."

The growing pressure for medical transition made Katherine nervous. She could not shake a nagging sense that the therapist's narrow and exclusive focus on her daughter's gender as the source of Maddie's problems was missing the broader picture of a troubled inner life. Her daughter's autism—the social awkwardness and habits of rigid thinking—went completely unaddressed.

Katherine transferred her daughter to a gender clinic that specialized in autism. "That's when I was told, okay, we needed to put her on puberty blockers"—medications that induce chemical menopause to artificially halt puberty. The gender clinicians stressed that puberty blockers were a way to "buy time" by pressing the "pause button on puberty," until they could all decide whether Maddie should resume normal puberty as a girl or go straight to cross-sex hormones and become a "man." They assured Katherine that puberty blockers, such as Lupron, were "perfectly safe" and "well studied."

Katherine once again found herself anxious and alarmed. She couldn't believe a medicine strong enough to induce chemical menopause wouldn't pose long-term health risks to her daughter. She decided she wouldn't do it—not until she knew more about puberty blockers and what they did to the body. Of the group of parents at this gender clinic, she believes she was the only one who hit a pause button of her own.

Katherine began reading everything she could about Lupron. Originally used in cancer treatment and in kids with precocious puberty, it is now prescribed off-label to prepubescent kids to halt the onset of puberty before beginning cross-sex hormones (typically administered up to two years later). The goal is to block the secondary-sex characteristics that would make eventual "passing" as the opposite sex more difficult if one continues on the path to medical transition.

But the more Katherine read, the more disturbed she became. When the medical papers she read cited studies, she tracked down those and read them, too. "So first of all, the studies show that when a kid is put on puberty blockers, almost 100 percent will go on to do cross-sex hormones."

This is true, though the reasons are not entirely clear. One possibility is that a young person would only go on puberty blockers in the first place if she was reasonably certain of wanting to lead a transgender life. Another is that, after years of socially identifying as a person of the opposite sex, the social costs of taking it all back are quite steep. It's hard to change your mind about something you've been insisting on for so long—even if you might wish you could.

But it was the next thing she learned that sent Katherine spinning. "When you've stopped puberty with puberty blockers and go straight to cross-sex hormones, you absolutely guarantee that you will be infertile." When the gender clinicians pushed Katherine to start her preteen child on hormone blockers, they were proposing that she put Maddie on a path toward infertility. Her faith in the gender therapists fell apart.

Katherine could not understand how psychologists would encourage this, how doctors would allow it, or why medical professional standards would permit parents to consent to eliminating such a vital human capacity on behalf of their minor children. And yet, right in front of her, schools were encouraging it, parents were going along with it, the media was celebrating it, and everyone was acting as if this were perfectly kosher. It was enough to make her think she might be losing her mind.

What's more, even if her daughter did not start puberty blockers and instead waited puberty out and then began cross-sex hormones (testosterone), this carried all sorts of risks of its own. Endometrial and ovarian cancer. Hysterectomy.

Katherine was beside herself. Horrified, she concluded that she should never have started her daughter down this path. She told her husband and daughter what she had learned and began scrambling to take it all back. But in certain respects, it was too late. "We didn't know she told the school and the school didn't tell me."

For her seventh grade year, without discussing it with Katherine, the school had reintroduced Maddie to her class as "Kyle" and informed her classmates and teachers that she was now a boy. On an overnight trip, Maddie had even been allowed to sleep in a boys' bunk. No one had informed Katherine, much less asked her permission.

Aghast at what she had begun, Katherine began casting about for anyone who could help or at least share her pain and horror. But those who would raise public objection to transgender ideology were hard to come by; in Katherine's progressive circles, they were nonexistent. She began posting what she had learned on discussion forums about transgender-identified adolescents, alerting parents to the risks of the medications, sharing her own experience—Maddie's psychological entrenchment in her boy identity after having been "affirmed." Her posts, she says, were deleted, and she was banned from discussion boards. Whenever she read an article in the mainstream media celebrating transgender teens, she posted her concerns; several times, she says, her posts were removed.

Katherine's research eventually took her to TransgenderTrend, a UK-based website, and 4thWaveNow, its American counterpart—"gender critical" forums for parents who are skeptical of their adolescents' sudden identification as transgender. 4thWaveNow is one of the largest consortiums of information for those who believe that medical transitioning is neither salutary nor appropriate for most adolescents.

Brie Jontry, the public face of 4thWaveNow, is one of the few moms who was willing to speak to me under her own name, partially because her own daughter, who briefly fell into this craze, has since desisted. "I'm kind of insane in that I believe that the truth protects you, and I'm not ashamed of anything I have to say," Brie told me, adding, "And I gave up my full-time faculty position already." But she did much more than that.

Like Maddie, Brie's daughter had suddenly decided she was transgender after extended internet use. Like Katherine, Brie had taken her daughter to gender therapists. She had even attended a gender conference with Jazz Jennings. Brie Jontry, like Katherine, decided to do her own research after puberty blockers were suggested for her daughter.

Brie called a doctor friend who said, "You know, stopping puberty is going to stop her brain development." That was enough to prompt Brie to halt all talk of medical transition and begin scrutinizing the information the gender clinicians were doling out.

When she realized her daughter seemed to be experiencing more distress as a transgender-identified adolescent than she had before, Brie quit her job and spent a few months traveling with her daughter, to remove her from the social environment in which she'd identified as a boy. Her daughter's friends seemed to be fortifying the trans identity. To undermine that identity, Brie needed to get her away. They moved across the U.S., to the Southwest, where her daughter could start life, redux, once again as a girl.

Brie became active in 4thWaveNow. Everything she learned about sudden trans-identification among adolescent girls, Brie posted to the site: the dangers of Lupron, the known and unknown risks of testosterone, and a deeper look at the suicide statistics that are often used to pressure parents into transitioning their children.

With the help of sites like 4thWaveNow, Katherine Cave began to realize that her daughter had become caught in a cultural current, and she wasn't alone. Katherine had already noticed that a very high percentage of the kids in her daughter's school seemed to be coming out as trans—far more than prevalence numbers for gender dysphoria would have suggested. She rushed to inform Maddie's school of all she had learned, before the teachers encouraged more adolescents along this path. "I thought I was being quite reasonable and giving them evidence and whatever. They treated me like I was the biggest transphobe."

She gave up on the school and decided to focus her efforts on helping her daughter see the harm of transitioning. If she couldn't entirely pry Maddie from the ideological grips of its fanciful science, perhaps she could at least persuade Maddie against self-harm. She got nowhere. "When you have a daughter that's really indoctrinated—and it's almost like a cult really—and it's part of who they think they are, and you yourself have been affirming, the school's been bending over backwards, she's had therapists going along with her new name, that's all solidifying to a young person," she said. Even the medical advice Katherine found online seemed to support Maddie's new identity and the urgency of medical transition. "She has everybody on her side. I mean, I don't have a leg to stand on."

Katherine eventually founded the Kelsey Coalition, an organization devoted to opposing transgender ideology; it's named for Dr. Frances Oldham Kelsey who, back in 1960, had warned the world of the dangers of thalidomide. Katherine has also drafted legislation that would make it illegal for adults to consent to eliminating the future fertility of their children, and has even managed to get some lawmakers to sponsor it. But like most of the mothers of suddenly trans-identified adolescents, she continues to work under a pseudonym, and her sense of isolation is keen.

Many of the mothers of suddenly trans-identifying teenage girls have grown disillusioned with progressivism and disaffected from the Democratic Party, which they believe has abandoned girls for the sake of the transgender cause. Several have been betrayed by progressive friends who went behind their backs to buy their daughters a binder or to give the girls encouragement in what their mothers viewed as a regimen of self-harm.

"This whole thing has shifted how I read, what I believe, the whole concept of an expert," Katherine told me. "I used to think association guidelines were based upon consensus or experts, I just don't believe anything anymore. I can't tell you what my politics are anymore."

○ ○ ○

Katherine can't always be the most effective advocate for her cause. A seemingly tireless worker with a formidable mind, she has read virtually every relevant study and considered every argument. But like most of the mothers—Brie Jontry of 4thWaveNow, as we have seen, being a rare exception—she is handicapped by her need to remain anonymous. She says her relationship with Maddie depends on this. Fair enough. Then again, it's hard to get your message out if no one knows who you are.

Katherine Cave finally agreed to meet me in August 2019, in a rural Southern town to which she and her husband had relocated the family in a desperate attempt to outrun the forces that had ensnared their daughter. Her need to maintain anonymity is ferocious. We met in a hole-in-the-wall coffee shop apparently run by one distracted employee.

I was there to interview her about the subject most urgent and painful to her in the world. But as she strode in, trim and serious, her hair pulled back tight as her nerves, I had the keen sense that I was the one being interviewed. She wore sunglasses propped up along her hairline, light makeup, and a navy halter-top sundress. On Katherine, it might as well have been a power suit.

The fear that her daughter would self-harm haunted Katherine. It struck at odd times and stalked her about her day, like a beeping digital watch buried in the lining of her purse. In the months I'd spent chasing down her claims about the dangers of gender transition—every one of which I was able to verify—I'd become impressed by her smarts, her resourcefulness, the tenacity that fills the hollow of her bones.

In some ways she was a lot like every mother I talked to. Listening to their stories wore me out. These women rose early to take their daughters to practice, abandoned lucrative jobs to homeschool or address any emotional need their children had. They searched out every specialist, shared their daughters' every enthusiasm, and chased down their daughters' interests and talents to afford their girls a moment on stage, a chance to succeed and shine. These women listened—dear God, did they listen—to every tremulous worry and spent nights up late, guessing at those their daughters withheld. They knew the name of every boy their daughters fell for, and every teacher who gave them a hard time. If *these* women had raised daughters who vanished down the rabbit hole of gender ideology, what chance was there for the rest of us?

None of the parents I spoke to was naïve about the pressures or hardship of adolescence. They knew the rigmarole: one day the little girls they had tended through countless flus and rushed to the hospital for casts and stitches would transmogrify into teenagers and curse their love. Every one of the parents I met had been prepared to be hated for a while. They knew their daughters would mock their fashion sense, even reject their values for a time. What they were less prepared for was the macabre spectacle of their daughters' sharp turn against themselves.

Most of the time, I marveled at these women's intelligence, conscientiousness, their breathtaking desire to understand and help their daughters. Occasionally, I wondered whether they hadn't unintentionally inspired their daughters' deep dive into an ideology that seemed inseparable from teenage rebellion—the irresistible chance to stick it to mom.

The mothers had worked so hard to meet their daughters where they were—to share their fads and enthusiasms, from emo to anime. They embraced their daughters' announcements of allegiance to atheism, communism, and their epiphanies about being gay. They needed their daughters to be happy and successful—and maybe, looking back, they needed this too much.

Sometimes I wondered whether all this open-mindedness hadn't robbed their daughters of the rebellion they so badly seemed to want. Maybe if they had put up monstrous opposition to, say, their daughters' joining the Gay–Straight Alliance in middle school, maybe if they hadn't been there with camera and hugs when their daughters wore a tux to prom—maybe if they'd faked horror or moral opprobrium they didn't feel and unleashed a tirade or lecture or fit of exasperation worthy of a John Hughes movie, maybe their daughters would have declared victory and deemed their War of Independence a success.

When Angela and I first spoke, her daughter was in her junior year of high school and had suddenly come out as "trans." Seven months later, when I talked to Angela again, her daughter had walked away from her "trans boy" identity and settled on "non-binary." In fact, she had a boyfriend.

I asked Angela about her daughter's sexuality—whether she thought her daughter was straight or gay. She laughed and said that she remembered when her daughter was very young, she had chased a boy around a playground, trying to kiss him. And, of course, Angela's daughter had a boyfriend now, though Angela suspected he might consider himself "queer" or some other member of LGBTQ. "They all do," she said, referring to her daughter's high school classmates.

Complicating the issue of her daughter's sexuality, now that she thought about it, was the fact that when she hit middle school her daughter had "developed a crush or two on girls."

Then Angela said this: "But I also have heard from psychiatrists who say that, especially for girls around that age, early adolescence, it's very common to develop crushes on their friends. In fact," she told me, "when I was a kid, I believe that I had had crushes."

I was intrigued that Angela would need to consult a psychiatrist about whether adolescent girls who seemed to have had crushes on other girls could eventually emerge as heterosexual. This was something she had known from her own experience, as I knew from mine. Angela had even recently found a letter she herself had written to another girlfriend when she was an adolescent, so saccharine, she said, that she could only describe it as a "love letter."

This is so common an experience that it hardly seems worthy of mention—as inseparable from adolescent girlhood as braces and training bras. Stirred by romantic feeling, filled to the brim with love, girls of twelve and thirteen cast their gaze toward those adorable, ridiculous sops—boys of twelve or thirteen—who are entirely emotionally unprepared to receive it. Disappointed, sometimes rejected, they transfer all that feeling—so much affection and loyalty, so many assurances of devotion—to their girlfriends, who stand in as placeholders, while they wait for the boys to grow up.

Angela concluded, "So I think that my daughter is maybe bi, but right now, she seems to have a boyfriend."

I marveled over that conversation for days. What Angela was content to dismiss as a meaningless phase in herself became evidence of an outré sexual identity in her daughter. So many of the mothers I spoke to seemed to feel the need to decide—right then—what their daughter "really was," sexually speaking, as if anything important hung on this.

We are, all of us, so quick to diagnose ourselves in every way—including sexually and, now, in gender terms; it is a habit the next generation has picked up. Were it not for this compulsion to categorize and diagnose, minor bouts of anxiety, depression, obsession, romantic impulse, sexual inclination, and all manner of good and bad feelings might be left to grow, develop, change course, or die off.

RICHARD

In January 2019, my piece on the sudden spike in transgender identification among teenage girls appeared in the *Wall Street Journal*. I was flooded with emails and calls. Most of those who contacted me were mothers. Many said they had witnessed the phenomenon I had described at their own adolescents' schools and had no idea it was playing itself out across the country. They noticed that the incidence of trans-identification among their children's friends seemed much higher than anything they might have imagined. As one mom said, *all* of her daughter's friends "identify as transgender, or lesbian or gay or bi."

Nearly all of these parents were highly educated, upper-middle-class, white, and politically progressive, but I also encountered a few religious people and coastal conservatives—those who vote Republican but support gay marriage; those who believe in small government, but have no real interest in seeing *Roe v. Wade* overturned.

Richard was among them, and he first contacted me through LinkedIn after he read my piece, excited for the first time to recognize what his daughter was going through. His daughter, Joanna, had been a feminine girl, even boy crazy off and on, before announcing a pansexual, non-binary, and then trans identity in her last year of a progressive private high school. Richard and his wife Rachelle agreed to allow her to attend the top-tier university to which she was admitted on the condition that she promise not to medically transition while at college.

It was a promise Joanna broke almost immediately. With the help of a college mental health counselor, she obtained a prescription for testosterone covered by her school health plan. Although she talked to her mother nearly every day, she only informed her parents that she had started testosterone after she had been on it for months.

"She thinks she looks like a guy," he told me. "She's got the hair on her arms and everything, but she's beautiful. They were actually calling her 'sir' [on our vacation], which was crazy. To me, she doesn't look like anything but my daughter."

By the time his daughter came home that summer, she had legally changed her name. "She's done all this stuff without telling us," Richard said. "And the top surgery thing, she went in for a consultation with the doctors and then submitted a request to the insurance company, so I come home with it, and I see, I opened this letter, it's addressed to her from the insurance company. . . . So I saw it and I was like, oh wow. . . . [T]here's a whole different world of stuff that's just being done secretly, surreptitiously, and it's so damaging to the relationship." He told his daughter flatly that if she went through with this, their relationship would never be the same.

At times, his voice hardened to fury. He sounded ready to break walls. He blamed his daughter's foolishness, her "echo chamber" of friends, her enabling psychologists, so many trans "friends" she had made on the internet, the mental health counselor at college—a "wrecking ball for families"—and the trans-embracing culture that pervaded her top-tier university and allowed his daughter to become a campus leader by virtue of her trans identification. But really, these were just stand-ins for his real punching bag. "My feeling is one of pity and failure. Pity for [my wife] and failure for me."

Four months later, I received this text from him: "Well we lost the battle. Daughter had breasts removed last week. Thought we had seen her position change. I sent my kid an impassioned commentary on all the reasons not to harm herself further and plan obstacles to her professional success. . . 3.8 Gpa . . . yet zero job offers or interest. Announced it on Instagram I'm told. Total fail for me."

That was how Richard cloaked his anguish—in a series of assertive, sometimes aggressive factual statements, which alternately expressed despair, contempt, fury, and gruff indifference. Richard is a partner at a prominent international law firm, prone to tough talk, head-on confrontation with other men, chivalry with women. I met him at a cafe downstairs from his office. He asked for my parking card and had it validated. We were on his turf, and he seemed to assume it was his job to take care of me. When I fumbled for a moment with the cellophane wrapping on my cookie, he took it from me, opened it, handed it back. It was the sort of thing another generation might have called good manners, but I think it was at least partly a diversion.

He couldn't bear talking about his daughter but also couldn't stop himself—his blue eyes going watery at the mention of her name—talking about her brilliance, her academic success, her beauty. By the end of our first conversation, I knew, beyond doubt, what he never expressly said: She was the person he loved most in the world. She had broken his heart.

He told me about all he had done to find her a good, safe apartment and to provide the down payment. He was also subsidizing her rent. He called her "my kid" over and over. There was no trace of the relationship breakdown he had threatened if she went through with the double mastectomy. She had called his bluff and won.

I met with Joanna's parents separately and expected their stories to diverge a little, based on which details of Joanna's life each considered most salient or explanatory. What surprised me was that, for all of their discrepancies about how best to handle their daughter, different inclinations as to what had gone wrong and why, they were in complete agreement that their daughter wasn't on a good path. That none of this gender journeying had done their daughter very much good.

Rachelle filled in many more of the details of Joanna's life over the years—exactly which grade she started therapy, when she got her first prescription for Prozac. What boys she had liked, that she had had sex with a boy, and when, in her junior year, the switch to girls came.

Rachelle and Richard had different approaches to something they both saw as a problem. Richard tried hard to reason with Joanna, since his daughter was, as he said over and over, one of the smartest people he knew. Rachelle merely stayed close to her. When Joanna was in high school, Rachelle committed to going through all of Joanna's phases with her—emo, goth, girly girl. Even toward the end of high school, when Joanna decided she was non-binary and then trans, Rachelle and her daughter remained emotionally close. "My belief has always been, if I loved her enough, she wouldn't do this. And then I came to the realization, after she started the testosterone, that she was going to do this."

Rachelle has always been a progressive. She grew up in the fashion industry because her father worked in jewelry. Her family was, for generations, always very comfortable with homosexuality, long before many Americans were. The thing that Rachelle can't seem to get past is how different homosexuality is from being transgender.

Homosexuality has always been around, she assured me. But this transgender epidemic—this is new. "This trans thing? I feel like it came up five years ago and everybody jumped on the bandwagon. And to tell me that it's always been there, when I grew up in the heart of the fashion industry—it wasn't."

THE THERAPY LANGUAGE GAME

Like a lot of the moms, I once believed therapy a good exercise, the sort of thing that promotes self-awareness and discourages the punching of walls. But in the course of writing this book, I became aware of just how much therapy the next generation is receiving, for matters big and small. We Gen X moms consider ourselves more psychologically healthy than our parents. We believe in therapy like we believe in working out—something one does to build strength and maintain balance.

One side effect may be that the next generation is coming to see all human emotion as a sign of mental illness—something to medicate, curb, give therapy for, or otherwise blot out. As Jungian analyst Lisa Marchiano has observed, "When we construe normal feelings as illness, we offer people an understanding of themselves as disordered."[2]

Nearly all of the mothers I spoke to offered me diagnoses of their daughters provided by therapists, the internet, or a book. They suspected their daughters might be a touch autistic or have auditory processing issues or agoraphobia. They may all be right, but I couldn't help wondering whether the process of diagnosis wasn't itself altering the outcome, helping to convince suggestible daughters that there really was something wrong with them.

By the time they reached adolescence, self-focus and self-diagnosis had become an ingrained habit, a way to handle feelings that confused them. With the rest of the culture, they had been reared to participate in a therapy language game, in which everyone has *some* mental illness and the only question is what code to offer insurance.

In listening to the mothers, I could not help wondering what diagnoses I would have received, had my parents been a little more forward-thinking, psychologically speaking. Social anxiety? Without question. Generalized anxiety? There too. But my parents, being boomers, applied a moral vocabulary instead of a psychological one. What might now be catered to or treated as "social phobia," my parents admonished as "rude." And they enlisted me in a treatment of their own devising: As a child of seven or eight, I was compelled to order off the menu from waitresses myself, ask for help from sales clerks, and hand over the money to the cashier, counting the change. By middle school, I was compelled to recite this little speech every time I phoned one of my friends: "Hello, Mrs. Pevenstein, this is Abigail. How are you? May I please speak to Deborah?" I can't say I particularly enjoyed any of those moments.

What is more, the mothers' penchant for diagnosis does not seem to confine itself to the psychological realm but extends to the sexual one as well. With similar deliberateness, they described daughters as young as eleven as "pansexual" or "bi" or "probably gay." They seemed to assume that their prepubescent daughters' sexualities were already fully formed, and that careful observation would reveal it.

One mother, Angela, an editor from the Washington, D.C., area, was a case in point. Strikingly intelligent, utterly devoted to her daughter—an only child—Angela possessed an abiding belief in the power and constructiveness of talk therapy. She first took her daughter to a therapist at age three, when the little girl started to show signs of the obsessive-compulsive personality disorder that had plagued Angela as well. The therapist told Angela that her daughter was "within normal range" and sent her home. By her daughter's second grade year, Angela had her back on the couch, this time to help her daughter deal with the anxiety brought on by the death of a kitten.

I'm not doubting that the little girl's anxiety was real, that therapy was a caring response, or that her psychological struggles worsened over time. Indeed, by middle school, Angela's daughter's anxiety had risen, and she was engaging in minor cutting.

But it is worth noting that a generation ago, mothers' reactions to their daughters' anxiety would likely have been to ignore, dismiss, or perhaps admonish. As in, "Don't you ever hurt yourself. If you're feeling sad, just tell me." Or, "Why don't we take you to the mall for some ice cream?" Or even, "You're making a big deal out of nothing."

In small children, sadness and dread may naturally worry us, depending on the severity and duration. But with teens, careening between doldrums, rage, and euphoria was long understood to be relatively normal, the psychological analog to puberty itself.

Today's adolescents, practiced in therapy, have assimilated its vocabulary. They can tell you what sorts of social situations they find emotionally challenging and the precise contours of the psychological problem that's to blame—"social anxiety," "testing anxiety," "panic attack," and so forth. Such diagnoses have a way of reifying the problems they describe.

Therapy is predicated on the conceit that our thoughts and feelings must always be monitored. That any swing to one side is cause for alarm, and that even minor disturbances ought to be listened for and deciphered, like faint signals from a distant planet. Almost by definition and certainly in practice, therapists lead adolescents deeper into the forests of their minds. Is it any wonder, then, that it's so hard for them to find a way out?

Having long ago accepted that something must really be wrong with them, the only task left is to diagnose it.

CHAPTER SIX

THE SHRINKS

A woman walks into a therapist's office, dragging her teenage son. "Doctor," she says. "Please help! My son thinks he's a chicken."

The son says: "If there is one thing I can tell you about chickens, it's that we know who we are."

"Where is your proof?" the woman demands of her son. "You have no feathers."

"True," the son replies. "I went through the wrong puberty."

The woman turns to the therapist: "You see what I mean? He's lost his mind!"

The therapist replies: "You're the one arguing with a chicken."

Yes, it's an absurdist joke. But this is, roughly, the scenario created by "affirmative care," the prevailing medical standard for the treatment of transgender patients. The standard asks—against much evidence, and sometimes contrary to their beliefs on the matter—that mental health professionals "affirm" not only the patient's self-diagnosis of dysphoria but also the accuracy of the patients' perception. The therapist must agree, in other words, that a male patient with gender dysphoria who identifies as a woman *really is* a woman.

There is nothing particularly outlandish in feeling discomfort in one's own body or in suspecting that one might feel better in another. There are so many things about our physical forms that cause us distress and regret. We lug around bodies we would never have chosen. Anyone who has ever had the unpleasant sensation of looking in the mirror and being startled by the age of the woman staring back—the blanching, the slack, the lines that stole their way in while you slept—is well acquainted with our bodies' ability to confuse and shock and disappoint.

For those with gender dysphoria, this unpleasantness must be excruciating, and we should expect mental health professionals to be respectful of it, sympathetic to those who bear it, and understanding of their pain—even perhaps by supporting medical transition. I have spoken to several transgender adults who are living good, productive lives, in stable relationships and flourishing in their careers. I believe there are instances in which gender dysphoric people have been helped by gender transition.

But the new "affirmative-care" standard of mental health professionals is a different matter entirely. It surpasses sympathy and leaps straight to demanding that mental health professionals adopt their patients' beliefs of being in the "wrong body." Affirmative therapy compels therapists to endorse a falsehood: not that a teenage girl feels more comfortable presenting as a boy—but that she actually *is* a boy.

This is not a subtle distinction, and it isn't just a matter of humoring a patient. The whole course of appropriate treatment hinges on whether doctors view the patient as a biological girl suffering mental distress or a boy in a girl's body.

But the "affirmative-care" standard, which chooses between these diagnoses before the patient is even examined, has been adopted by nearly every medical accrediting organization. The American Medical Association, the American College of Physicians, the American Academy of Pediatrics, the American Psychological Association, and the Pediatric Endocrine Society have all endorsed "gender-affirming care" as the standard for treating patients who self-identify as "transgender" or self-diagnose as "gender dysphoric."

As the World Professional Association for Transgender Health (WPATH) standards, consulted by nearly every field of medicine, advise, "Health professionals can assist gender dysphoric individuals with affirming their gender identity, exploring different options for expressing that identity, and making decisions about medical treatment options for alleviating dysphoria."[1] Notice whose medical judgment is in the driver's seat. Hint: it isn't the doctor's.

GENDER-AFFIRMING CARE

The American Psychological Association's Guidelines for Care of Transgender and Gender Nonconforming (TGNC) patients defines "transgender affirming care" as "the provision of care that is respectful, aware, and supportive of the identities and life experiences of TGNC people."[2]

Respect and support doesn't seem like so much to ask; in fact, it would seem a standard *all* patients ought to be afforded. But the APA guidelines go much further, mandating that mental health professionals adopt gender ideology themselves.

The guidelines state, "Psychologists are encouraged to adapt or modify their understanding of gender, broadening the range of variation viewed as healthy and normative. By understanding the spectrum of gender identities and gender expressions that exist, and that a person's gender identity may not be in full alignment with sex assigned at birth, psychologists can increase their capacity to assist TGNC people, their families, and their communities."[3]

Imagine we treated anorexics this way. Imagine a girl—5'6" tall, 95 pounds—approaches her therapist and says: "I just know I'm fat. Please call me 'Fatty.'" Imagine the APA encouraged its doctors to "modify their understanding" of what constitutes "fat" to include this emaciated girl. Imagine the APA encouraged therapists to respond to such patients, "If you feel fat, then you are. I support your lived experience. Okay, Fatty?"

Or what about a black girl who has internalized the racism of her peers? Suppose Nia, twelve years old, informs her therapist that she desperately wants to become white. She wasn't sure about this for a while, but then she saw these white girls on YouTube who were just so amazing, and that's when she knew what she was supposed to be. "Call me Heather," the girl pleads. "I want my ugly nose narrowed," she says. "And I hate my hair; I want it to be straight and blonde. I want my skin bleached. There are creams; I know—I've read about them. I was never meant to look this way. Anyway, I don't *feel* black. I find white boys cute. I'm not good at basketball or singing; I'm more into hiking and playing acoustic guitar. I like the TV and food that white girls like. I'm basically white already."[4]

Imagine if the therapist said, "Okay, Heather. Nobody knows who you *really are* better than you. So based on what I'm hearing today, I can absolutely affirm that you are Caucasian. See, sometimes white people are born with black bodies and features. I can bring your dad up to speed on the medical interventions, but even if he doesn't agree, you should know this is a safe space. I will always respect who you *really are*. We'll talk about how to procure those creams at our next session."

We wouldn't think such a therapist was compassionate. We might think she was a monster. Nia has offered meaningless stereotypes as evidence that she's not "really" black. We would expect any half-decent therapist to challenge these ideas she has, to push back on their substance, to expose their source. Who put this rot into this child's head? How had she tragically come to ingest and internalize these racist archetypes? Body dysmorphia has grotesquely exaggerated her features in the image staring back at her from the mirror. The problem's in her mind, not her face.

Race is a far more trivial biological feature than sex. Unlike male and female—of which there are statistically insignificant abnormal variations—race really does admit a spectrum.

And yet the moment a girl like Nia presented herself to a therapist, we would cry out for the therapist not to encourage the girl's distorted perception. There's nothing wrong with her nose, any more than there was for the numberless Jewish girls who rushed to get nose jobs in the 1960s, hoping to achieve a different ethnic beauty ideal. Nia is beautiful just as she is, and anyway, she's a teenager. We wouldn't tolerate any therapist encouraging her to make irreversible body modifications while she was still sorting herself out. We'd expect a therapist worth her salt to challenge Nia's self-destructive intentions. We'd want that therapist to gently probe, to get to the root of her unhappiness: Why on earth did Nia start believing there was something wrong with being African American? It's a wonderful, beautiful thing to be.

Was it something someone said to you, Nia? When did you start hating your nose, can you remember? What's wrong with it? Have I shown you this picture of Beyoncé? She has hair like yours—do you think she's ugly? Have you heard of Naomi Sims? Does she look ugly to you in this photo? Because she didn't to millions of Americans; she was an inspiration. What is your idea of African American that makes you feel you aren't really one? Did you know there are African Americans who have shared your interests, your hobbies, your passions, too? Do you think that made them any less African American, merely because they bucked a few stereotypes? They didn't think so.

Truly the last thing any of us would countenance from therapists is this response to an anorexic: "If you think you're fat, then you are, and we can talk about weight-loss programs and liposuction." Or, to Nia: "If you say you're white, then you are. There are treatments that we can explore to fix your coloring. I have a great plastic surgeon for you."

We would expect compassion from any therapist who works with adolescents. We would demand that they listen. We would hope that the therapists achieve understanding. But we would never want them to automatically agree with the patient's self-diagnosis—both because that is so likely to strengthen the patient's flawed self-perception and because agreeing with the patient's self-assessment has never been a mental health expert's job. In fact, it still isn't the mental health professional's job with regard to any other psychiatric condition.[5]

But it is undeniably the current professional mandate of therapists and psychiatrists and even endocrinologists and pediatricians to accept and "affirm" the self-diagnosis of gender dysphoric patients. The American Psychological Association guidelines even recommend that mental health professionals take "affirmative involvement as allies" in the transgender community,[6] insisting that what trans-identified patients need is "respectful treatment that addresses their gender identity in an affirming manner."[7]

Interestingly, although the only relevant medical diagnosis is "gender dysphoria," the APA guidelines talk about the treatment of "transgender" people. In other words, the APA has given up the vocabulary and perhaps even the methods of medicine in dealing with this population and entered the world of politics. It is worth asking whether a standard guided less by biology than by political correctness is in the best interest of patients.

THE THERAPISTS

Randi Kaufman isn't the only gender-affirmative therapist I spoke to, but she is undoubtedly the most prominent. An expert in both gender identity and gender expression, she works with kids age ten and up at the Gender & Family Project of the prestigious Ackerman Institute for the Family in New York City. She has determined gender-nonconforming youths' fitness for medical intervention at Boston Children's Hospital/ Harvard Medical School. And in 2004 she founded the Transgender Health Program at Fenway Health in Boston to provide mental health and medical care to transgender adults.

As for the affirmative-care model, if Dr. Kaufman didn't quite write the book, she certainly contributed a chapter. You'll find hers in the canonical work on gender-affirmative therapy, *The Gender Affirmative Model: An Interdisciplinary Approach to Supporting Transgender and Gender Expansive Children.*

In researching the theory and practice of gender-affirmative therapy, I spoke with a number of psychotherapists specializing in gender issues, including some who are transgender themselves. More than one told me it was not their job to question an adolescent patient's stated gender identity, but instead to facilitate the patient's range of options. One therapist's website, I discovered, promises he will never serve as a "gatekeeper" between patients and their gender hormones or surgeries; he guarantees a same-day first-consultation letter of fitness for gender medical interventions.[8] Another informed me that if I wanted to know anything about gender-affirmative therapy, I needed to speak to Randi Kaufman.

So what does Randi Kaufman believe transgender-identified teenagers need from their parents and therapists? "Well, what I would say is that there are certain things that transgender and non-binary adolescents really need for good mental health—and I'd say the single most important factor is to start with family support and acceptance," Dr. Kaufman said. "There are studies that show that adolescent children who are supported by their family, the suicide rate drops dramatically and mental health increases and that gets borne out over time."

Suicide rates are often cited by gender therapists as a reason to immediately affirm a child or adolescent's stated gender identity and sometimes even as a reason to allow them to medically transition. Of course, the very prospect that their child might self-harm would bring all but the coldest parents to their knees. If adopting her new name and pronouns and buying her new opposite-sex clothing is what it takes to keep her alive, most parents would leap aboard the gender train. According to gender-affirming therapists, this is not only advisable, it is the bare minimum required for parental support.

"[P]art of the acceptance means now understanding that this child is going through a gender journey, whatever it may look like. And you know, many kids and adolescents do transition, but not everyone does," Dr. Kaufman told me. "And transition can look different for different people. Some people do social transition only, some people do social and medical transition, some people do surgical not medical. So it really varies what people choose to do or not do but the most important thing is to recognize that someone who feels like they're not cisgender, in whatever way they identify, they need to be supported and affirmed in that gender."

Asking your daughter, *Are you out of your mind?* is clearly off-limits, then. So is, *No, I will not call you "Clive."* And *We don't even eat hormone-raised beef, for God's sake!* Put out of your mind every manner of very understandable parental interjection. You don't want your child to hang "himself" in the garage just because you accidentally referred to her as "Rebecca."

But according to gender-affirmative therapists, offering a trans-identified teen appropriate support requires not merely getting the terminology right. It requires the mental feat of *believing* it. Your daughter is gone; you now have a son. *Mazel tov!*

To support and affirm their child's journey, Dr. Kaufman told me, parents must "believe what their child says, while also understanding both that it may or may not change over time and that part of that journey means staying in step with their child each step of the way and seeing where it goes."

It's worth noting how different this is from being the parent of a gay adolescent. An adolescent who comes out as gay asks her parents to accept her for what she *is*. An adolescent who is transgender-identified asks to be accepted for what she *is not*. Even the most loving parent might be forgiven for failing this mind-bending test.

If an adolescent's understanding of her gender "may or may not change over time," how can a parent possibly support body modification? Why would parents permit their daughter to "socially transition" in school if the next year she may wish to take it all back? "By adolescence, most adolescents have a pretty good sense of how to discern the differences between things like gender identity, gender role and gender expression, which is how you express your gender with your dress, your hair, your mannerisms, your names, your pronouns, things like that," Dr. Kaufman assured me. "It's pretty rare by adolescence for people to change their mind."

But how rare is "pretty rare"? When you're contemplating injections that may permanently alter your daughter's facial features, enlarge her clitoris, leave her covered in body hair, and perhaps render her infertile, is the "pretty rare" chance that she might change her mind rare enough?

Here's when, in my various conversations with gender-affirming therapists, they typically told me to slow down. No one said we had to jump to medical treatments, did we? This is fundamentally a wait-and-see approach. The important thing to do when an adolescent comes to you with a new gender identity is to listen to them, believe them, employ their new names and pronouns, buy them new clothes, and ask whatever else you can do to make their lives easy. "I would say being attuned and supportive means you follow the child's lead. So if the child wants to go by a new name and pronoun, then you follow that. And names and pronouns—the importance of them cannot be over-emphasized," Dr. Kaufman told me. "That is something that really shows support. And even if it's challenging for the parent to change names or pronouns, it's very important that they work at it."

"Why?" I asked her—wondering if these poor parents hadn't already been troubled enough.

"Imagine if someone started to call you by a male name and pronoun," she said. "It wouldn't feel like it's you, and it would feel disrespectful, right? We don't really think about that. What if suddenly someone was calling you 'Andy' instead of 'Abigail,' and you'd be like, *'What's up with that?'*"

Try as it might, this notion had trouble working itself through the crusty loam of my cisgender brain. But wait. This is an adolescent we're talking about. She's been called, say, "Rebecca" her whole life. In what sense would this be a shock and trauma for her parents to continue to do what they'd always done—use the name they'd given her? Refer to her as their "daughter"? It wasn't *they* who had changed the rules.

I was beginning to feel like a rotten student, and I could sense Dr. Kaufman expertly exercising her considerable patience with me on the other end of the line. "Well," she said, "because the child feels like the parent hasn't understood or recognized who they are, which they haven't. If a little boy grows up believing that he's actually a little girl and the parents are calling him John and he wants to be known as Julia, and he realizes 'I'm really Julia and this is all wrong,' and the parents say, 'No, we know better than you,' I mean, think about it: We don't question an eight-year-old girl who says she's a girl. Why would we question an eight-year-old who says they're actually a boy even though they're assigned a girl at birth, when the child was too young to know or articulate who they are?"

We had landed somewhere new: Dr. Kaufman seemed to be introducing an ontology—one in which chromosomal DNA is no more determinative of identity than the ineffable feelings of an eight-year-old. "Doctors make an assignment based on external genitalia," Dr. Kaufman informed me. "But we know that anatomy does not necessarily line up nicely and neatly with someone's gender identity. A majority of people feel their anatomy lines up with how they identify, but some people do not and that's a normal variation on the human experience."

But wouldn't all the variation and inconstancy of a "gender journey" seem to provide reason to keep calling your kid what you always have? No, gender therapists will tell you, because adolescents know who they are—even if they later change their minds. "I think the most important thing to know about gender is that for some people, it's really fluid and it can remain fluid throughout life," Dr. Kaufman told me. "We don't really think about it that way. We think about it being fixed and for some people it is, and for some people, it's not," she said.

"I think as a society, if we get more comfortable with the idea of gender being fluid and not necessarily being binary, and we allow for people to shift over time, some people will do more of that and it won't be considered such a problem if someone wants to transition one way at one point in life and maybe transition another way at a different point in life. And there are people who want that."

As for the parents, Tennyson once wrote about another group of battle-worn soldiers doomed to failure: "Theirs not to make reply / Theirs not to reason why." So what if they can't understand it? Their job is not to challenge their adolescents or put the brakes on their gender journey, or even to question it. They are there to follow their teenagers' lead. To "listen to" their children. To do as requested. To adopt a new worldview, one that regards biological sex as "gender assigned at birth"—something as malleable as "name assigned at birth."

But what about all those parents who can't get these ideas through their thick skulls? What about, say, religious Christians or Muslims or Jews who insist on a gender binary, merely because people have done so for thousands of years?

"I tell them that we can't change the mind and so we have to change the body," Dr. Kaufman said. "That's sort of the nutshell. I would let them know that if someone identifies this way, it's pretty rare that they would change their mind. We have known that we can't socialize someone into or out of a gender."

In this way, being transgender is like being gay, Dr. Kaufman explained to me. We know you can't convert someone out of being gay. "So I would tell these parents, we can't convert someone to being cisgender. They are who they are. And your choice is to learn to accept this and support your child, or if you don't, what I see coming in the future is, this child is going to be very mentally unhealthy and unhappy and will likely—if they're not already—become depressed, anxious, not function well, not being able to get on with life; not do well in school, not have friends. May be suicidal—may try to commit suicide. May be self-harming. May kill themselves. That's what you can expect."

It's a gun to the head: do as your kid says, or she just might take her own life. Again and again, I heard this question from gender therapists and also from parents to whom they had spoken: "*Would you rather a dead daughter or a live son?*"

THE THEORY OF GENDER AFFIRMATION

The weltanschauung of gender-affirmative therapy rests on several key claims. A great many irreversible medical outcomes depend on it being good theory. Is it?

1. *"Adolescents know who they are."*

For those of you who have ever been an adolescent or attempted the toe-curling, hair-whitening endeavor of raising one—hold your laughter. Resist the urge to squeal out loud at the preposterous notion that a teenager in any sense knows who she is with the level of certainty sufficient to entrust her with life-altering decisions.

Exponents of gender affirmation often argue that, unlike childhood gender dysphoria, which shows very high rates of desistance when no affirmation or transition is made, adolescent dysphoria has higher rates of persistence into adulthood.[9] It's hard to evaluate this claim since there is no long-term study to prove it. Those studies that exist are based largely on samples of adolescents whose onset of gender dysphoria began in early childhood.[10]

What studies *do* show is that nearly all adolescents who identify as transgender *and are put on puberty blockers* go on to take cross-sex hormones in adulthood.[11] Of course, that does not prove that these adolescents "knew who they were"; at most, it proves that if you *medically halt a kid's puberty so that they do not obtain secondary sex characteristics*, while also socially affirming their new gender identity, that adolescent will be less likely to later reverse course.

Teenagers test boundaries. They press limits. They question authority. Erik Erikson called identity formation the key task of adolescence for a reason: identity isn't already formed. More than adults and even young children, adolescents typically engage in a profound period of tumultuous self-discovery. So why on earth would we presume they have already discovered everything about themselves?

A funny thing about wanting body modifications—small changes, like a tattoo, or more invasive ones, like a nose job, liposuction, or even a double mastectomy: we're often sure that if we just had that thing, we'd be a lot happier. We're very good at knowing what it is we want right now; far less good at predicting whether the object of our desire will produce the satisfaction we take for granted.

The reason we typically discourage teenagers from making significant alterations to their identities or bodies—religious conversion, name changes, tattoos, and so forth—is not only because they so often fail at predicting what they will want in the future, when their identities are more fully formed and their hormones have calmed down. Even adults regret major decisions they made about their lives post-adolescence. And yet, as a society, we tend to trust adults to make them. What teenagers fail at so miserably is avoiding risky behaviors that their peers approve of.[12] Turns out, adolescents really care what their friends think—quite a lot, in fact—and this distorts all kinds of choices they make.

Teenagers take more risks than any other age group. They may even be neurologically inclined toward risk, especially where peer approval is on the line.[13] It isn't just that teenagers do dumb things. It's that, when faced with their peers, they almost can't help themselves. The prefrontal cortex, believed to hold the seat of self-regulation, typically does not complete development until age twenty-five.[14]

But what about those sober teenagers, the careful, thoughtful ones? The ones who did their homework, studied hard, got into good schools, occasionally even made sense? For most of my teenage years, I fell into this awkward camp, the ones who took "internships" and did our homework without being asked, maybe even enjoying it (though we were always careful to deny it).

By my freshman year of college I had come to realize a few things about myself, including this: I hated the way my clothing pulled and puckered, the way the center button on every shirt looked ready to pop. I could never wear sleeveless shirts without exposing a moon slice of bra. I hated that I couldn't wear normal bathing suits, without the built-in shelving. I could never own a sexy bra. I was confined to the more industrial apparatuses, those that involved feats of engineering and came in various shades of drab. Each so hideously practical, so wholly impervious to fun. I discussed it with my best friend, and she heartily agreed: things would be much better for me if I went down a cup size or two. I informed my parents: I had decided to get a breast reduction.

I knew my mother might put up some protest, what with her genetic bequest at issue. What I hadn't anticipated was my father's opposition. He said absolutely not. No way. He said there was nothing wrong with me, that I looked like a woman should, even if I couldn't see that now. He added that I might want to breastfeed one day. This needless surgery could put that capacity at risk, and for what?

I assured him there was no chance I would want to nurse any babies. (At the time, I was utterly failing to rouse myself for 9:00 a.m. Hebrew class. I was pretty sure my future children's lack of access to breast milk would be the least of their problems.) Besides, breastfeeding? Did I look like an imbecile? I felt certain bottles and formulas had been developed for a reason.

I had neither the money nor the imagination to plow ahead with a breast reduction without my parents' buy-in, so my plan more or less ended there. (The "like a woman should" comment, which I had pretended to ignore, comforted me—as only reassurance from my father could—that one day, just as I was, I would capture the right man's attraction and love.) But even a year or two later, as I grew more comfortable in my body, or at least resigned to it, I was still sure my father was wrong: there was simply no way I was going to want to breastfeed a child. This wasn't the Middle Ages, and I would no more forego the magic of baby formula than I would that of vaccines.

More than a decade later, I would nurse three children—one of the most profoundly tender undertakings of my life. There are other ways of transmitting comfort to a newborn, of course, but nursing is among the most effective. It facilitates communication with the most vulnerable creature imaginable, who knows no language but is mercifully programmed to imbibe a mother's calm. Nursing, I discovered, is its own kind of lullaby, a private mother-and-baby song. But the thought that forgoing it would be any kind of loss was as foreign to me in adolescence as it is obvious to me now.

I offer this personal story as a reminder of how imperfect our knowledge of our future desires is, how cavalier adolescents often are with risks they are in no position to assess, especially when faced with the encouragement of friends. This is not a reason to proscribe all identity alterations or body modifications for teenagers—it is merely cause for hesitation. A reason to be skeptical of the idea that teenagers' self-diagnoses should be automatically accepted, especially when the terminus of that new identity involves dangerous surgeries.

Even gender therapists—for those paying attention—effectively concede that adolescents' knowledge of their gender identities is imperfect. Dr. Kaufman described identity formation for teens as a "journey," noting that many adolescents turn out to be "gender fluid"—that is, tending to change their minds about what their gender really is or should be. And, according to her, there is no way of knowing ex ante which distressed teenagers claiming gender dysphoria will likely turn out to be not "trans" but "fluid."

The many desisters and detransitioners already writing and talking about their own experiences, some of whom we'll meet in Chapter Ten, provide proof enough: some percentage of adolescents who claim certainty of their transgender identity will change their minds. We have no way at this time of predicting which of them will fall into this group. In the absence of mental health professionals' ability to predict this, it would seem obviously unwise to encourage teenagers to make any significant life changes on behalf of a feeling that may soon flip or subside.

This is not to say that a therapist shouldn't explore a teenager's ideas about gender identity and expression; that would seem a role of therapy. But affirming is the endorsement and encouragement of a feeling. Affirming is likely to reify and harden an idea. In the absence of the ability to predict which teenagers will prove "fluid," it seems worth asking how psychological and medical associations could mandate that doctors immediately assent to these patients' (or any patients') self-diagnosis.

2. *"Social transition and affirmation is a 'no lose' proposition."*

A common response to the problem I just raised is that therapists and parents might as well affirm trans-identifying kids and adolescents because affirmation causes no harm. In response to my question of whether there was anything to lose by social affirmation, Dr. Kaufman said flatly: "No, there's nothing to lose."

Parents often worry that if they permit their children to socially transition, something irrevocable will have occurred. "Let's say . . . they change names and pronouns and they go to a different bathroom and they change their hairstyle and their clothing," she said. "And let's say in three years they start to go through adolescence and puberty and they decide, 'You know what? I'm gonna go back to being a boy,' and it's really fine. And then they need to sort of transition back."

Dr. Kaufman explained that there is "not a lot of data out there" on the effects of social transition on adolescents. But she still maintains, "Generally, it's a lot more harmful to a child to not go with a transition in the first place, even if they transition back, than it is to wait and say, 'No, you can't make this decision. You're not old enough' or 'You don't know your own mind.' Those can be very damaging things for children and adolescents."

Faced with this dire prognosis, many parents understandably give in. Any parent who has ever refused an adolescent knows how much strength such stands require. The most persistent street hustlers have nothing on the average teen faced with something she wants.

Commence the rewriting of history: your daughter is not only a boy, she somehow *always was*. So fine, call Grandma, and tell her Janet is now Jorge. Let her use the boys' bathrooms and play on the boys' teams—the therapist said it was riskier not to. And if she later changes her mind—no harm, no foul? That's gender therapists' claim: that social transitioning can always be readily and harmlessly undone.

Is this right? "The truth is that our identities are socially negotiated," said Lisa Marchiano, Jungian analyst and an outspoken critic of gender-affirmative therapy.

It's a heckuva point: Social transition, by definition, is a communal activity, requiring the buy-in of others. It insists on the community's participation in this new identity. It requires that others accede to certain practices, if not entirely adopt the belief themselves. And it may even increase an adolescent's dissatisfaction with her body: Once you've cemented her belief that she really *is*—or is supposed to be—actually a boy, her given body can only be an endless source of disappointment to her.

Years ago, I was writing a Holocaust-era work of historical fiction that required me to spend many hours in the basement of the Los Angeles Museum of the Holocaust and at the Shoah Foundation, listening to testimonies of survivors. I heard stories about Jews from all over Europe and Asia, representing every level of religiosity, social class, and education. I heard stories of brutal psychological torture, of starvation and beatings and the torment of those watching their loved ones starved and beaten in front of them.

I walked away with several distinct impressions, including this: Of all the brutality and psychological scarring inflicted by the Holocaust, among the most abject of its survivors were those who spent years living under an assumed identity. I remember one woman's testimony, in particular. Her parents had hidden her with a Catholic family who had agreed to take her in for a fee. Hastily taught the rosary and the Our Father and given a saint's name—I think it was "Mary"—for the duration of the Holocaust, she pretended to be someone else, never telling a soul who she really was. The artifice worked, and the girl survived.

Many years later she was invited to Israel and welcomed as a Jewish Holocaust survivor. But as she explained in her piteous testimony, she did not know what to make of the odd embrace. She felt detached from other Jews and survivors and wasn't entirely comfortable with Christians, either.

It was hard to explain, though she tried: having had to pretend for so many years to have nothing to do with the Jews—to see Jews through Christian eyes—she didn't feel like a Jew anymore. She was at least half Christian. She had managed to be both and neither, never entirely fitting in with either community. The Jewish girl who survived the Holocaust emerged as a woman with no natural community, no home, no family—and no idea who she was.

What struck me about the story was that in many ways Mary had it easy. She never saw the inside of a camp. She never knew hunger. She never weathered physical abuse or torture. She was surrounded by playmates, hosted by a good family.

And yet, unlike so many of the other Holocaust survivors I've known, she had never married nor had children. She remained in perpetual isolation, marooned on her own island. What had been stolen from her left no physical trace, but the psychological lacerations were profound; her identity had been eroded by the deceptions of a mind that had finally managed to fool itself.

Of course, unlike the girls who come out as trans, Mary hadn't chosen her new identity; it had been forced upon her. She had wanted to stay with her family, to be her parents' daughter, to be known by the name they had given her. But after years of living in a community in which everyone regarded her according to her new, Christian identity, she had managed to expunge who she once was. The erasure was so complete, she couldn't recover what she had lost, even when she might have wanted to.

We are, by nature, social animals—as Aristotle once observed. We absorb ideas about ourselves from our surroundings more often than we realize and more deeply than we know. If we attend a school or live in a family in which we are made to feel stupid or told we are, some number of us will come to believe it. If a boy is placed in a school in which the other boys tease him for being gay, he may come to internalize their homophobia. He may turn his anger inward, at himself.

All of which is to suggest that social transition is not nothing; it is, in fact, an extremely potent and consequential act. It provides what world-renowned gender psychologist Kenneth Zucker—no fan of affirmative therapy—called an "experiment of nurture" when he spoke to me. It places a child or adolescent in an environment in which the entire school is asked to participate in affirming this child's identity as the opposite sex. If the adolescent wasn't entirely convinced of her new identity before the experiment, she may be much more so after it is underway.

In fact, a team of Dutch clinician-researchers who pioneered the use of puberty blockers found just that: Social transition is a significant intervention. In a 2011 journal article, they warned that early social transitions proved sticky. Given that girls who had been living as boys for years during childhood "experienced great trouble when they wanted to return to the female gender role," they cautioned, "We believe that parents and caregivers should fully realize the unpredictability of their child's psychosexual outcome."[15]

Once you've been insisting to everyone that you're one thing, it isn't easy to announce to all your friends, classmates, acquaintances, teachers, and family that you might have made a mistake and change your mind. "You're worried about losing face," Lisa Marchiano explained. "First of all, you're going to get treated like a traitor to the trans community if you step away, but also you're going to look like an idiot. Like, you made all these people change your name and pronouns. You were up presenting at school for the Trans Day of Visibility—and now you're not? Who can do that as a teenager?"

So "social transition" and "affirmation" are not without risk—for the patient or for the doctor. It's worth wondering if a therapist who has adopted wholesale the perceptions of her patients is able to provide them with objective guidance. In the case of gender dysphoric adolescents, the perception that a teen is "born in the wrong body" is the very reason for seeking therapy in the first place. It is the cause of distress. One would think that if there were any aspect of the patients' assessment about which a therapist should maintain objective detachment, it would be the nature of the ailment that led the patients to seek therapy in the first place.

3. "If you don't affirm, your child may kill herself."

For a long time, I had a habit of reading Philip Roth's *Goodbye, Columbus* once a year, just for the pleasure of it. At the back of most editions, there's a collection of stories, and one—"The Conversion of the Jews"—pops to mind nearly every time I hear parents recite the suicide narrative.

The story goes something like this: Ozzie Friedman is a twelve-year-old boy preparing for his bar mitzvah, who can't seem to stop hectoring the rabbi at Hebrew school with challenging theological questions. Ozzie wants to know how the rabbi is so sure that Jesus isn't the Son of God, why he's so complacent in his belief in Judaism. Ozzie doesn't let go, and when his brazen defiance pushes the rabbi too far, the rabbi loses his temper and strikes him. The story ends with Ozzie on the roof of his Hebrew school, threatening to jump unless the rabbi, his mother, and all the Jews gathered below get down on their knees and pray to Jesus. They do, just before Ozzie leaps from the roof, landing safely in the firemen's net awaiting him.

In a sense, this is every adolescent's fantasy: to expose the hypocrisy of adults—in this case, their stubborn insistence on the rationality of their own theology compared to the alleged nonsensicalness of others'. The chance to declare one's independence in a good fight. Ozzie's leap from the building is his real bar mitzvah, as much a coming of age as any.

But the story also exposes the vulnerability of adults in the face of teenage defiance. There is one way any adolescent can bring parents to surrender: with a compelling threat of self-harm. So many parents I spoke to in the course of writing this book seemed to go blank with fear at the mention of it.

Given the power this has to disarm and disable parental judgment, there is something a little disturbing about the fact that so many therapists feel comfortable trotting it out. There is, after all, no other life decision a teenager might make, no other identity proclamation, that would likely lead a therapist to blithely suggest to parents that if they didn't go along with it, they might have a dead kid on their hands. It's a weapon so highly coercive, one would think a mental health expert would only brandish it, if ever, in a grave emergency.

But is it true? Are transgender-identified youth likely to kill themselves? And are they less likely to do so if parents and teachers and therapists drop to their knees and affirm?

The rates of anxiety, depression, self-harm, and suicidal ideation for transgender youth, adolescents, and even adults are indeed startlingly high.[16] Nearly every study confirms this. In 2014, the Williams Institute put out a widely cited study that reported the suicide attempts among transgender and non-conforming adults at 41 percent. If true, this would be a ghastly statistic. For the U.S. population as a whole the rate of attempted suicide is 0.6 percent, and 10 to 20 percent for lesbian, gay, and bisexual individuals.

There are a few problems with the study, however. One is that it is entirely based on self-report. As a writer at 4thWaveNow, a consortium of parents who oppose medical transition for young people, pointed out in an excellent blog post, "More careful and rigorous studies always follow-up with in-person interviews, and when self-harming behaviors (not intended to end life) are controlled for, the actual suicide rate is typically halved—meaning the suicide attempt rate could be as low as 20%."[17]

That is still horrifically high. And there are other studies that seem to corroborate a very high rate of suicidal ideation and self-harm from transgender-identified kids. It's fair to assume that this is a deeply troubled population and that it is suffering acutely.

In order to justify the peculiar mandate that therapists immediately accept patients' self-diagnosis when presented with someone claiming gender dysphoria, we must answer two questions: 1) Is the gender dysphoria *causing* the suicidal ideation? And 2) Do we have any evidence that affirmation ameliorates mental health problems? The answer to both questions, it seems, is no.

In a recent academic study, Kenneth Zucker found that the mental health outcomes for adolescents with gender dysphoria were very similar to those with the same mental health issues who did not have gender dypshoria. In other words, we have no proof that the gender dysphoria was responsible for the suicidal ideation or tendency to self-harm. It may have been the many other mental health problems that gender dysphoric adolescents so often bear.

Still, even if the gender dysphoria were not responsible for the suicidal ideation, it might be worth "affirming" these youths if doing so would cure their depression and lift their suicidal fantasies. Unfortunately for proponents of affirmative therapy, there is no evidence that this is the case. There are a few important studies on point, though none is definitive here, since the current craze is so new. One is a long-term study of adult transsexuals (the term in use at the time) showing a rise in suicidality after sex reassignment surgery.[18] Another, more relevant to today's gender-crazed girls, comes from a leaked 2019 report from the Tavistock and Portman Trust gender clinic in the UK, which showed that rates of self-harm and suicidality did not decrease even after puberty suppression for adolescent natal girls.[19] The report was so damning that a governor of the clinic, Dr. Marcus Evans, resigned. He told the press that he feared the clinic was fast-tracking youths to transition to no good effect and in some cases to their harm.[20]

The most commonly cited report purporting to show the mental health benefits of social transition for children, authored by academic psychologist Kristina Olson,[21] collected mental health data for kids aged three to twelve at an unspecified time after the children had socially transitioned. It never looked at the mental health of those children *before* social transition.[22]

4. *"Gender identity is immutable: You can't convert a child out of a transgender identity."*

Dr. Kaufman told me this explicitly: "We know that we can't convert someone from being gay to being straight. So, conversion theory has been debunked and it's outlawed in certain states; you can't socialize someone into or out of being heterosexual or gay. Sort of, *who you are is who you are*. And the same thing with being transgender or cisgender."

But it is not true that gender dysphoria or "being trans" is similarly immutable. We know this, because before "affirmative therapy" was the vogue, gender therapists practiced "watchful waiting," a therapeutic process whose goal was to help a child grow more comfortable in his or her biological sex. As we'll see in the next chapter, watchful waiting was remarkably successful. Several studies indicate that nearly 70 percent of kids who experience childhood gender dysphoria—and are not affirmed or socially transitioned—eventually outgrow it.[23]

There are no long-term studies of desistance rates among those who had no childhood history of dysphoria, identified as transgender in adolescence, and underwent no social or medical transition. But there are a growing number of desisters and detransitioners among those who identified as transgender in adolescence, all of whom were quite passionate about their transgender identities until, quite suddenly, they weren't. Many of the desisters and detransitioners believe that they were influenced by their peers to identify as transgender. Later, once peer influence subsided or their own sense of self matured, they realized that they weren't actually transgender at all.

But there is something else, too: We know that homosexuality can't be eliminated through socialization—because it hasn't been for thousands of years, in all kinds of cultures that specifically attempted to repress it. And we have voluminous records, throughout history, of gay writers, poets, leaders, and philosophers living under repressive regimes, even battling their own homosexuality, unsuccessfully. We don't have any similar weight of history telling us that we can't treat gender dysphoria.

Finally, many affirmative therapists argue, as Dr. Kaufman did to me, that we know gender identity is immutable because of the famous case of David Reimer.[24]

David Reimer was an identical twin (born "Bruce Reimer") whose badly botched circumcision at seven months left him without a functioning penis. Under great pressure by Johns Hopkins psychologist John Money, David's parents renamed him "Brenda" and acquiesced to full sex reassignment surgery to "transform" David into a girl. On the strict advice of John Money, the parents never told Brenda she had been born a boy. For years, many hailed this experiment as a triumph of nurture over nature: unlike his identical twin, Brenda Reimer had actually become a girl.

But John Money's experiment failed miserably, as later follow-up studies and reports showed. David never felt comfortable as a girl, was unalterably boyish for all of his life, aggressive and unhappy. By adolescence he was so troubled and depressed that his parents reluctantly told him the truth. He abruptly renamed himself "David," underwent masculinizing hormone treatments and surgery and presented himself, once more, as a boy, then a man. David went on to marry a woman. But David, who was never able to fully regain physical functionality as a man or to escape the tortured years he spent treated as a girl, eventually committed suicide in 2004.

Transgender activists and gender-affirmative therapists often point to the David Reimer case, somewhat incredibly, as proof of the immutability of gender identity. After all, they say, David Reimer's gender identity had been "male." All the efforts by David's parents, teachers, friends, family, and therapists to convince David otherwise failed because you can't change someone's gender identity.

But of course, this case just as readily proves the opposite. After all, David's *biological sex* was also male. It was arguably David's biology that he couldn't escape—that not-so-minor detail stamped on every cell of his body—not the ethereal concept "gender," for which there is no scientific evidence.

Not every therapist agrees with the affirmative model, but those who don't are wise to keep their mouths shut. Nineteen states have now banned mental health professionals from engaging in "conversion therapy," not only with respect to homosexuality but even, specifically, with respect to gender identity. If a therapist in those states were to second-guess a patient's self-diagnosis of "gender dysphoria"—or even to suggest that whatever dysphoria there was is not the patient's most significant problem—it might be on pain of losing their licenses. Such therapists could be accused of trying to "convert" their patients out of a transgender identity. Even those mental health professionals who do not agree with the affirmative model today are loath to speak against it.

Some decry it anyway. They've lost their jobs over this, or retired, or live outside the nineteen U.S. states that have made "conversion therapy" illegal. They have conducted pioneering research into gender dysphoria, authored the *DSM-5* entry on "gender dysphoria," and devoted their entire professional careers to the treatment of gender dysphoric patients. They are giants of psychiatry or world-renowned experts in gender dysphoria, now fallen into sudden disfavor with their colleagues. They believe their professions have become badly politicized. They consider the current approach dead wrong.

CHAPTER SEVEN

THE DISSIDENTS

Until the 2015 controversy that cost him his job, Kenneth Zucker was universally recognized as an international expert on child and adolescent gender dysphoria. As psychologist-in-chief of Toronto's Centre for Addiction and Mental Health (CAMH) and head of its Gender Identity Service, he spent decades conducting research and practicing what he had trained to do—help children and adolescents with gender dysphoria grow more comfortable in their bodies.

In 2007, Dr. Zucker oversaw the writing of the definition of "gender dysphoria" for the *DSM-5*.[1] He also helped write the "Standards of Care" guidelines for the World Professional Association for Transgender Health (WPATH).[2] Until transgender activists rallied against him, most health professionals practicing in this area regarded Dr. Zucker as an international authority on what "gender dysphoria" was.

His philosophy was simple, though his understanding of gender dysphoria was anything but: a child or adolescent in distress is not reducible to one problem. To reach an accurate diagnosis, Dr. Zucker believes mental health professionals need to look at the whole kid.

Some children latch onto gender dysphoria as a way of coping with trauma or other distress. A therapist needed to question the patient's understanding of gender in order to determine why the patient might have fixated on that as a source of their problems. What beliefs did the patient have about boys or girls? Why did the child or adolescent come to believe changing gender would lead to a happier life? The goal of the questioning was often to challenge the notion that biological sex was the source of the patient's problem and, wherever possible, to alleviate the dysphoria.

He was stunningly successful. Zucker's colleague Devita Singh examined the outcomes in the cases of more than one hundred boys who had been seen by Dr. Zucker at his clinic.[3] In cases in which a child had not been socially transitioned by parents, she found that 88 percent outgrew their dysphoria.[4]

For decades, Dr. Zucker practiced a therapy that has been called "watchful waiting," a term that Zucker once applied to his own method but has since come to dislike. He finds that it is overly simplistic and implies a passivity that only sometimes characterized his approach. Zucker administered more or less active therapy—and sometimes recommended no therapy at all—depending upon what he thought the child needed. But in all cases a diagnosis of "gender dysphoria" was only the beginning for Dr. Zucker. It neither exhausted his range of diagnoses nor determined the treatment he recommended.

"There are different pathways that can lead to gender dysphoria, but it's an intellectual and clinical mistake to think that there is one single 'cause' that explains gender dysphoria," he said in a BBC documentary about his life's work.[5] In the case of one child he treated, the boy's desire to be a girl stemmed from wanting to connect with his single mother, who had briefly abandoned him, to keep her from leaving again. The therapy addressed his feelings of abandonment and only secondarily the child's gender dysphoria.

o o o

I spoke to Dr. Zucker several times, mostly over Skype. At sixty-nine, he has a close-cropped white beard, the gentle manner of someone who excels at working with kids, and a Talmudic habit of answering every question with a question. Although he has maintained a clinical practice for decades, when he talks about his work he is the consummate academic—apparently incapable of providing a straightforward answer to any question without considering every nuance, drawing all sorts of fine distinctions, and reaching for every caveat that will make his ultimate statement precise.

He is—in other words—a journalist's nightmare. But his even-handed, nonjudgmental approach and genuine open-mindedness seem to lend themselves to academic inquiry and therapeutic practice. It isn't hard to believe he's authored over 250 academic papers and book chapters or to imagine that his patients find him easy to talk to.

"I'll see a kid who will say, 'Well, I have a male brain in a female body' or a 'boys' brain in a girl's body.' 'I was born this way,'" he told me. Dr. Zucker doesn't dismiss this kind of talk out of hand. He acknowledges to me that interesting MRI studies have indicated that people suffering with gender dysphoria may have certain neural structures that more closely resemble those of the desired sex than the current sex.

But he also doesn't allow au courant gender theory to trump scientific research. "It's completely simplistic to say that there are 'male brains' or 'female brains,'" he told me. So he said to his young patient, "'Well, you know, [with] most traits, both physical and behavioral, there's a lot of overlap between boys and girls, or men and women.' I said, 'What if there is really no such thing as a male brain or a female brain?' The kid said, 'Well, then I would have to rethink whether I'm really trans, that maybe there's something else wrong with me.'"

According to Dr. Zucker, the mere fact that patients may have fixated on gender as a source of their problems does not mean that they are right or that transitioning will alleviate their distress. "I said to this kid, 'I don't care if you have a male brain or a female brain. This is how you're feeling currently and we need to figure out why you're feeling this way and what is the best way to help you lose this dysphoria.'"

His method certainly isn't "affirmative therapy," but it isn't quite the opposite, either. In cases in which gender dysphoria had persisted without change into adolescence, Dr. Zucker sometimes recommended medical transition. But transition was never his goal—if he could help a child or adolescent become more comfortable in their skin, he would. And he doesn't believe in taking a patient's self-diagnosis at face value, either. After a lifetime of study, he was the professional, after all.

By 2015, however, "affirmative therapy" fever had swept Canada, where it became the prevailing standard for therapists and doctors who work with transgender patients. That year, Ontario became the first province to ban "conversion therapy" even with regard to gender identity. Activists took the Ontario ban as a bill of attainder and headed straight for Dr. Zucker's door. On the basis of their claims that he had engaged in "conversion therapy," as well as specious accusations that he had denigrated and humiliated transgender patients (later proved false), Dr. Zucker was fired and his gender identity clinic shut down.[6]

Nearly five hundred mental health professionals from around the world signed an open letter to CAMH protesting Dr. Zucker's firing. It seemed obvious that the hospital had sacrificed an international expert on gender dysphoria and the families he served "for some real or imagined local political gain."[7]

But to any mental health professional paying attention, the message was clear: Not even the most prominent members of their profession were safe from the activist mob. Get on board with "affirmative therapy"—or lose your job and maybe your license.

o o o

There are, however, a few professionals who refuse to play ball and are nervy enough to say so. Many of them treated transgender patients long before such work was fashionable. They have earned international reputations as giants of psychiatry, sexology, or psychology. Some have authored major academic research on psychiatric disorders, sexuality, or gender dysphoria. Others are Jungian analysts and published authors. All have suffered professional setbacks and reputational smears for their stubborn insistence that "affirmative therapy" isn't really therapy at all.

They disagree with each other on plenty: they believe medical transition is appropriate only for some children, or only for adults, or never appropriate at all. They characterize gender dysphoria according to age of onset, or sexual orientation of the sufferers, or the idea on which the sufferer fixates. Each approaches the question of how best to treat it from a different angle, bringing different conceptual tools to the question, and often disagreeing on best treatment.

But they all believe gender dysphoria is, first and foremost, a psychopathology—a mental disorder to treat, not primarily an identity to celebrate. They all agree that the current epidemic of gender dysphoria among adolescent girls is atypical (some deny it meets the requirements for "gender dysphoria" at all). And they believe that "affirmative therapy" is either a terrible dereliction of duty or a political agenda disguised as help.

All of them read Lisa Littman's paper with great interest, believing she was onto something. All suspect that this epidemic may be the result of peer contagion. They also have all suffered ostracism, deplatforming, and public censure for having insisted that gender dysphoria ought to be treated—and not merely facilitated. They believe that it is wrongheaded to regard helping a patient overcome gender dysphoria as "conversion therapy." They are dissidents from the current order, by dint of therapeutic duty and the Hippocratic oath.

THE SEXOLOGISTS: RAY BLANCHARD AND J. MICHAEL BAILEY

In the world of research into sexual orientation and paraphilia, Dr. Ray Blanchard is a giant. If you've ever encountered the theory that older brothers increase the odds of homosexuality in later-born males—you're familiar with Dr. Blanchard's work. And he advanced the still-prevailing explanation of the phenomenon: giving birth to successive boys, some mothers produce antibodies that attack male-specific antigens, hampering sexual differentiation in the brain of succeeding male fetuses.

Blanchard has also conducted groundbreaking research into pedophilia. Using phallometric testing, he was able to demonstrate that men who say they are most attracted to pubescent children differ from men who say they are most attracted to prepubescent children and from those who say they are most attracted to physically mature persons. In other words, a man who pursues fourteen-year-old-girls may be a criminal, but he isn't a pedophile.

In the 1980s and 1990s, Blanchard developed a typology for understanding transsexualism (the term in use at the time) that is still actively employed and debated among academics today. In Blanchard's view, the "early onset" and "late onset" distinction for gender dysphoria is fine, but it doesn't, borrowing a phrase from Plato, "carve nature at its joints." Blanchard proposed dividing gender dysphoria into two categories: "homosexual transsexualism" (child-onset, effeminate boys or masculine girls who would grow into gay men and women; think drag queens) and "autogynephilic transsexualism" (adolescent-onset, heterosexual men who are aroused by the idea or image of themselves dressed as women; think men who transition to female in their fifties and are married to women). It was his discovery of "autogynephiles," a term he coined, that brought the outrage mob to his door.

In 2003, another academic psychologist and expert in gender identity disorders, J. Michael Bailey, publicized Blanchard's understanding of "autogynephiles" in a popular book, *The Man Who Would Be Queen*. Bailey offered a highly sympathetic portrayal of transsexualism—so sympathetic, in fact, that the book was a finalist for the Lambda Literary Foundation's transgender award in 2003. But then the mood swung.

Trans activists decided the book was unfavorable to them. "They calculated, and maybe correctly, that the general public could be sold a woman trapped in a man's body, but a more nuanced and realistic version of events would be harder to sell to the general public," Dr. Blanchard said, recalling the uproar. A man trapped might be sympathetic. A man aroused might seem shameful—possibly even dangerous.

Transgender activists collected thousands of signatures protesting the Lambda Literary Foundation's nomination. The foundation's judges quickly changed their minds, decided the book was indeed transphobic, and removed it from their list of finalists. Deirdre McCloskey, a prominent transgender woman and distinguished professor of economics, history, English, and communication at the University of Illinois at Chicago, said that including Bailey's book among the list of nominees was "like nominating *Mein Kampf* for a literary prize in Jewish studies." Within a year, the executive director of the Lambda Literary Foundation who had approved the nomination had resigned.

Stripping Bailey of the nomination for the literary prize was not nearly enough. Activist academics launched an aggressive campaign to persuade Northwestern University to revoke Dr. Bailey's tenure, accusing him of violating the university ethics rules—based on the pettifoggery that he had lacked informed consent from research subjects and that he failed to obtain permission from the Institutional Review Board (neither was needed for a non-academic book) and the much more serious charge that he had had sexual relations with a transsexual research subject.[8] The last grievous charge was never proven, but the public allegation was more than sufficient to tarnish his reputation.

One reason that the existence of autogynephilia matters has to do with women's safe spaces. If transgender-identified biological men are completely uninterested in women sexually, one might argue that however uncomfortable it may be, there is little danger in admitting them to women's private spaces. But if some transgender men are heterosexual, aroused by the idea of themselves dressed as women and generally by the female form, the nature of the debate shifts and the possibility of admitting trans-identified men into women's safe spaces begins to seem untenable.

Nonetheless, it is hard to deny that autogynephiles exist. Many transsexuals conduct romantic relationships exclusively with women. Suppressing or denying the fact of autogynephila, according to Dr. Bailey, doesn't help anyone, least of all autogynephiles themselves. "[I]t prevents us from learning things that would help them perhaps in planning their lives. I mean, we don't really have good follow up studies" on various surgical choices a transgender patient might make.

Blanchard has stuck by his typology. According to him, a simple overlap in some symptoms does not necessarily collapse two different conditions into a single disorder. The boy who wants to be a girl and find a boyfriend and the man who is sexually aroused by the image of himself as a woman both experience gender dysphoria, but that does not mean that their psychopathologies are the same.

By way of comparison, Dr. Blanchard offers the case of a patient who complains of swollen, painful fingers. There are at least two different causes of that. It could be osteoarthritis, a breakdown of joint cartilage, or it could be rheumatoid arthritis, an autoimmune disease. "All types of gender dysphoria culminate in a request for sex reassignment or culminate in a desire to live as the opposite sex. But there are different etiologies of transsexual impulses. And not only did they start out different, but even in the end, they preserve the flavor of where they started out. [I]f you compare Jazz Jennings to Caitlyn Jenner, you know, I don't see how anybody could say these are two people who are suffering from the exact same condition."

Blanchard believes sex reassignment surgery is appropriate for some gender dysphoric patients. He claims to have treated trans-identified patients whose dysphoria was largely alleviated by surgical intervention. As head of Clinical Sexology Services at the Toronto Centre for Addiction and Mental Health, Dr. Blanchard saw adult patients and recommended surgery for those trans-identified adult patients he believed it would help.

But—and here's the important point, in his view—he never recommended such measures merely on the basis of a patient's demand. Part of Dr. Blanchard's job was to determine whether patients were likely to succeed at presenting themselves as the opposite sex; he undertook this evaluation precisely because he hoped they would.

Dr. Blanchard emphasized to me the daily difficulties of trying to present as the opposite sex. It's psychologically wearing, sometimes much more than patients anticipate. "People who don't pass well are going to be subject to stares and possibly hostile comments from strangers. I'm sure it does take a toll on people to have to brace themselves for every trip to the store to get a quart of milk."

For this reason, his clinic only saw adult patients and insisted they spend two years living as the opposite gender in order to be eligible for sex reassignment surgery. The last thing he wanted to do was approve surgery for someone who would later regret it.

"I can't think of any branch of medicine outside of cosmetic surgery where the patient makes the diagnosis and prescribes the treatment. This doesn't exist. The doctor makes the diagnosis, the doctor prescribes the treatment. Somehow, by some word magic or word trickery, gender [activists] have somehow made this a political issue," he says.

But the management of transgender health is not a political issue—or shouldn't be. What irks him about the informed-consent model now in place in so many gender surgery centers is that it essentially "absolve[s] the physician, the psychiatrist, and the surgeon from the responsibility of making the decision."

His clinic's model was appropriate, he says, because patients "sometimes present with symptoms of gender dysphoria that are actually related to other psychiatric problems. Or they will present in a state of a kind of acute, fulminating gender dysphoria without having experienced what it would really be like to live in the world as the opposite sex." Psychiatric patients should not be their own doctors; as the saying goes, a lawyer who represents himself has a fool for a client.

It's an old idea: physicians are not merchants. The shop owner lives by the conceit that the customer is always right; the physician trains to acquire a critical understanding of a patient's needs. Giving in to a patient's request is appropriate only when it coincides with his professional judgment.

The erasure of this distinction has arguably enabled and accelerated the opioid crisis, with doctors behaving like vendors, rushing to meet an existing demand rather than evaluating its appropriateness and sometimes frustrating it. *"You're in pain? Here's some Percocet." "You're feeling dysphoric? Here's a script for testosterone. Here's a letter for surgery."*

It isn't hard to see parallels between the medical professionals in both instances: much like physical pain, gender dysphoria leans heavily on a patient's claim about herself. Any medical or mental health professional who fails to ask further questions is essentially handing over the prescription pad to the sufferer.

According to Blanchard, the issues surrounding transgender healthcare have become so politicized that the underlying mental health problem has become completely obscured. "The gender-critical feminists are using language like 'misogyny,' 'patriarchy,' 'male domination,'" he says. And the transgender activists "are happy enough to have the argument in this language, because any language is better than talking about mental illness and clinical management of symptoms."

○ ○ ○

One interesting feature of Blanchard's typology is that it completely omits the current crop of teenage girls with no history of gender dysphoria—now the largest group of patients at most clinics in America, Canada, England, and Scandinavia. "Autogynephilia" is an exclusively male phenomenon; researchers have never studied (or even discovered) women who claim to be turned on by the image of themselves as men. And most of the adolescent girls currently identifying as transgender had no history of childhood gender dysphoria.

In fact, Blanchard does not believe the adolescent girls who suddenly identify as trans in adolescence necessarily have gender dysphoria at all.

He believes they are likely a mixed bag of at least three groups: (1) some kids who are going to be transgender no matter what therapy they're given; (2) kids who would naturally have outgrown their dysphoria on their own and proceeded to live as gay adults; and (3) "some contingent of teenage girls who just have borderline personality disorders and who have a kind of faux gender dysphoria, which they have identified as the locus of their unhappiness."

Blanchard emphasizes that in the entire diagnostic history of gender dysphoria—dating back to the 1910s—there is no record of genuine transsexualism or well-established syndromes of gender dysphoria ever passing from one person to another. "People developed gender dysphoria in isolation from models." They didn't need prompting from a friend, a school assembly, or a YouTube influencer to realize their dysphoria; it simply was.

This is a view of trans-identified teenage girls that never fails to infuriate trans activists—much to Blanchard's surprise. "The activists could have gone the route of saying, 'Yeah, there might be some young people who falsely think that they are gender dysphoric, but that's got nothing to do with those of us who are truly gender dysphoric.' But for some reason, they felt the need to circle the wagons."

Although he has watched trans activists grow increasingly powerful and persuasive in the past decades, he does not fault them for it. "Trans activists do this kind of lobbying. I mean, they're activists, that's what activists do. They try to get as much as they can of their demands." What astonishes him is the members of his own profession. "That's where I'm always saying to my colleagues, yeah, yeah, that's what *patients* say. That's what *patients* do. *What's wrong with us?*"

Like Dr. Blanchard, after spending much of his career studying trans-sexualism and gender dysphoria, Dr. Michael Bailey has arrived at the conclusion that the current trans-identifying teenage girls are not suffering actual gender dysphoria. Their distress rests instead on the false beliefs that they are like transgender people of the past. "It's a mistaken identity," he said.

Dr. Bailey believes that for these teenage girls gender dysphoria is a hysteria much like multiple personality disorder, another historical example of disturbed young women convincing themselves they possess an ailment and then manifesting the symptoms.[9]

For academic psychologists like Dr. Bailey, the entire issue of gender dysphoria ought to be a matter of evidence. Rigorous empirical study should guide diagnosis, understanding, and treatment. Instead, today, the language swirling around the transgender debates has tended to make such science all but impossible.

○ ○ ○

Take, for instance, the issue of "immutability." Activists often claim that gender identity is innate and "immutable."[10] Attempts by mental health professionals to help gender dysphoric patients become comfortable in their bodies, therefore, amount to "conversion therapy." If gender identity is the sort of thing that will never change, irrespective of the environmental factors at play, then encouraging a child or adolescent to quiet or overcome the feeling would seem foolhardy, cruel, a form of torture.

But we have scant evidence that gender identity—a person's ineffable sense of her own gender—is immutable. In fact, we have very good evidence that in many cases it is not. Several long-term studies have shown that a majority of children with gender dysphoria have outgrown it.[11]

Why then would so many activists insist on innateness and immutability? Perhaps the answer lies in American anti-discrimination law. The Supreme Court has indicated that the Fourteenth Amendment's Equal Protection Clause protects certain traits such as race or sex but not, say, hair color, in part because the protected traits are "immutable."[12] You could change your hair color if you really wanted to—and you could do so without surrendering anything vital about yourself. That, at any rate, seems to be the principle underlying much of our Equal Protection Clause jurisprudence.

There is a good argument that this is a silly litmus test for offering the Equal Protection Clause's shield to those groups facing discrimination. But because "immutability" has long been a test for those seeking protection, transgender people are sometimes forced to argue that their condition is "immutable" in order to demonstrate that they merit protection, too.

But what is gender identity? It has no diagnostic markers, no measurable signs, no blood test to confirm it. It is a feeling—an attitude. That does not mean that it does not exist. But it does mean that, like many psychiatric ailments, it poses challenges to diagnosis and treatment. When the prospective treatment is an irreversible surgery, the slippery nature of the condition would seem to justify measured and careful evaluation.

If a therapist believes he might be able to help a gender dysphoric patient feel better in her body, Dr. Bailey believes he ought at least to be allowed to try. But the current gender-affirmative therapists leap straight to affirmation. "At best, they're keeping these girls from adjusting to their natal sex. And at worst, they're encouraging them to take these harmful and unnecessary medical steps."

If you're thinking Dr. Bailey might land himself into trouble for these views, I can assure you, he knows. "You know, there's a kind of progressive language police now and part of the function is to keep people off balance so that they're always apologizing and never asking questions and also to prevent people from being able to have clear conversations about things," he says. "I have heard even 'transgender' is problematic to some people. I don't know what the correct language is and I don't really care."

But he *does* care. I can hear it in his voice. What he won't do is alter the language he employs to render his professional judgment. He isn't above changing his mind in the face of evidence; scientists do that all the time. What he won't do is knuckle under.

THE NON-AFFIRMATIVE PSYCHOTHERAPIST: LISA MARCHIANO

Lisa Marchiano is a Jungian analyst, a social worker, and a widely published author. Like a lot of therapists in North America and Europe, she began to notice a surge in adolescents identifying as transgender in the last five years, apparently out of nowhere. But unlike most of her colleagues, she greeted this phenomenon with skepticism. She never doubted the distress of the teenage girls claiming gender dysphoria. But as a profound admirer of the power of the unconscious, she was also well aware of the mind's ability to deceive itself.

"I think the human psyche is very susceptible to these kind of psychic epidemics," she told me. "It happened with lobotomies. It happened with multiple personality disorder. It happened in Germany in the 1930s and 1940s. Human beings are susceptible to psychic contagion. We just are. Any of us."

When we feel psychological distress, she says, we want to explain it in a way that will prompt others to take it seriously. "So if you manifest [distress] in some novel way that no one's ever heard of before, the likelihood is you're going to be dismissed. But if it fits into a prescribed narrative, the unconscious latches onto that. It has explanatory value for you and you receive care and attention."

This is the idea developed by historian of psychiatry Edward Shorter, and popularized by journalist Ethan Watters: Patients are drawn to "symptom pools"—lists of culturally acceptable ways of manifesting distress that lead to recognized diagnoses.[13] "'Patients unconsciously endeavor to produce symptoms that will correspond to the medical diagnostics of the time,'" Watters credits Shorter with discovering.[14] "Because the patient is unconsciously striving for recognition and legitimization of internal distress, his or her subconscious will be drawn toward those symptoms that will achieve those ends."[15] Many social contagions are spread this way.

Hong Kong, for instance, had never experienced an epidemic of what Westerners call "anorexia"—girls, captivated by a belief that they are fat, engaging in self-starving. Not until 1994, that is, when local media widely publicized the story of a girl whose tragic death was interpreted by news outlets as an example of an unfamiliar Western ailment called anorexia nervosa. An outbreak of girls presenting with symptoms soon followed. It wasn't that no one in Hong Kong had ever thought to starve themselves before 1994; it was simply that only when anorexia became a "culturally agreed-upon expression of internal distress did it become widespread."[16]

Similarly, gender dysphoria has entered our symptom pool by way of the internet, *Vanity Fair,* and various popular television programs, like *I Am Jazz.* They have helped elevate gender dysphoria from something you might never have heard of to the first or second thought that pops into your mind when you see a boy clopping around the house in his mother's high heels. "Our early 21st century symptom pool includes the notion that children can suffer extreme distress as a result of being born in the wrong body," Marchiano wrote.[17] Once gender dysphoria entered the symptom pool by way of a few highly publicized cases—lo and behold—parents, therapists, and doctors began seeing much, much more of it.

A lone sympathizer with parents facing the predicament of suddenly trans-identifying teens, Marchiano began counseling them in 2016. She avoids conversion-therapy bans by not seeing adolescents. Very often, parents have told me she is the only therapist they could find who didn't insist they immediately affirm their daughters' self-diagnoses.

It's fair to say Marchiano has a love-hate relationship with her profession. She believes strongly in the power of therapy and analysis; the problem is that too few seem to be engaged in it. "The whole premise of therapy is that you explore," she told me. "It's that you open things up and you approach a symptom with curiosity. Affirmation is the exact opposite of curiosity. It's saying, *I already know what this is.* It's taking things at face value."

In fact, Marchiano says, genuine therapy pushes patients to question their own self-assessments. It does this with the explicit purpose of making the patient stronger. "If I work with someone who's really suicidal because his wife left him, I don't call the wife up and say: 'Hey, you just have to come back!' That's not the way we treat suicide," she said. "We don't treat suicide by giving people exactly what they want. We treat suicide first of all by keeping people safe, and by helping them to become more resilient." We ought to treat gender dysphoria that way, too.

This approach doesn't discount the possibility that a patient's self-diagnosis of gender dysphoria may be correct—it only requires that a therapist not stop there. Patients claiming gender dysphoria, she says, ought to be treated according to the same therapeutic principles as any other troubled patients. "When someone walks in and says, '*I think I want to leave my marriage, that's why I'm here.*' I don't know what's going on. We have to listen and find out, and the way that I work, that could take months of listening. This idea that a kid's going to come in and tell us that they're trans and that within a session or two or three or four, that we're going to say, '*Yep, you're trans. Let me write you the letter.*' That's not therapy."

Marchiano believes suicide statistics are often employed by gender therapists in a manner that is both irresponsible and unethical. "It's essentially emotional blackmail," she told me. "It's being used to force parents' hands to do something that they don't feel comfortable with." But there's something else she's even more worried about: Insisting that an adolescent who doesn't transition is likely to kill herself—that notion can also easily fall into the symptom pool, too. It may have already. "When you tell a group of highly suggestible adolescent females that if they don't get a certain thing, they're going to feel suicidal," she says, "that's suggestion, and then you're actually spreading suicide contagion."

○ ○ ○

I met Lisa Marchiano at Vedge, a trendy vegan restaurant in Philadelphia, a few blocks from Rittenhouse Square, near where she practices. It isn't hard to see why her patients like her. She has an obvious lack of pretense about her, right down to her unvarnished gray curls. Although she has a string of Ivy League degrees to her name, and a number of highly respected publications under her belt, they don't impel her to jargon, nor to curry favor with the gender ideologues who seem to be guiding her profession. She makes no effort to break and bind the arc of her thought merely to conform to current cultural standards.

She has spoken with hundreds of parents whose teenagers suddenly identified as transgender, and she has much to say on the subject. For one, being a teenager—perhaps especially a teenage girl—is never easy. Adolescence comes with the mandate to strike out on your own, form your own identity, and detach from your parents. "So the thing about a trans identity is it kind of does double duty because it allows you to separate from your parents," she said. "Like, 'I'm so different from my mom that I'm not even female.'"

At precisely a cultural moment when American parents are maximally disinclined to allow their children ever to experience negative emotions, here come their shaky teens, beset by them. Unprepared to weather the trials of adolescence—romantic relationships, the pressures of schoolwork and parental expectations—teens scramble for any excuse to duck them. "Parents become so worried about the kid that they no longer expect them to do well in school. Like, 'Oh, you're feeling anxious or dysphoric today? Stay home.'"

Why then are so many gender-affirmative therapists insistent that they are doing good? Many claim to be saving lives when they encourage a child or adolescent toward gender transition. Marchiano explains the mentality of these affirmative therapists this way: "You cannot let yourself imagine that it might be a mistake because then you'd have to accept that you've been participating in something truly awful."

But, Marchiano believes, they are. In fanning the flames of an epidemic, mental health professionals are withholding the independent judgment and therapeutic help that confused adolescents desperately need. If anything, "affirmative therapy" encourages a confused adolescent's most dangerous impulses.

Marchiano considers the implications for a moment. "I think the last holdouts in all of this are going to be the parents who transitioned their children," she says. "They'll never be able to admit that maybe they did something wrong."

THE PSYCHIATRIST: DR. PAUL McHUGH

By this point you may be wondering, what *is* gender dysphoria? Yes, it's a feeling of profound and persistent discomfort with one's body—but that simply restates the question. Surely psychiatry has more to offer than the *DSM*'s list of symptoms, which amount to this: gender distress is distress about gender.[18]

Johns Hopkins University distinguished professor of psychiatry and behavioral sciences Paul McHugh has an answer. Gender dysphoria is an "overvalued idea" or ruling passion. This is "an idea held by many people in the world, but held intensely by the patient or the person, who is making a life of that idea," Dr. McHugh told me. Many people believe that it is good to be thin, for instance. Many adolescent girls believe it's better to be a boy. But for anorexics and those with gender dysphoria, those ideas become all-consuming.

Dr. McHugh does not doubt that those under the sway of an over-valued idea are suffering real distress. What he doubts is that they have accurately located its source. An anorexic, for instance, often becomes taken with the notion that if she simply lost more weight she would at last be happy with her body. But in fact, she'll never get there—not by starving herself, at any rate. Pursued this way, happiness will forever be like the beach ball caught in a current, always bobbing out of reach.

No amount of subtracted weight will deliver the bodily comfort the anorexic seeks because her weight was never the real problem. In Dr. McHugh's view, mental health professionals must endeavor to change the anorexic's wrong view of her body—not the body itself. "Policy makers and the media are doing no favors to the public or the transgendered by treating their confusions as a right in need of defending rather than as a mental disorder that deserves understanding, treatment and prevention," he wrote in 2014.[19] From this statement alone, one might guess that Paul McHugh has won his share of detractors.

For decades, Dr. McHugh was psychiatry's most prominent scourge. In 1979, as psychiatrist in chief at Johns Hopkins Hospital, Dr. McHugh shut down the gender identity clinic, which performed sex-change operations. In his view, the hospital had "wasted scientific and technical resources and damaged our professional credibility by collaborating with madness rather than trying to study, cure, and ultimately prevent it."[20]

This is a controversial view. Drs. Zucker, Blanchard, and Bailey, for instance, all believe sex reassignment surgery is worthwhile and salutary for at least some adult patients. The problem with gender surgery, according to Dr. McHugh, is not that it can never satisfy a patient or alleviate dysphoria. The problem is that doctors have no way of knowing who will be healed and who will be harmed by it. "Well, I know this," he told me. "That some people are satisfied and live happily ever after. And some, of course, get suicidal, depressed, and regretful. And nobody can tell the difference between the ones in the beginning that will and will not regret it."

Even Dr. McHugh's critics admit that scientists have yet no reliable means of predicting who will be helped and who will be hurt by a gender surgery. For Dr. McHugh, that alone is sufficient reason to pull the plug, and limit these surgeries to controlled experiments overseen by an institutional review board. The medical profession should never have flung open the gates of surgery merely to appease a clamoring public.

○ ○ ○

I met Dr. McHugh in his book-laden Baltimore home, a white brick American Moderne set in the leafy Guilford neighborhood abutting Johns Hopkins Medical School. At eighty-eight he is stunningly sharp and erudite, able to quote long passages of Matthew Arnold from memory and scan his considerable mental microfiche of psychiatric literature, never failing to provide an accurate citation.

In the 1980s, Dr. McHugh became a leading opponent of recovered-memory therapy, in which psychoanalysts claimed to have discovered the latent source of patients' multiple personality disorder in past childhood abuse. Dr. McHugh believes multiple personality disorder is a phony ailment and recovered memories are iatrogenic—a Greek word meaning "brought on by the healer"—implanted by the therapeutic process that purports to discover them. Often the fake memories were of childhood abuse, and Dr. McHugh traveled to Rockville, Maryland; Manchester, New Hampshire; Providence, Rhode Island; and Appleton, Wisconsin, offering expert testimony to exonerate wrongfully accused defendants.

Dr. McHugh believes the current transgender craze is similarly encouraged and improperly treated by a psychiatry profession overtaken by fad. Whereas in all other areas of medicine experimental procedures performed on human subjects must be overseen by an institutional review board, gender surgeries are not. And they *are* experimental, Dr. McHugh insists, pointing to the poor evidence quality of the studies on which they are based.

One key difference between this and past psychiatric crazes is that the transgender epidemic seems primarily induced by peers and the media and schools. Today's teens don't wait to talk to a therapist to find out what's wrong with them. They simply park themselves in front of a screen, Google "Am I trans?" and self-diagnose from the list of symptoms. If anything, therapists are merely exacerbating or encouraging a problem already begun.

But Dr. McHugh believes the transgender craze will likely end as the multiple personality craze did: in the courts, with patients suing their doctors. Some of these teenage girls, he says, "will wake up at age twenty-three, twenty-four, and say, 'Here I am. I've got a five-o'clock shadow, I'm mutilated and I'm sterile, and I'm not what I ought to be. How did this happen?'"

Of course, even if this transgender epidemic does represent yet another psychic craze, that doesn't explain *why this?* So many crazes have come and gone. Serial killing is vanishingly rare; mass shootings, on the rise. Bulimia may be in decline, while cutting and suicide sharply spike. Other fads died off, while this one took root. Why? What's in the national drinking water?

CHAPTER EIGHT

THE PROMOTED AND THE DEMOTED

In May 2019 I got a call from a friend who had just taken her thirteen-year-old daughter for a first bra fitting at Nordstrom. It went badly, my friend said, and my mind leapt to the typical reasons—so much dressing room exposure, the icy hands of a lingerie specialist, this stranger who eyeballs cup size and fit before delivering her verdict loud enough to be enjoyed by the other occupants of the changing room.

But it turned out that the problem had come in a slightly different package: six feet tall, pancake makeup blurring a stubbled jaw, two breasts grafted onto a muscular torso like add-ons. Weeks later I headed to the Nordstrom to confirm my friend's story. The employee was elegant, attentive and professional, fluttering around the floor in a tulle skirt, pink manicured nails trailing her every gesture like streamers. But there was no mistaking that this lingerie specialist was male.

"What would have happened if I hadn't been there?" my friend asked me, again and again. "What if I had sent her into the dressing room alone, and she was too embarrassed to say anything?"

○ ○ ○

A man may find it hard to imagine just how much mortification attends a typical teenage girl's experience of her changing body. Even in a private dressing room with only women present, teenage girls cling to their clothing, terrified their perfectly normal bodies might actually be hideous and worthy of scorn. If urinals were made to accommodate female micturition, girls would still never use them.

This anxious modesty only increases at the prospect of being spied on by the opposite sex. It could not have been much of a surprise to women when British news reported in October 2019 that girls whose school bathrooms had turned coed were skipping school to avoid the shame of using those facilities during menses. The horror of handling a period, even in a closed stall, was too much when next to a boy.[1]

Over time that embarrassment dissipates. The shame that stalks most girls like a chaperone, warding off early sexual encounters, relaxes its watch. A girl's body begins to feel less alien to her. If she is not pressured to share it too early, she will learn to wield it with pleasure. Mortification will no longer attend her every trip to the bathroom.

But even after the shame of adolescence fades, many women refuse to see a male obstetrician. It is, in fact, quite typical for women to prefer that another woman handle their pap smears, annual physical, post-rape exam—to want only a woman to execute any touching that might, in another context, feel sexual. My friend's reaction to the Nordstrom lingerie experience was utterly standard for women of my generation. But it is also quickly becoming outdated.

We have entered a "transgender moment," as CNN called it in 2015—or perhaps the transgender moment has barreled into us. In 2015, Laverne Cox became the first transgender person to win an Emmy. In 2018, in a first for a film with a transgender lead actor, *A Fantastic Woman* won an Oscar. At the 2019 Emmy Awards, Patricia Arquette gave a teary and heartfelt tribute to her late transgender sibling, Alexis, pleading that we end the persecution of trans people. HBO's hit show *Euphoria* has a transgender star.

Even *Cosmopolitan* magazine—*Cosmo!*—ran an article in May 2016, "A Complete Beginner's Guide to Chest Binding," advising girls on the "safe" and best way to use chest compressors to flatten their breasts.[2] "[Binding] offered me the ability to shove something that was bothering me to the back of my mind and not have to worry about it," said biological-girl-now-trans-man Jackson Tree, according to the article. And *Teen Vogue* routinely educates girls that gender is a social construct. "The truth is, not all women menstruate and not all people who menstruate are women," one article blithely informs readers, as if that were factual.[3]

One can argue that this is how it should be: movies and television and magazines reflecting the entire spectrum of humanity, the gender dysphoric included. But one can't argue that transgender individuals haven't received, in airline parlance, a "status upgrade"— or that adolescent girls haven't noticed.

Transgender people are living today with less shame or stigma and less fear of violence than at any point in living memory. That fact should gladden all decent people. Caitlyn Jenner should feel free to pursue a life of her choosing—that most American of wants.

But this cultural shift also bears on the current epidemic gripping adolescent girls. A decade ago one might have wondered, "Why would anyone except the most excruciatingly gender dysphoric pursue gender transformation?" That question can no longer be asked. The person who would pose it isn't living in 2020.

My friend who took her daughter to Nordstrom may have been upset to find a biological male offering to measure her daughter for a first bra. But for her daughter and her daughter's friends, this is already normal.

But don't take my word for it. To discover whether and to what extent the stigma surrounding transgender identification has lifted in the last decade, I spoke with transgender adults, lesbians, and radical feminists. Here's what I learned.

UNWELCOME PUBLICITY

Kristal is a male-to-female transgender person in her late fifties, born to a mother who had suffered three miscarriages trying for a girl. "When a boy popped out, she basically disowned me," Kristal told me. "I was not a welcome member of the family." An older relative has filled in many of the details Kristal couldn't know at the time, and Kristal prefers not to rehash them, except to say this: hers was an unhappy childhood, pockmarked by abuse. "Until I was six years old, I thought I was a girl. I never knew any different. I was raised with female cousins."

Although she had been cross-dressing privately in adulthood whenever she had an opportunity, she only began to do so publicly in 2015. By that time, Kristal was single, in her early fifties, working as a property manager in British Columbia. "I simply decided it doesn't matter how crazy it appears to other people. I'm single, I have a job, I have nothing else to worry about. I don't give a crap what people think. And so that's what I did. I went and got information on how to use makeup and how to measure myself for women's clothing. I started dressing and living as a woman. That, for a while, was enough, and it relieved a lot of stress."

A few months later, following years of therapy, Kristal began taking hormones. Eventually, she would undergo a surgery, though she has no plans to undertake the "final" one. She insists living as a woman is in many ways far easier than it was for her to live as a man. "Like I put a lot of effort into being a man and I didn't realize how much effort I put into being a man until I let that all fall away."

For a few months, Kristal was truly happy, able more or less to pass as a woman or at least get by without harassment. "So my life was good, I had no complaints. I was just doing my thing," Kristal remembers. "And then Caitlyn happened and suddenly, I was under a microscope. I mean, every trans person was. We couldn't walk down the street, you know."

For many classic sufferers of gender dysphoria, celebration of their trans identity is anathema. They aren't looking to show off a "costume," they want to be accepted as the real thing. "I knew I looked like a man in women's clothing," Kristal said. "But it became a freak show. I couldn't have dinner in a restaurant without strangers hugging you. It was really bizarre. It was a really strange experience. So I felt that something weird was happening, and everywhere I went, people were asking my opinion on Caitlyn Jenner and, you know, it was just, it was awful."

Kristal's gender dysphoria has been an unrelenting source of discomfort. She doesn't want to be celebrated and she certainly doesn't want to make other women uneasy. In fact, she says, transgender people's ability to use the bathrooms of their choosing was really no issue until the activists politicized it. "I mean, they're cubicles, you walk in, you do your business, you walk out."

She abhors what she sees as efforts by trans activists to make biological women feel unsafe, and she says the gender ideologues' "pseudoscience is nuts." Kristal knows that she is biologically male; she simply feels most comfortable presenting as a woman. "I don't think you can throw out the science of DNA just because of people's feelings."

o o o

Nearly every transgender person I've spoken to on the record (and several others off) points to Caitlyn Jenner's appearance on the cover of *Vanity Fair* in June 2015 as a tipping point, a thunderclap heard all over the Western world. Many describe the stigma of being transgender dropping away—but also the possibility of quiet toleration, the chance to get by without inviting spectators. Kristal met anti-trans hate for the first time after Caitlyn's announcement, from Canadians incensed by the efforts by biological males to push into women's-only spaces. But she felt equally harassed by the sudden, emphatic embrace she received. "What was bothering me was the people literally—I'm not exaggerating—literally crossing the street to hug me and saying 'I support you.'"

CHRISTINE, CAITLYN, AND FALLEN HEROES

Caitlyn Jenner was not the first American transgender celebrity. That would be Christine Jorgensen, a Brooklyn-born ex-GI who served in

World War II. In 1953, George William Jorgensen Jr. began hormone therapy in America and then traveled to Denmark to undergo a full sex reassignment surgery. The Hearst Corporation contacted her while she was still in Copenhagen's Royal Hospital, offering to purchase her story as a series of five articles to be run in its eleven newspapers.[4] According to LGBTQ Nation, "In 2019, her 1952 fee from Hearst would amount to over $240,000. And virtually every other paper in the country was publishing articles about her."

The articles seem to have been largely flattering, praising her grace and beauty. Christine became an instant celebrity. She returned to America to great fanfare—beautiful, blond, and "everybody's idea of the 'all-American girl.'"[5] She was invited onto television and radio shows and profiled favorably in dozens of periodicals. The New York *Daily News* announced "Ex-GI Becomes Blonde Beauty" and referred to her as "a striking woman."[6] The *LA Times* reported, "Former GI transformed into lovely woman in long series of treatments."[7]

Today we think of the 1950s as an era of unrelieved sexual prudery, but Christine Jorgensen seems to have returned home to a warm media reception. "She was a tireless lecturer on the subject of transsexuality, pleading for understanding from a public that all too often wanted to see transsexuals as freaks or perverts," one much-quoted obituary put it in 1999. "Ms. Jorgensen's poise, charm, and wit won the hearts of millions."[8]

Thanks to the Hearst Corporation, Christine Jorgensen became a household name, and "sex change operation" entered the American lexicon. But gender dysphoria did not make it into the symptom pool, and for all the polite congratulation, few Americans seemed ready to imitate her. Christine Jorgensen, in other words, "came out" to a very different America.

○ ○ ○

By 2015, it's fair to say that America had absorbed a great many cultural knocks, her heroes a sad lot of castaways as deeply disgraced as they had once been beloved. Take Bill Cosby, for instance.

For most of the 1980s and decades after in reruns, Bill Cosby and his television alter ego, Dr. Heathcliff Huxtable, served as a shining example of the best sort of American man—married to a strong woman, raising good kids, meeting life's tribulations with endless patience, his love as sturdy as his cable-knit sweaters. As kids, my brother and I rarely missed a *Fat Albert* episode, we ate his Jell-O Pudding Pops, and sat with the rest of America every Thursday evening for an airing of *The Cosby Show*. We knew he wasn't actually our father—but for the length of a weekly episode, while he admonished his children or listened to their dilemmas, it wasn't hard to believe that in some sense *he was*.

In 2014, allegations that Bill Cosby had drugged and raped a series of women were piling up, increasingly impossible to disbelieve. In 2015, networks took the reruns of his famous show off the air. He had served as America's dad for decades; now we could hardly stand to look at him.

By 2010, one could hardly feel pride in Lance Armstrong's seven Tour de France titles, as proceedings were begun to strip his awards for doping. Michael Jackson's name could hardly be mentioned without reference to those boys. Lance was a cheater; Michael Jackson, a pervert.

Onto this worn-out stage glided Bruce Jenner, America's beloved Olympian and a regular guest on the popular television show *Keeping Up with the Kardashians*. Audiences had watched him quietly transition on the show. Hormone therapy gradually softened his features and made sleek his jaw, but never seemed to interfere with the love he received from his family.

In May 2015, the person we'd known as Bruce Jenner came out as transgender to American audiences in a *20/20* interview with Diane Sawyer. He hadn't hurt anyone. He had made America proud, having taken on one of athletics' most brutal competitions—the Olympic decathlon—and won gold. He had never doped or cheated to get ahead. Nor did he overwhelm us with his pain. All he wanted was acceptance. It didn't seem like too much to ask.

In fact, by 2015, we were happy to hand it to him, relieved at the chance to celebrate a celebrity who struck us, suddenly, as rather wholesome. So he wanted to be a woman. So what? What was so wrong with that? Americans couldn't come up with a good answer. Maybe there isn't one. Maybe, in the scheme of things, transgender is a great thing to be.

"Gender dysphoria" still appears in the *DSM*, but it is already on the way out—no longer called "gender identity disorder," which emphasized the psychopathology. "Homosexuality" was once classified as a mental disorder, too; most of us no longer believed homosexuality was an impediment to a full and happy life. Maybe appearing in the *DSM* doesn't mean anything so bad; maybe it won't be there for long.

In any event, by 2013, one in six Americans was taking a psychiatric drug. Who's to say what counts as "normal"? Maybe we were all a little nuts.[9]

THE FORGOTTEN 'L' IN LGBTQ

One might have thought that this current era of transgender acceptance would benefit all members of LGBTQ, but many lesbians insist that hasn't been the case. In the last decade, lesbians have seen the disappearance of their bars, their publications, women's-only colleges, and single-sex bathrooms and locker rooms. Convicted rapists who suddenly "identify" as women are housed in women's prisons,[10] and natal males demand access to battered women's shelters.[11] "If you look at Smith College, Wellesley, those are no longer specifically female institutions," Pippa Fleming, an African American lesbian performance artist, told me. In 2015, Smith College decided to open its doors to biologically male students who identify as women.[12]

But lesbians and radical feminists who object to the idea that identification should grant biological men an all-access pass to women's rights and safe spaces are openly derided as "TERFs" all over social media—that is, "trans-exclusionary radical feminists."[13] This might confuse those who have been led to believe that "LGBTQ" is one community with one set of interests. In fact, gender ideology puts transgender individuals into direct conflict with radical feminists who believe sex is the defining feature of one's identity. Radical feminists like Pippa tend to regard gender, on the other hand, as trivial—the set of stereotypes society senselessly assigns. They do not believe short haircuts or mannish clothing makes one any less a woman. Women can wear anything they like, they say; clothing does not make the woman. Nor does it make the man.

In the mid-'90s, Pippa told me, lesbians were thriving in America and lesbian culture was enjoying a heyday. Now, she says, lesbians have "gone underground." Lesbian organizations have either disappeared entirely or they use vetting and background checks to bar trans women from forcing their way in on the grounds that they, too, are "lesbians." Many other lesbians have confirmed for me that these "underground" meetings are taking place around the country. This, they say, is the only way lesbians have been able to keep their meetings restricted to biological women.

More than one adolescent girl I interviewed told me that whereas "trans" is a high-status identity in high school, "lesbian" is not. It is, in fact, openly derided as a lesser identity—masculine girls who can't admit they're supposed to be boys.

In her all-girls' high school in Britain, in which many of the girls in her class identified as "transgender," sixteen-year-old Riley told me that "lesbian" was a dirty word. "In a very superficial way, it's just not very cool," she explained. "It's a porn category."

TRANS RIGHTS BEAT GIRLS' RIGHTS

If the last decade has witnessed a rise to prominence for transgender Americans, it has also seen the demotion of women and girls.

Biological boys identifying as girls are already overpowering the very best high school girl athletes across the country. Female runners,[14] swimmers,[15] and weight lifters[16] are being routed by trans-identified biological boys, many of whom were only middling athletes on the boys' team.

Those who object to the unfairness are either dismissed or accused of bigotry.

All of which is to say, girls have likely noticed that they've lost favor in the broader culture. Their private spaces turned coed; their sports records stolen; their protestations of unfairness shouted down as bigotry. In February 2019, tennis great and proud lesbian Martina Navratilova wrote for the *Sunday Times* that allowing trans athletes to compete in women's sports was unfair to biological women. She was labeled a transphobe and dropped by her sponsor Athlete Ally.[17] "The trans community is under attack," Athlete Ally declared, "and we firmly stand opposed to any and all people who perpetuate attacks against them—regardless of who they are or their accolades."[18]

If Navratilova, perhaps the world's most prominent gay female athlete, could be branded an anti-LGBT bigot for having stood up for girls, how could unknown girl athletes object? What chance did they have to be taken seriously? For so long, sports have offered women and girls the chance to excel, to gain scholarships and professional opportunities and to feel rightful pride in all they could do. Suddenly, it seemed the game was fixed. If they had objections, no one really wanted to hear them.

WHAT IS A WOMAN, ANYWAY?

If "women" can no longer be defined according to physical characteristics or biology, how are we to define them? Prominent transgender author Andrea Long Chu has an answer: "Female is a 'universal existential condition' defined by submitting to someone else's desires."[19]

A more offensive or insipid definition of womanhood could hardly be imagined. But in order to redefine womanhood to include trans women, this sort of "solution" has become typical. Bereft of biological markers to explain who counts as a woman, trans activists rely on social stereotypes, many of them archaic or insulting.

In this way, women's biological uniqueness is denied outright—all reference to our specialness stripped with the acid of intersectional language. Pregnant women are increasingly referred to as "pregnant people," and the word "vagina" replaced with the hideous phrase "front hole"; the more "inclusive" language strives to whitewash the feminine nature of anatomy that trans-identified biological women would prefer to forget.[20]

The mainstream media has cottoned on to this newspeak with the wet-lipped, wide-eyed excitement of toddlers. In an October 19, 2019, tweet, NPR announced, "People who menstruate spend an estimated $150 million a year just on the sales tax for tampons and pads."[21] In the service of trans-inclusive language, "women" become "people who menstruate." Why would any young girl look forward to joining this group?

But this sort of trans-inclusive derogation of womanhood is increasingly common. Women are referred to as "breeders" or "bleeders."[22] Those who use the terminology claim it offers a more sensitive way of referring to biological women, so that trans women do not feel excluded. But what does it offer actual girls, except membership in a group so grotesquely described that they could hardly wish to belong to it? Our biological gifts so downgraded, a young girl can only look toward the future with distaste, if not outright dread.

And then there is the internet porn.

If women my age have seen any pornography at all, they likely picture the videos their brothers and boyfriends once watched: a woman's face frozen in an expression of startled ecstasy, as if she were cresting a hill on a roller coaster, into which she had voluntarily strapped herself. Breasts bare and bouncing, stealing the show. She may not have been the picture of dignity—but at least she seemed to be having a good time.

Pornography has always been shocking and offensive to young women who first encounter it. But today's internet porn adds a layer of menace. Choking has become so common among all categories of viewing on Pornhub that there is no separate rubric for it.[23] As *The Guardian* noted of commonly depicted scenes, "Women are choked with anything from a penis to a fist to the point of gagging, and in some cases almost passing out." At the end of the scene, the woman "says, often in a hoarse voice, how much she 'loved it.'"[24]

"In my experience, the kids that I work with are often pretty freaked out by porn," Sasha Ayad told me of the trans-identified adolescent girls she sees in her practice. "In some cases, you know, porn did play a big role in their new adopted identity."

Violent porn not only terrifies young girls about men and the prospect of sex with them, it is changing the expectations and behavior of boys. Sex researcher at Indiana University School of Public Health Debby Herbenick found that nearly a quarter of adult women say they have felt scared during sex and "13 percent of sexually active girls ages 14 to 17 have already been choked."[25] If you have trouble seeing the appeal of transgender life, consider that the typical dating life available to young women today doesn't look half as great as it used to.

Young women are intruded on by biological men in locker rooms,[26] trounced by biological boys on sports teams, and told work life will never offer them fair rewards. Intersectional language denies all their biological specialness. Hollywood—no longer in the rom-com business—offers them no fantasy on which to hang their girlish hopes. The gifts and presumptions of this culture make it hard to imagine why anyone should want to be a girl.

TRANS AS INTERSECTIONAL SHIELD

Remember that the overwhelming majority (over 90 percent of the parents) of the girls suddenly identifying as transgender—according to Littman's surveys—are white.[27] They belong, in other words, to perhaps the most reviled identity on today's campuses. What to do about it?

They can't choose to be people of color. Most can't choose to be gay. Nor can they choose to be disabled (though they might be inclined to milk whatever setbacks they have endured).

"Of all of these badges of victim status, the only one that you can actually choose is 'trans,'" Heather Heying, visiting fellow at Princeton

University, pointed out to me. "All you have to do is declare 'I'm trans' and boom, you're trans. And there you get to rise in the progressive stack and you have more credibility in this intersectional worldview."

But are students really identifying as a member of LGBTQ in response to peer pressure? How would we know?

Heying points out that otherwise the numbers don't make sense. By the time she left Evergreen State College in 2017, 40 percent of students were answering yes to campus surveys asking, "Do you identify as LGBTQ?" "So that's obviously insane," she said. "There's simply no way that 40 percent of any student body" is LGBTQ, "when across cultures, LGB consistently comes in at around 10 percent, and probably even that is high. There's just no way." (By 2020, 50 percent of students at Evergreen were identifying as LGBTQ or "questioning."[28])

If you are a college freshman looking for friendship, hoping to be included, there's perhaps no more expedient means of obtaining a social life than signing up as "LGBTQ." (In the fall of 2019, Yale University offered eighteen LGBTQ social events in just the first two weeks of September.)

Virtually everything that transgender activists hope to achieve in the broader culture has already been achieved on college campuses. While the broader American culture endures constant flogging, LGBTQ identities enjoy a nonstop parade. The universities revile privilege and facilitate emancipation from it, too. All they ask is a de minimis sacrifice to the intersectional gods. Your birth name is a good start.

If you were born "Allison" but think you'd be taken more seriously as "Aiden," the modern university can't wait to help. Universities like UCLA offer simple instructions and provide forms for making this change campus-wide (ensuring your parents won't know) or legal (adding that serious touch).[29] "Any student, including transgender, gender nonconforming, gender variant, and non-cisgender students, who wish to designate a preferred name should fill out the Preferred Name Change Form," invites the University of Pennsylvania website. The college offers easy steps for changing one's "sex marker" as well. In the time that it takes to fill out an Amazon review, colleges offer the chance to give your identity a quick update.

A college freshman may be just three months more mature than a high school senior, but at eighteen—and in some states younger—she sits before a feast of new powers.[30] For those undergrads ready to prove that a trans identity is more than a name and pronouns, the university is a well-stocked discount pharmacy. Over a hundred universities now cover transgender hormones under their health plans, including every Ivy League school.[31] At least eighty-seven colleges and universities cover gender surgery. At Yale, the cost of a course of testosterone for a natal girl under the student health plan is ten dollars a month—less than a standard Netflix subscription.[32]

Still, most young women head off to college with no thought of transitioning. However effective a shield from their classmates' intersectional anger, the whole idea of gender transition, to many coeds, still seems a little extreme. You're eighteen years old, you had a boyfriend in high school; you may not know everything about yourself, but you're pretty sure you're a woman.

Ah, but then a mental health crisis visits. Perhaps it is that old habit of anorexia, or cutting—the one that plagued you in high school. Perhaps, in the face of all these exams, your anxiety dances out of control. Maybe you have a fight with your roommate and you lose your friends and everyone else is so stressed out and strange. You're texting your mom constantly, but she can't really help, and you have no idea how you're going to make it through the next four years this way.

And this is where the story takes a strange turn. Because you've been in therapy for years, ever since middle school, when your mother first signed you up. And you know anti-anxiety pills are your truest friends, and talking about your troubles with a mental health professional really is the best way to proceed.

Realizing that today's coeds are, to put it mildly, psychologically fragile, colleges have hired a battalion of mental health counselors. (Columbia University has fifty-six.) They specialize in things like "eating disorders" and "trauma support" but also "sexual and gender identity issues." In fact, it's possible to sign up with a college counselor wanting to talk about, say, depression, and discover that her other expertise is "LGBTQ." So you're feeling sad. What could be the source? Spoiler alert: you're probably trans.

As we have seen, one parent described his daughter's college mental-health counselor as a "wrecking ball for families." (The counselor works at a very top university and specializes in anxiety and depression while also serving on the university "Gender Team.") With just a little encouragement, therapists like these might point your daughter in the direction of a course of testosterone, for which many coeds no longer need to leave campus. Many universities, like Rutgers University, now disburse testosterone directly—some on an "informed consent" basis, the very day you walk through the door, without so much as a therapist's note.

MEREDITH

Never tomboyish in childhood, Meredith had a steady boyfriend in high school, was captain of her athletic team, and academically precocious enough to win admission to an Ivy League university. She struggled socially her freshman year and came home for Christmas noticeably depressed, having made few friends. Her parents hoped she would cheer up and things would improve by sophomore year, but the social success she had achieved in high school never resumed, and the academic pressure she had heaped on herself proved too much.

According to several students and parents I've talked to, Ivy League schools today are much more of a grind than they were a generation ago—kids never leaving the library, pulling all-nighters not only in exam period, but all semester long. The lesson of so many millennials who struggled to find jobs with humanities majors and mountains of debt seems not to have been lost on today's college students.

When Meredith could not get out of bed for days on end, her roommate walked her to the health clinic, where she would be treated for a nervous breakdown. Her alarmed parents drove to campus and brought her home for the balance of that semester. Meredith wanted to spend the summer taking a course at her university to make up some of the credits she had missed, and she promised to take things easy. This time she returned home with a shaved head and a new penchant for secrecy. Her parents couldn't tell what was going on, but they were leery of pressing. They hadn't even been sure she should be doing anything more than resting. They hoped that whatever this rebellion was would pass; hair grows back, after all.

When she returned to school that fall, she joined an academic club where another participant suggested to her that she might be transgender. Meredith later informed her parents that she realized then that student was right. Within a year she had changed her name to "Micah" and begun a course of testosterone. (That wasn't hard to do; her college gave it out to students on an "informed consent" basis.)

Her parents were unnerved by the sudden change and told her so, but they were also fearful for her precarious psychological state. When she informed them that she would no longer be speaking to them, they became alarmed. They considered driving to campus and physically collecting her, or at least confronting her, but by this point they had met other parents in their situation and they knew the drill: show up on campus against your daughter's wishes, and campus security escorts you out. They considered cutting off tuition, so that she would be forced to come home, but they feared that if she dropped out and remained in the college town, they would lose her for good.

Her mother and father reached out to the university, reminding administrators that only the year before Meredith had been admitted to the health clinic with severe depression. Surely she was in no position to decide to begin a course of testosterone; she wasn't yet stable.

The head of the university health service wrote back cheerily. We employ "a gender-affirmative" model, he told her. "[W]e do what we can to remove obstacles to care for transgender students."

Students like "Micah" are only given hormones if they are at least eighteen and demonstrate ability to give "informed consent," he assured Meredith's mother. "[I]f significant medical or mental health concerns are present, they must be well-managed, including demonstration of an ongoing relationship with a medical and/or mental health provider, as appropriate." Since "Micah" met all the criteria, there was nothing to be done, and little to worry about.

But Meredith was physically altering her body in permanent ways, with her Ivy League school's help and blessing. Her parents knew she was psychologically unstable; Meredith's mother offered the dean of students evidence: "We have seen pages upon pages of texts where [Meredith] claims to hate us, says she cannot breath [sic], cannot get out of bed, is beside herself with anxiety, followed by messages saying she is sorry and loves us, followed by threats to cut us off completely."

Meredith's mother knew her daughter was technically an adult, legally able to make these decisions; only she wasn't in the best frame of mind to do so. "We are not opposed to her transitioning," she pleaded to the dean of students. "We are opposed to her doing it NOW."

"I appreciate that this situation is an extremely difficult one for you and your family and that it gives you great concern for [Micah's] health and well-being," the dean of students wrote back. "However, neither the decision to transition nor the timing of this process are in the University's hands to determine. It is our policy, guided by current medical standards, to allow the students to make these decisions." And, of course, to furnish all the hormones without hesitation. Best of luck!

○ ○ ○

Meredith's parents had no legal recourse against the Ivy League school they had hired to educate her, only despair over the course she had chosen, and a lingering sense of betrayal. So many adults were aiding Meredith's medical transition, as if she were merely changing phone plans, not pursuing an irreversible course to disfigure her body.

"I feel like we're paying for them to ruin our daughter's life," Meredith's mother told me. The school in question is the sort of place whose logo parents dream of placing on their car's rear window. Now Meredith's mother would prefer to watch the place burn.

Then again, that wouldn't help her daughter. Meredith's metamorphosis was already underway. All who had known her at the start of college would find her unrecognizable by junior year.

CHAPTER NINE

THE
TRANSFORMATION

In 2005, Fox kicked off what would become its longest-running television drama, *Bones*. The brains-meets-brawn team of intellectual yet smoldering forensic paleontologist Dr. Temperance Brennan (Emily Deschanel) and hunky yet full-of-heart FBI Agent Seeley Booth (David Boreanaz) spent their days solving murders (obviously). Apparently, there are enough skeletons strewn along the murky banks of the Anacostia to fill another Smithsonian.

If the show had all the structural limitations of its TV decade—every supporting character existed only to serve the goals of its dynamic duo—its 11 million fans seemed not to care. *Bones* was rom-crime perfection.

Each episode was more or less the same. An unidentified skeleton is dredged from the Potomac, found rotting in a submerged refrigerator in Fairfax, or charred by a car bomb on Capitol Hill. Agent Seeley secures the perimeter and hunts for typical homicide-investigation clues; Dr. Brennan "reads" the bones.

Decaying, broken, splintered, or wiped clean by flesh-eating beetles, the bones seem to bear no resemblance to their deceased former owners.

And yet—even before she returns to the lab to run her chemical tests, with only the benefit of naked-eye observation—Dr. Brennan can tell the age, sometimes the hobbies, and occasionally the race of an adult victim. But the very easiest determination Dr. Brennan ever has to make is whether a skeleton belonged to a man or a woman.

Millions of viewers found this plausible. Turns out, they were right. I interviewed three forensic anthropologists, and each confirmed for me that with an adult skeleton, sex is easy to spot. Men's bones are not only much bigger—they have on average 50 percent more bone mass than women's—but many bones, including the pelvis, femur, and skull, also have a sex-specific morphology, meaning they are shaped differently, too.[1]

Think about a man you know who is said to look "*just* like his mother." The resemblance may be remarkable. But it's also limited. He may have her coloring, general face shape or body type (tall, stocky, or bird-boned). But he also looks very much like a man, as she does a woman. This isn't merely because his genitalia differ, nor because testosterone has bequeathed him much more body hair and, on average, 36 percent more muscle mass.[2]

At the skeletal level, the differences are profound: His forehead is thicker and more sloped, culminating in a ridge. The mastoid region behind his ears is more pronounced. His jaw, squarer. His pelvis is narrower, and his legs attach at the hip in a more parallel manner, at less of an angle than a woman's—meaning he stands differently too.

We may not always realize it, but we humans are pretty good at picking up on these differences, and we are always scanning each other, sorting men from women. It's the reason we do a double take when our initial read on someone's sex doesn't seem quite right; reflexively, we return to correct ourselves.

As any biologist will tell you, sex in humans is much more than a few spare parts. Long after our organs have liquefied, skin begun to recede, our cells converted to nitrogen, and ligament casings have surrendered our teeth—when everything that made us identifiable to those who knew us is gone—maleness or femaleness remains.

Gender transformation is, by any measure, an uphill battle. And yet, this is precisely where transgender-identification leads. After all, you can only insist that you're "trans" for so long before so many doubtful looks from peers silently prod: *prove it*.

Remember that for all the cultural purchase of a transgender identity, it comes tethered to an underlying psychological discomfort in one's sexed body. Sufferers of gender dysphoria can find their bodies endlessly distressing. There are treatments and surgeries to meet every physical fixation. Since the motivating ailment is not physical and observable, but mental and vague, there is no natural end to the series of medical treatments that call themselves remedies. Like the distress itself, the cure runs on and on.

LUPRON: CHEMICAL CASTRATOR TURNED PUBERTAL "PAUSE BUTTON"

Remember "Katherine Cave"? She's the mom whose daughter came out as "trans" at twelve after a school presentation, and Katherine—not knowing what else to do—took her daughter to a gender clinic. One of the first things the counselors pushed, as an essential first step, was that her daughter be put on "puberty blockers."

Puberty is a sweeping metamorphosis. If your kid's pretty sure she's going to want to be a trans man, why make her travel there by way of breasts, hips, and menses? Gender doctors like to insist that halting puberty at onset (typically, ages eight to thirteen) is a neutral intervention, or "pause button,"[3] since if the blockade is withdrawn, normal puberty should resume. Like freezing your eggs, blocking puberty is presented as simply allowing a young woman to put nature on hold while keeping her options open.

Once used in chemical castration of sex offenders,[4] Lupron is the go-to puberty blocker, FDA-approved to halt precocious puberty. If your four-year-old daughter is spontaneously developing breasts, Lupron shuts off part of her pituitary to slow puberty down, until her brain and peers catch up.

What the FDA has not approved is using Lupron to halt normal puberty in anyone—transgender-identified or otherwise. In general, doctors don't like to interrupt healthy endocrine signaling based on the say-so of minors, and gender dysphoria has no observable diagnostic criteria. There are as yet no reliable studies that show Lupron is safe for these kids. All available studies note the "low quality" of evidence, or contain similar caveats. Nevertheless, endocrinologists have been administering Lupron "off-label" to gender dysphoric minors in ever-rising numbers for a decade.

But is Lupron actually a neutral, low-risk intervention? Imagine you're a fifteen-year-old girl. But unlike all of your friends, you have no pubic hair; you've never had a period; you have no breasts; you've never experienced orgasm. In terms of size and function, you have the vagina of a pre-pubescent girl. Sound like a neutral intervention?

We wouldn't consider a drug that stunted your growth in height and weight to be a psychologically neutral intervention—because it isn't one. It's psychologically taxing, to say the least, to proceed through high school with dwarfism, remaining the size of a much younger girl. And yet the change in height brought on by growth hormone is arguably far less profound than that caused by puberty's years-long flood of hormones, which transform our bodies into sexual adults.

Sex hormones like testosterone don't only target the sex organs. They also shower the brain. There is good reason to believe they participate in an adolescent's neurological development.[5] Why on earth would doctors liberally prescribe drugs that block it?

"I think the whole area has become politicized," said psychotherapist Marcus Evans, who resigned from England's national gender clinic, the Tavistock Foundation, over the lack of careful protocols in its treatment of transgender-identified children. "The drugs, you know, the hormone blockers, first of all, they say it's a neutral act. What are they talking about? You're going to powerfully interfere with a person's biological development," he said to me over Skype. "I'm not saying you shouldn't do it. . . . But you don't say it's a neutral act. . . . They're not with their peers anymore."

Even if those peers are perfectly sensitive and supportive, surely the girl on blockers will be acutely aware of her strangeness. Other girls her age have breasts, hair under their arms, struggle to manage their periods, say things that indicate sexual awakening—all things she knows little about. She is likely to feel more alienated from womanhood—not less—after she's been cut from the team, endocrinologically speaking.

No surprise, then, that in a clinical trial 100 percent of children put on puberty blockers proceeded to cross-sex hormones.[6] That is a stunning statistic, especially considering that when no intervention is made, roughly 70 percent of children will outgrow gender dysphoria on their own.[7] Far from being "neutral," the psychosocial effects seem closer to radical.

Suppression of normal bone density development and greater risk of osteoporosis, loss of sexual function, interference with brain development, and possibly suppressing peak IQ are all risks puberty blockers carry.[8] The degree and level of certainty of each is anyone's guess, since we have no good long-term studies on children who were given puberty blockers for gender dysphoria. What we do know is that these risks increase dramatically if an adolescent moves straight from puberty blockers to cross-sex hormones. In that case, infertility is almost guaranteed—and sexual development and potential for orgasm may be foreclosed for good.[9]

Adolescent and adult endocrinologist Dr. William Malone is one of the country's most outspoken critics of administering puberty blockers and cross-sex hormones to minors. He told me that the risks of shutting off the pituitary without observable medical justification are dire. "After a certain period, basically the way to think of this is that the system 'goes to sleep' and at some point it may not wake up," he said.

It's worth noting how great a departure this is from normal medical protocol. When we allow parents to consent to medical procedures for teens or tweens, it is typically to permit doctors to save, cure, or alleviate an observable medical problem.[10] But in the singular instance of transgender medicine, we allow a parent to consent to intervention that halts normal, healthy biological functioning—essentially, introducing the "disease state" brought on by a pituitary tumor—all based on self-reported mental distress.

GETTING SERIOUS ABOUT TRANSITION: CROSS-SEX HORMONES

If, as Arthurian legend would have it, self-determination is every young woman's fondest desire, then testosterone is not a bad way of obtaining it. Testosterone suppresses anxiety and even lifts depression.[11] It makes young women bold and unafraid. For the socially inhibited, the freedom it offers can feel like nothing short of a miracle.

Of course, it can also lessen short-term memory and increase moodiness and irritability, but that's someone else's problem. Was I rude or pugnacious? Sorry. It's just that I *feel so good.*

And then there's the hateful mirror, every adolescent girl's foe. Testosterone redistributes a young woman's fat, away from all those places that give her so much consternation—thighs, hips, bottom. That cruel pageantry of online body shaming no longer holds relevance for her. No one examines a boy's photos for thigh gap, muffin tops, cottage cheese. Within the first few months of injections, as body and facial hair begin to sprout, it'll be clear that she's done serving up her body for ridicule. She's on the boys' team now.

Testosterone comes in a variety of forms, including gels and patches. But if you're up for something really edgy, there's also the self-administered intramuscular shot. This testifies to the world, loud as Stentor, that you're nothing like your mother. You're not even a girl. And you're not messing around.

As over six thousand YouTube videos on "how to inject testosterone" readily attest: for a trans-identified girl, T is a joyride. Shortly after starting a course of T, euphoria hits and you absolutely can't wait to tell all your friends—nay, the world—how absolutely amazing it feels.

As YouTube female-to-male influencer Alex Bertie puts it, "Taking testosterone is the best decision I've ever made. I'm so happy within myself. It did not solve all of my problems, but it's given me the strength to make the most out of life and to battle my other demons like my social issues." Self-sovereignty, at last.

In 2007, there was one gender clinic in the United States. Today, there are well over fifty; Planned Parenthood, Kaiser, and Mayo all disburse testosterone, too. Many do so on a first visit on an "informed consent" basis; no referral or therapy required. The age of medical consent varies by state. In Oregon, it is fifteen.

One young woman, Helena, told me that after she came out as "trans" to her mother in her senior year of high school, she couldn't wait to start T. "So I told my parents that I was going to be on a sleepover and then I just drove to Chicago," where the nearest "informed consent" clinic was located. She walked out of the office the same day with a course of testosterone, without even having had to present a therapist's note.

Sure, the clinic informed her about some of the risks (though not the painful vaginal atrophy she would suffer). But how do patients ever assess the risks? Does anyone read those forms? In any case, most trans-identified adolescents are more than happy to accept them.

As YouTube influencer Chase Ross said to me, "I think that some people think that it's dangerous. It's going to make you have worse cardiovascular health, and you're at risk of heart attack and all of these things. But what we need to keep in mind is that the risk I am at right now for cardiovascular disease and things like that is the same level as men." Chase believes testosterone merely took him to the level of cardiovascular risk that that he should have been born with—had he been born in the right body.

Put another way, health risks are another perk, like that tattoo that brands you a member of the gang. If you want to become a man, you have to expect being strong like one, horny like one, and, yes, prone to a heart attack like one.[12]

As for the gratification, you don't have long to wait. After only a few months, body and facial hair will sprout. A "happy trail" appears on your stomach. Weight drops away from your thighs, hips, and bottom. Sure, testosterone renders you "cloudy"-headed, as more than one woman who had been on it told me—less able to evaluate your decision to use it in the first place. But in the place of mental sharpness, it offers the compensatory gifts of mood elevation and a satisfying spurt of heedlessness. A newfound sense of bravado, but also punchiness, descends. Anxiety that shook you and depression that wrapped you in chains have relaxed, relented, drifted away.

Many of the girls caught up in this epidemic may be unconsciously self-medicating. They call their distress "gender dysphoria." But what they may be treating is anxiety and depression; most have battled one or both.

After some number of months on T, a young woman's voice will start to crack. She'll develop acne. She may experience male-pattern baldness. Her nose will begin to round, and her jaw will square, and her muscles will grow too. She studies these changes in the mirror, the way an anorexic would her thinning form. But unlike the anorexic, she's growing stronger; she can feel it. She begins to resemble a very small man; a beard rushes in to establish her virility. Her sex drive intensifies. Even her clitoris begins to enlarge; it may grow to the size of a baby carrot.

But her new eroticism may be limited to the do-it-yourself sort. One of the major side effects of testosterone is vaginal atrophy—dryness, cracking, and recession. Intercourse becomes painful. Young women in transition often become so hyperconscious of the dramatic changes to their bodies that they are afraid to approach, much less undress in front of, a sexual partner.[13] Whatever euphoria these girls are chasing, it stops short of helping them achieve physical connection with another person.

The greatest thrill of all may be that of disguise. Remember the boy who dumped her? The ill-considered nude selfie, which made its way to his several hundred best friends? All those stupid things she did back in middle school, captured in digital images and spread among her peers? The clique that locked her out, then tormented her with an endless online exhibition of how much fun its members all have without her? The doctored photos of her some kid created as a prank—and made sure everyone saw? The hand that mocked her, and the heart that fed.

Well, the joke's on them. She's done feeling bad. Everyone can see— that's not her anymore.

TESTOSTERONE: THE RISKS

Chase Ross wasn't quite right. The nine years he has spent on testosterone may have conferred something more than the cardiovascular frailty of a biological man. In fact, it may have made his risk of cardiovascular disease much worse.[14]

Testosterone thickens the blood. Transgender-identified women are given a dosage of testosterone ten to forty times greater than their bodies would normally bear to produce the changes they seek.[15] There is some indication that biological women on these doses of testosterone may have nearly five times the risk of heart attack that women have, and two-and-a-half times that of men.[16]

Since dosage is driven by desired physical appearance—rather than the alleviation of a physical illness—it is guided by aesthetic principles, not medical ones. Testosterone is typically justified as a treatment for "gender dysphoria," but the endocrinologists who administer it rarely seem even to be evaluating its progress with the patient's dysphoria. What they examine instead are blood levels to ensure that testosterone stays within normal range for a man.

This seems to place endocrinologists (and just as often, nurse practitioners) in the position of hair stylists, who aim to satisfy, rather than medical professionals who seek to cure. Transgender medical guides are fairly open about this. The *Guidelines for the Primary and Gender-Affirming Care of Transgender and Gender Nonbinary People,* put out by the University of California at San Francisco's Center of Excellence for Transgender Health, straightforwardly states, "The goal of masculinizing hormone therapy is the development of male secondary sex characteristics, and suppression/minimization of female secondary sex characteristics."[17]

Although alleviation of gender dysphoria was supposed to be its justification, doctors administering T very often seem less interested in treating "gender dysphoria" than in giving trans-identified patients the look they want. As long as the hair is growing in and the blood work shows that testosterone is maintained at men's levels, the dosage is unlikely to be questioned or altered.

Shortly after cross-sex hormones are introduced, permanent changes result. If a biological girl regrets her decision and stops taking testosterone, her extra body and facial hair will likely remain, as will her clitoral engorgement, deepened voice, and possibly even the masculinization of her facial features. While massive doses of testosterone must be maintained to continue the full effects of transition, eliminating testosterone doesn't whisk an adolescent back to where she started.

There are also pains and inconveniences that come with testosterone. We've seen that vaginal atrophy is a problem. There are also muscle aches, painful cramping due to endometriosis, increased sweating, moodiness, and aggression. The long-term effects include heightened rates of diabetes, stroke, blood clots, cancer, and, as we've seen, heart disease. In general, mortality risk rises.

There is one last but inevitable risk, brought on by the fact that no patient on earth takes every dose of her medicine precisely on time: at some point, a young woman on T will give herself a shot a day or two after she was supposed to.

In a woman not on testosterone, the fast-growing uterine lining is managed by her pituitary, which either halts its growth for the sake of a placenta or directs the lining to be shed in a period. Testosterone shuts down this signaling, turning a woman's menstrual cycle off. When a woman forgets to take her testosterone on time, her ovaries will stimulate sudden spurts of fast-growing uterine lining. This could heighten risk of cell mutation—and endometrial cancer.

Because of this suspected risk of uterine cancer, after a woman has been on a course of testosterone for five years, many women find themselves contemplating a prophylactic hysterectomy and oophorectomy (removal of uterus and ovaries), often with the encouragement of their physicians.[18] Whether by way of Lupron, or straight to T, the end of this story is sterility. These young women have wagered their identities, names, and bodies on the promise of a fresh start, and testosterone arrives like a Rumpelstiltskin to claim their fertility for good.

After all this risk and untold sacrifice, *at least* her dysphoria is gone, right? In fact, there are no good long-term studies indicating that either gender dysphoria or suicidality diminishes after medical transition.[19] Often a young woman's dysphoria increases with testosterone, as it occurs to her that even with a man's voice, body hair, squarer jaw, rounder nose, and full beard, she doesn't look exactly like a man. She still has breasts, after all.

By now, she has likely been binding for months or years, flattening her breasts in a compression sleeve. The binders aren't comfortable, and they pose risks of their own: back pain, shoulder pain, chest pain, shortness of breath, bruised and fractured ribs.[20] Binding can also permanently damage tissue,[21] leaving breasts looking like deflated balloons, flat and wrinkled. Binders aren't a long-term solution. At some point, she may want to wear a pair of guy's swim trunks to the beach.

"TOP SURGERY"

There's a video, infamous to parents of trans-identifying adolescents, featuring one of the country's most prominent pediatricians specializing in gender, Dr. Johanna Olson-Kennedy. Medical director of the Center for Transyouth Health and Development at Children's Hospital Los Angeles, the largest clinic of its kind in the country, Dr. Olson-Kennedy is the one of the country's best-known advocates for early medical transition in children and adolescents.

Shot at a weird angle by a camera likely half-hidden in a mother's purse, Dr. Olson-Kennedy is still recognizable. Her blonde hair is messily tied back in a loose bun. She's wearing a stretchy outfit—camouflage green shirt and black pants—that could pass for pajamas. She looks more like a coed caught prepping for finals than the recipient of the National Institutes of Health's first grant, $5.7 million, to study the outcomes of medical treatment of transgender youth.[22] Her spunky alto and rap-session manner are cool, fun, reassuring. Her words, hair-raising as a fire alarm: "So what we do know is that adolescents actually have the capacity to make a reasoned, logical decision," she says. "And here's the other thing about chest surgery: If you want breasts at a later point in your life, you can go and get them."[23]

It's a shocking statement, the sort of thing parents of these girls send around to each other to prove what sort of monstrous ideology they're up against. Doctors can't really be that flippant about recommending girls for double mastectomy, can they? Surely someone who believes in recommending girls as young as thirteen for top surgery—as Dr. Olson-Kennedy does[24]—takes that responsibility quite seriously. (Yes, thirteen-year-old girls can undergo "top surgery" in California.[25]) Surely such doctors recognize the patient's profound loss, even if they ultimately recommend it?

I will save Dr. Olson-Kennedy's response to my questions for the chapter's end. For now, it is enough to note that until I began researching for this book, I assumed her comment was more or less on the mark: Breasts could be given, and taken away, and given again. Couldn't they?

According to plastic surgeon Dr. Patrick Lappert, the answer is an emphatic no. "I can reverse masculinizing your nose, I can reverse masculinizing your jaw; I can reverse masculinizing your hairline," Dr. Lappert told me. "But I cannot reverse a mastectomy. All I can do is make you a new breast mound, but it's not a breast. It's a lump on your chest which looks like a breast."

A breast, it turns out, is not a lump of fatty tissue, but a series of fibro-glandular structures roughly dividing into quadrants. Within these quadrants are a number of lobules connected through ducts. The whole breast structure works like a rainwater cistern, running milk through the ducts and out the nipple, which also serves as an erogenous zone, exciting the brain.

The difference between a healthy organ with biological capacities— in this case, erotic sensation and milk production—and a lump of flesh that resembles it turns out to be pretty significant to doctors bound by the Hippocratic oath. The two forms may seem fungible to a layperson. But according to Dr. Lappert, eliminating biological capacities merely for the sake of aesthetics is wrong and—in virtually all other areas of medicine—strictly verboten.

"To completely overthrow a natural capacity would be like a person desiring to be blue-eyed, and you deciding the best way to do that is to gouge their eyes out and give them glass eyes that are blue. Now, they've got blue eyes, but they're not working. You've robbed them of the capacity," he told me. "That's an extreme example, but it's an instructive example because we are talking about a cosmetic change." He finds no excuse for the members of his profession who are engaged in this sort of destruction.

One might respond that, in fact, plastic surgeons do this all the time: perform surgeries and introduce risks for the sake of aesthetic or cosmetic goals. But according to Dr. Lappert, even cosmetic surgery has professional ethical limitations.

"There is no other cosmetic operation where it is considered morally acceptable to destroy a human function. None," he told me. "There is no cosmetic operation that I could propose in front of a room full of my colleagues where I could say, 'Hey, listen, I'm going to improve this guy's nose but take away his ability to smell.' Or, 'I'm going to improve the appearance of this boy's ears but he's going to be deaf.' They'd say, 'Sir, we'd like to see your credentials.' But in the case of an adolescent girl, surrendering her capacity to breastfeed so that she can appear to be a boy, that's considered morally correct. Forgive me for my skepticism."

A great many plastic surgeons, however, seem not to agree. Top surgery is a very popular procedure for natal female adolescents who identify as men. I spoke with Dr. Hugh McLean, a prominent "top surgeon" in Toronto, who's been performing masculinizing mastectomies on biological women since a patient first requested one in 1999.

"The most gratifying thing seems to be seeing all the smiles," he told me. "You know, it's a group of patients that's so eager to have their surgery, it just seems to be gratifying in terms of their positive results, their happiness and their well-being." Dr. McLean told me he has personally performed "way over a thousand" top surgeries in total, on patients as young as sixteen.

Dr. McLean actually feels pretty great about what he's doing for patients. So good, in fact, that his practice's Instagram account features a picture of his associate top surgeon wearing a Santa's cap and holding up two white vats, each labeled "breast tissue"—apparently, just removed from his patients. Delivering Christmas joy, it seems, two mastectomies at a time.

According to proponents, these surgeries are the only effective means of curing a patient's dysphoria. Without giving these young women the chance to "become a man"—or, at least, the chance to convincingly appear as such—these patients will be lost to sorrow.

Interestingly, Dr. McLean and other top surgeons like him offer masculinizing double mastectomies to natal females who do not even identify as men. He provides them to those who claim to be "non-binary," too.

Wait a minute, I pushed back. I thought the point of the surgery was to turn a woman into a convincing man? What is the justification for cutting off a woman's breasts to turn her into a—*neither*?

"You know, I long ago stopped trying to totally understand this," he conceded. "I think more than understanding, you need acceptance of this is how the patient is, how the person feels about themselves, and they need to be understood that this is how they feel."

How they *feel?* But surely a drastic medical intervention like this one would be backed, at least, by a therapist attesting that a young girl really has actual gender dysphoria? We wouldn't want to give top surgery to a girl who was just, say, having a nervous breakdown.

Top surgeons like Dr. McLean do not require a therapist's referral; their patients are admitted for surgery based on their own desire to appear more like a boy (or a "non-binary" person). His website states, "For us, the diagnosis is made by the patient, not the doctor, in the same way that a patient seeking breast enlargement is the one who diagnoses her own breasts as being too small."

But surely there are girls who misdiagnose their own gender dysphoria? They aren't doctors, after all. His patients, as we have seen, come as young as sixteen. "Have you turned patients away?" I ask him. "Yes," he said, "but so rarely that I can't actually think of specific cases."

There are two main procedures for "top surgery." One sacrifices the nipple sensation but places (not entirely convincing) constructed nipples in the desired location; the other preserves nipple appearance and sensation but placement is not exactly on target. Both often result in slashing scars across the chest, just below where breasts used to be. For many of these girls, the scars themselves are a kind of stigmata, signaling to those in the know that you may look like a man, but you weren't born that way. Passing often seems far less important than establishing membership on the "trans" team.

Results vary. Some of the surgeries provide a fairly impressive rendering of a male chest, albeit on a smaller body than most men would possess. The desired effect is easier to achieve if the patient bulks up the muscles of her upper body. Less attractive outcomes abound too, usually resulting in a saggy boy chest. The procedure comes with risk of infection, seroma (fluid accumulating under the skin), pain, bleeding, oozing, skin flaps, and nipples that resemble cooked hamburger meat.

For some adolescent girls, top surgery does seem to alleviate gender dysphoria—at least in the short term. I spoke to one young woman, Erin, who had been sexually abused by her mother in childhood. While she regretted her gender transition, she told me she never regretted her double mastectomy. Her breasts, she said, simply caused her too much distress, and she felt much better without them.

But then, when Erin later decided that she had made a mistake by identifying as transgender, contending with her double mastectomy wasn't easy. "I don't have nipples," she told me. "I just have like a huge scar tissue which superficially resembles nipples. And since I'm not on testosterone, I still have nipple discharge and sometimes it can't get all the way out and that's kind of annoying."

Erin also misses some of the sexual function she'd lost. "There's some numbness, yeah, it's just different. Like, sexually, I used to enjoy that part of my body when I was being intimate, but that's not a thing for me anymore."

In the course of writing this book, I studied dozens of images of adolescent women bearing masculinized chests. They're plastered all over the internet. In some, I noticed, the result wasn't quite right.

I wrote to Dr. Lappert about what I had noticed: hips. Once you remove a young woman's breasts, her hips look even more pronounced. To translate this into trans language, after top surgery, couldn't a woman be "even more dysphoric?" Dr. Lappert replied, "If a girl has wide hips, and you remove her large breasts, she is going to look out of proportion. If she is slender with small hips and small breasts, the effect would be less dramatic."

Not to worry. I checked with a plastic surgeon. If she becomes dysphoric about her hips, there's a surgery for that.

"BOTTOM SURGERY": PHALLOPLASTY AND METOIDIOPLASTY

Relatively few female-to-male transgender people pursue "bottom surgery"—which probably is a good thing. I have talked to enough transgender-identified people who have suffered a botched phalloplasty (or had friends who did) to fuel a lifetime of nightmares. Whereas 36 percent of biological females identifying as "trans men" have had top surgery and another 61 percent desire it, according to the U.S. Transgender Survey of 2015, only 3 percent have had phalloplasty and only 13 percent even want it.[26]

Metoidioplasty—another form of "bottom surgery"—is a less significant procedure. It involves shaping a clitoris into something that dangles and resembles a tiny penis. It is not meant to harden or penetrate, though the urethra can be run through the clitoris so that it urinates like a tiny penis as well (assuming everything goes just right).

Phalloplasty, the construction of a penis, is not for the faint of heart. To produce a penis shaft and urethra, a surgeon must take a skin flap from the body, most often by de-sleeving the forearm (peeling off the skin, fat, nerves and blood vessels). The surgeon must then connect nerves to restore sensation to the graft site.

When the best microsurgeons in the world do this, I am told, the result can be impressive. But most surgeons are far from the best in the world. Very often, even today, this surgery is beset by complications.

Getting a penis-like flap of skin to successfully graft is no simple task. Creating the function of urination, much less stiffening, is a challenge. Enabling it to harden enough to penetrate, yet another. A subsequent surgery is necessary to insert implants into the grafted phallus to produce an erection-like effect.

Even just connecting all the veins and arteries to allow blood flow to the new appendage demands microsurgical skills that would abash a master watchmaker, so much delicate piecing of miniature parts. The radial artery that supplies blood to the neophallus must be connected to the artery in the groin area under a microscope, using sutures about one-fourth the thickness of a human hair. The same suturing must be done to veins alongside the radial artery, to direct blood flow into the groin.

Blood clots are common, since even trivial injuries to the lining of the vessels will cause platelets to stick. A clot can cause the graft to fail, creating an open wound that, because of inflammation, cannot be sutured closed.[27] The newly fashioned urethra comes with its own risks: leaks internally and to the outside world. An internal leak can produce scar tissue and strictures, resulting in urine that will not stream but fans out in a spray. And then there is the donor site of the forearm—sometimes left frightfully disfigured by de-sleeving.

One female-to-male trans adult told me about a nineteen-year-old friend whose phalloplasty resulted in gangrene and loss of the appendage. The friend is dispossessed of normal genitalia for either sex—and tethered to a catheter that empties into a urine bag, strapped to her leg.

BLAKE

Blake did not transition as a teenager—but he knows a thing or two about bottom surgeries gone awry. Five years ago, Blake was a successful saleswoman and account executive in her forties living as a lesbian, recently divorced from a woman. Then, he decided to transition.

He began with a course of testosterone, which he loved. "I suffered from depression and anxiety my entire life. Testosterone has just knocked it out. I don't know why. But for me, testosterone is awesome." His depression suddenly under control, he underwent mastectomy and hysterectomy (a procedure that took two tries, since the first time the surgeon nicked his bladder). He underwent a Centurion, a form of metoidioplasty, and was pleased with the result. But to participate in vaginal intercourse as a man would require penetration. That meant phalloplasty.

One of the alarming aspects of transgender medicine today is that, as doctors have rushed to meet the demand of patients and activists, the standards of care have fallen. In 2012, WPATH altered its standards to permit even minors to receive hormone treatment on the basis of "informed consent," meaning that neither diagnosis of gender dysphoria nor therapist's note would be required.[28] Plastic surgeons expanded their practices to incorporate gender surgeries, but without the technical expertise. One prominent microsurgeon at one of the premier hospitals in the country told me that gender surgeries are such moneymakers, his hospital hires doctors to do gender surgeries who, in his opinion, are not qualified for the work. They're plastic surgeons who haven't done fellowships in microsurgery and have no expertise in transferring peripheral nerves. They simply haven't attained the level of skill required to accomplish these enormously complex surgeries with a high degree of success.

Blake's attempted phalloplasty was a disaster. The implanted urethra developed strictures, which required additional surgery to insert a suprapubic catheter to divert the urinary stream so that the wound could heal. The suprapubic tube developed sepsis. A blood clot—a common risk of phalloplasty—led to pulmonary embolism, from which he nearly died. A team of doctors saved his life, but he was left with wrenching pain.

His forearm mangled by de-sleeving, he could no longer lift objects, and even a breeze was enough to send painful shocks through his arm. "My arm is handicapped for life," he told me. "I can't hold things. I can't hold a fork."

Sepsis bloomed in his urethra. It turned out that the skin flap taken from the arm was sprouting hair inside of him. "Just imagine an ingrown hair in your beard or on your leg and multiply that by a thousand." His urethra failed; he has to sit down to urinate. "I have a big mound of nothing," he said.

Blake lives with so much anger, much of it directed toward his surgeon, but also toward a culture he says slathered so much gloss on the notion of transition that it amounted to a lie. Even his therapist, he says, pushed him to transition. After his failed phalloplasty, he returned to confront his therapist, but she seemed to think he had no reason for regret because transgender was what he was supposed to be.

"That's the thing that scares me about our youth. It scares me because [transition] is so glamorized in the news right now. It's so easy to do, it's not that big of a deal," he said. "And it is, it's a huge deal. And at forty-two, if I thought it was that easy, how is our youth going to be able to overcome something like that? That scares the hell out of me. So, for me, was it easy transitioning? No, it wasn't."

In some cases, of course, phalloplasty succeeds. But the surgery is so difficult to perform, there are many things that can go wrong. As elective surgeries go, this is certainly not one to take lightly. I'm no doctor. But the grisly stories I've heard from plastic surgeons and phalloplasty patients themselves have been more than enough to convince me: if there is any way on earth to alleviate your gender dysphoria without phalloplasty, it'd probably be a good idea to pursue the alternative.

HOW DID THIS HAPPEN?

Testosterone is a Schedule III controlled substance, full of long-term health risk. Top surgery is an elective procedure that destroys biological capacity, and phalloplasty is full of serious risk. And yet, in the last decade, doctors and clinics began providing gender treatments like these without even requiring a therapist's note. Why?

Part of the answer lies with the Affordable Care Act of 2010, which indirectly forced health insurance companies to cover hormones and surgeries by barring health insurance companies from discriminating based on sexual orientation and gender identity. This meant that if insurance companies provided hormones (like birth control) to the nontransgendered, it had to also provide the expensive cross-sex version to the transgender-identified. If health insurance companies were going to cover breast reductions for anyone, they had also to cover double mastectomies for the gender dysphoric; anti-discrimination law all but required it. [29]

Suddenly, expensive hormones and surgeries became free or of minimal cost to the patient. As one man, "Jade," who medically transitioned to a woman and now has transitioned back, pointed out to me, "[W]hen you hide the cost [of hormones and surgery], it makes it seem simpler and safer than it actually is." Jade now deeply regrets the cross-sex hormones he took and the orchiectomy (testicle removal) surgery he underwent during the few years after college when he believed he was transgender. "If something is really expensive, it gives you pause to accept just how important it is. But if it's free, it's just like, 'Sure, I'll have that.'"

Some states, such as Oregon, now cover transgender hormones and surgery for low-income patients through Medicaid.[30] Homeless residents and troubled adolescents who run away from home can be eligible to receive these expensive surgeries and treatments. The demand that followed was only natural. What is perhaps more surprising is that so many heirs to Hippocrates have rushed to meet it.

Then again, in the last two decades, doctors have fallen in social status. The now ubiquitous talk of a "human right to medical care" implies a patient's right to demand a doctor's labor. No longer seen as men and women of science, they are now commonly referred to as "health care providers"—a diminution of prestige that makes them out to be little different from nannies and preschool teachers—that is, "child care providers." With little scientific status to safeguard, their Hippocratic oath becomes less compelling than the patients right in front of them.

I have heard from several doctors that transgender medicine has become unlike any other field of medicine. Take WPATH for instance, the medical organization that sets the standards of care for transgender people. Once it represented the most serious scientific inquiry into the cure and care of transgender patients. Today, its conferences are hotbeds of activism, where even physicians and surgeons offering scientific evidence are shouted down.

Dr. Lisa Littman attended her first WPATH conference in 2017. "It was like an infomercial for early transition," she told me. Whereas most medical conferences involve dry lectures on the benefits and risks of any treatment, the one she attended was a benefits-only zone. If the treatments discussed carried risks, none of the organizers seemed prepared to tolerate discussion of them.

When I decided I might refer to Dr. Johanna Olson-Kennedy's lecture in this book, I contacted her. I thought it only fair to give Dr. Olson-Kennedy the opportunity to provide context and add nuance to her remarks (or perhaps retract them). I explained in my email to her that I was writing a book on the sudden spike of transgender-identification among adolescent girls with no history of gender dysphoria.

She wrote back almost immediately.

"Hi Abigail, you write for the Federalist, is that correct?"

The Federalist is an online conservative political journal in which I published three pieces two years ago. I said that no, I don't currently write for them. I am a freelancer; I write most often for the *Wall Street Journal*. I reiterated my request to come to her office, to gather her perspective—to hear why the video of her lecture failed to capture her actual view and why I might have gotten things wrong. I never heard back.

But far more interesting to me than her one-line response was her professional signature, which bears the images of two flags, each about the size of a postage stamp: one the LGBTQ Pride flag; and the other the Transgender Pride Flag.

It isn't only teachers who have become activists. Sex-change operations are now commonly referred to, even by doctors and medical centers, as "gender *affirming* surgeries"—as if doctors had given up the business of curing altogether and instead offered patients mere support and encouragement.

Most hormone-dispensing doctors provide no brakes and no reality check on these distressed patients. They are awash in unreality themselves. There are vanishingly few gatekeepers. The very idea that doctors should ever "gatekeep" is widely derided by trans activists, who seem to want the medicine cabinet left always open and fully stocked. The absence of sufficient oversight of access to this medication is precisely the precondition for substance abuse. Confused and suffering adolescents cry out—all of them certain that the next hormone or surgery will be the one that delivers relief. Doctors rush to appease.

The consequence of satisfying the young patient's demands can easily be the creation of a lifelong medical dependency, the introduction of profound health risks, and a succession of dangerous surgeries with unpredictable long-term results. All of which would suggest that medicalization should be a last resort, not an initial suggestion. Perversely, those who promote caution and restraint about transition are demonized.

The dangers are legion. The safeguards absent. Perhaps the greatest risk of all for the adolescent girl who grasps at this identity out of the blue, like it is the inflatable ring she hopes will save her, is also in some ways the most devastating: that she'll wake up one morning with no breasts and no uterus and think, *I was only sixteen at the time. A kid. Why didn't anyone stop me?*

CHAPTER TEN

THE REGRET

Benji has a pixie cut, an eyebrow stud, a fondness for loose T-shirts, and a girlfriend. As a high school student, her skill with the viola propelled her through level 10, the top tier of high school music performance in Canada. At twenty-three, she has re-embraced her biological sex and identifies as a lesbian. Having spent ages thirteen to nineteen identifying as a trans man, she may also be the canary in the coal mine.

Benji is one of a growing number of young women uniquely capable of warning girls in the grips of gender fever that it might be a good idea to turn back. But Benji doesn't believe she merely avoided personal calamity. What she escaped—she insists—was a cult.

Like a lot of the young women who suddenly identify as trans, Benji was both an intellectually precocious and highly anxious girl. At five she began playing the violin and took to it immediately, soon adding harp, piano, and viola. She was a voracious reader, but at nine, she began developing breasts, which made her terribly uncomfortable and self-conscious. She became anorexic, sometimes passing out in class. Her parents bought her Ensure and begged her to eat. She was diagnosed with depression. But her talent and smarts proved resilient. Like her younger sister, she was admitted to one of the best public arts schools in Canada.

Her parents' relationship was rocky. She and her sister were occasionally the target of physical abuse. Her sister weathered their childhood by smoking pot, cutting, and tipping into periodic bouts of depression.

Benji fell into YouTube and Tumblr. At thirteen, she discovered videos of women enthusing over their transformation into men. Feeling unfeminine, awkward in her body, and unhappy at home, Benji found the possibility of escape enrapturing. She never doubted the accuracy of the purely positive accounts of medical transition.

Kids her generation may be sophisticated when it comes to utilizing technology, Benji told me, but they are strikingly naïve about the truthfulness or completeness of the content. "They think that the mainstream news is full of lies and garbage, but when it comes from an independent person, that must be more realistic or something, more authentic in some way," she said. Postmodern queer theory regards experience as more valid than fact, she said, and her generation imbibes endless streams of this ideology from the internet. "So when you see somebody [on Tumblr] talking about their experience and their opinions, that can trump data and facts because experience is more authentic than data or something."

Benji decided privately that her story matched the video accounts of trans men online: She was trans, too. She set up her first Tumblr account and quietly announced herself as trans to viewers. She wasn't sure anyone would notice. To her surprise, she received an overwhelming "love bombing" from strangers.

You "get people direct messaging you that you've never spoken to before, being like, 'Wow, this must be so hard for you, how can I help you?' or like, 'You're so brave.' Like that kind of thing," she told me. "There's just so much positive reinforcement that there's just no room at all for any criticism or any thought that something bad could be happening."

At first, she explored her new identity exclusively online, interacting with trans adults—people she came to think of as her "real friends," the ones who actually knew her. Not only could she be freer online than she ever managed to be with people in real life, her online "friends" knew her secret. They were unconditionally supportive, showering her with praise. "If I lost my phone or my parents took it away from me, I would like have a breakdown because I was completely dependent on [my online 'friends']."

Often, various adults—mostly, men identifying as trans women—would ask to "sext." By fourteen, she was too curious and far too agreeable not to comply. On the occasions when she demurred, they accused her of "kink shaming," making them feel bad about their sexual predilections—a mortal sin in these online communities. Often, when Benji tried to assert a sexual boundary, her adult interlocutors would accuse her of transphobic oppression. The last thing she ever wanted was to upset them.

In high school, she joined the Gay–Straight Alliance. In 2012, at fifteen, she changed her name and pronouns at school, ditching her old name "Eva," for "Benji"—without telling her parents. "At school, I was Benji, he/him, and then I would go home and I was, Eva, she/her. It was like super complicated."

She became president of her GSA, which held a ceremony for her, where she was named "Captain Dialogue" and presented with a rainbow flag cape. Her secret life as a boy, the life her parents didn't know about, was the one that seemed to be going well. Her grades began to fall apart and her depression increased, but at least her GSA and online trans community seemed to appreciate her.

That year, in response to a domestic dispute, the police were called to her home. A social worker in Toronto began checking in on Benji and her sister and arranged for them to see a therapist. Benji told the therapist her secret. "So the moment that I said I was trans, there was no question whatsoever. And it was like, 'Yes, you're definitely trans' because I think that's probably their policy. But I also think she was biased."

Though it exacerbated her asthma, Benji began wearing a binder. She cut her hair shorter and shorter, and began wearing only men's clothes. She started taking the subway by herself to the therapist's office once a week. The therapist arranged for her to get a prescription for sertraline (Zoloft), and her grades continued to deteriorate. Benji and another friend from her GSA began traveling after school to LGBTQ youth groups in Toronto, where they would hang out for hours. When her parents were away, she hosted gay movie nights at her house, as "Benji" the "trans man" and eventually just as a "man."

The gender ideology world she inhabited was a "cult," she insists, because "when you're inside, you believe non-reality and you disbelieve reality. It literally got to a point where if I was in a queer space," she said, "I would look at someone, and I couldn't tell if they were male or female until they told me because I had trained myself to think that way. I would look at somebody and be like, 'I don't even know what their sex or gender is because I haven't asked them their pronouns yet.' I was so brainwashed."

Her parents were very disappointed in her grades and upset that she seemed so insistent on presenting in a mannish way. At some point, her mother tossed a razor at her in the shower and said, "Shave your fucking legs." Benji now believes the stress and academic pressure she felt at home was a key instigator of her escape into a trans identity.

"I think it helped me dissociate from the person my parents thought I was or the person I was expected to be within my family," she said.

When she complained online about her parents, queer adults often coached her on running away from her family. At the time, she believed that *these* adults—not her parents—had her best interest in mind, and that they were generally helping her to escape mentally and physically from a tumultuous home. But she no longer sees it that way. They were "weaponizing it against me to kind of draw me into their community more, and draw me away from anyone who would give me rational ways of thinking about my life."

She came to believe, in fact, that the only people she could trust were trans-identified. That, she says, is a mantra you hear frequently in the gender ideology world: you can't trust "cis" people—you can only trust trans. "They tell you that you cannot emotionally or psychologically depend on your family or any cis-hets [cisgender heterosexuals] or non-queer people because they can't possibly understand you or empathize with you or love you for who you really are."

But instead of providing a sense of well-being, Benji's trans identification and embrace of gender ideology increased her gender dysphoria and her depression. "My parents had to seriously drag me out of bed to get me in the shower. Like physically put me in the shower and be like, you have to go to school."

She knew her parents would never allow her to go on cross-sex hormones, and she was frightened of what would happen to her if she began taking the drugs while living in her parents' house. She asked her therapist to recommend "coping mechanisms" for dealing with her dysphoria as a next-best alternative. "She was confused about the question because she was like, 'We just put people on T.'"

Benji came to equate cross-sex hormones and gender surgery with salvation, the necessary precondition of a happy life. She devoted massive amounts of time and energy to contemplating the day when she would finally obtain them. Testosterone came to feel inevitable. "I think for a lot of people it's like they build it up in their mind for so long, like multiple years before they actually get it. And then once they get it, they're like, wow, this must be great. When they inject it, they get a sense of euphoria," she said. "They become addicted to it."

Erin, another detransitioner I spoke with, also described her own experience with testosterone as "addictive." By the time Erin began a course of testosterone in her twenties, she no longer suffered gender dysphoria. But because she was still trans-identified, she felt a lot of pressure to take it. "People actually started to bring me testosterone," she said. She realized she would never be fully accepted as a member of the transgender community without it.

At twenty-seven, Erin got a prescription. She hated it. "It made me feel nauseous and cloudy-headed and angry. And I told my trans friends about it, and they said, 'Well, maybe you should try taking more.'"

Even at the time, Erin knew it was crazy to continue an elective treatment that made her feel that bad. But she didn't seem to be able to stop. "Even though it's making me sick, a couple of months after taking it, I would be thinking about it all day and be like, 'I can't wait to put on the gel when I come home.' I just got obsessed with it. And I noticed in the support groups, people were talking about it. And it just made me think, 'Is this dysphoria or is this addiction?'"

In the transgender social scenes both Benji and Erin frequented, testosterone was the coin of the realm, and top surgery a coat of arms. Older trans people at the LGBTQ center in Toronto, Benji said, would offer their testosterone to teens to try, and provide advice about which doctors were trans friendly, or trans themselves, and willing to see the kids after hours. One adult visited the center to coach the adolescents on convincing therapists to sign off on their top surgery. "So they basically concocted a bunch of stories as to why they needed top surgery. And it was like any lie is okay if it leads to surgery because you need surgery. That was like the mentality we had. The same thing with hormones."

Benji decided she absolutely wanted to obtain hormones and undergo top surgery as soon as she left her parents' house. But given her health problems, she was also afraid. For years, she had battled chronic pain in her arms that would cause her muscles to spasm and ache, something she knew testosterone exacerbated.

In fact, the more friends she watched transform under the influence of testosterone, the more unsettled she became. "T makes people really irritable and often very depressed and it makes you gain weight, and a lot of people already had eating disorders before. And it makes your appetite uncontrollable. And it makes you sweat and smell like a man, which is kind of disgusting if you weren't expecting it." In addition, Benji's own chronic pain, asthma, and severe digestive problems made her leery of taking testosterone.

Questioning the panacea of medical transition was strictly verboten. At one point, Benji tried to "follow" a gay man on social media whose bio indicated that he was "homosexual—not homogenderal," meaning he didn't buy into gender ideology. She wanted to ask him questions and listen to what he had to say. According to Benji, one of her queer friends snapped a screenshot revealing that Benji followed this man and had allowed him to follow her back. The screenshot was then posted online, and Benji's queer friend implored their mutual friends to "cancel" Benji and block her, she says. "Just because I allowed this person to follow me without blocking [him] immediately was proof that I should be excommunicated."

Benji was angry with her friend, and she let him know. He didn't back down. "He was like, 'If you talk to these people, what they have to say to you will make you suicidal. You will lose your identity, you will stop being trans. You will literally die if you talk to these people.'"

Online shaming—she says—is pervasive in the gender ideology world, and a key mechanism for controlling the behavior of the suddenly trans-identified. If your friends catch you failing to use the correct terminology, they will attempt to reeducate you. They believe they are helping. They don't want you to be called out. They don't want to have to cancel you, too.

After high school, Benji moved out of her parents' house and in with her grandmother. She got a job at a coffee shop and took extra courses to improve her chances to get into a good university. She succeeded, but it would prove a confusing freshman year. She began to realize she was attracted to women, which surprised her. She made plans to undergo top surgery, as soon as her other health problems let up.

But then, Benji visited a gay male friend who was undergoing chemo for leukemia. "He had had so much chemo that his liver was failing," she told me. Her friend needed a transplant. "And also he was having bone marrow extracted, radiated, and then reimplanted. And he was having all these medical procedures that were non-optional."

He said something that stuck with her. "He was like, 'I'm literally going to die if I don't have this medical procedure,' and he was like, 'Why would you put yourself in the position to be like under the knife and under anesthesia and with like all these possible complications when you're not literally going to die from having breasts?'"

It was a turning point for Benji. She knew her friend had suffered body dysmorphic disorder for years; he could empathize with her gender dysphoria. She didn't have a satisfying response to his question. What was she doing?

She was afraid to leave the trans community cold turkey; she didn't think she could afford to lose its support without replacing it. So she found another online community—"gender critical" radical feminists and lesbians, like herself. Once she began to accept herself as a lesbian, she realized that she was no less a woman for being attracted to women or for failing femininity tests.

She soon learned that a lot of young lesbians are uncomfortable with their female parts as they wrestle against internalized homophobia and come to terms with their emergent sexuality. Gender dysphoria, she decided, did not necessarily make her "trans."

At nineteen, she unfriended all the gender extremists and made a new announcement: she was keeping the name "Benji," but she was a woman. She knew a lot of gender extremists would dismiss her desistance, claiming it proved she was "never really trans." This is the circular logic that pervades trans ideology: if you desist, you were never trans to begin with. Thus, no real transgender people ever desist. It's an unfalsifiable proposition.

"I would like to ask those people under what conditions do they think a lesbian can go to a gender therapist and be told, 'No, you're not trans, you are a lesbian.' Because I have never heard of any situation where that happens ever. How is it possible for any medical condition that every single person who walks in the door definitely has it?"

Benji dropped out of college and moved back in with her parents, determined to get her life back on track. Now twenty-three, she lives with her father, who has separated from her mother. She has returned to the viola and is applying to conservatories in England and Quebec.

The more she reads and reflects on her own experience, the more convinced she has become that trans-identified teens are being hurt by a medical system that fast-tracks their demands without regard for their actual welfare. "That's another thing too that I think about a lot. There are varying degrees of dysphoria, but there are not varying degrees of treatment. If somebody has anorexia, the first move is not to put a feeding tube down their throat. But why is it for trans, the first move when somebody has dysphoria is to be like, 'You need hormones.'"

She believes that mental health professionals ought, instead, to present an array of treatment options to meet the range of severity of dysphoria. Therapy alone should be the treatment for more mild cases. Transition, a much more drastic measure, should be treated as such; therapists should not so readily encourage patients to undertake the daily grind of having to "pass."

This type of thinking has made Benji an outcast among many of the people she once considered her "real friends." She has been put on 125 Twitter block lists, so that those who subscribe can't see her profile. "Basically I'm blocked by all these people so that they never have to interact with me," she says.

Twitter and Medium happily lend their help: Benji has been kicked off of both for her allegedly "hateful conduct." She believes her specific crime was "misgendering": she referred in a tweet to biologically male trans activist Katy Montgomerie as a man.[1]

In her volte-face on trans-identifying, Benji is far from alone. In 2017, another detransitioner I spoke with, Jade, created a Reddit forum for detransitioners who wanted to ask questions or share their experiences. Today, it has over seven thousand members.[2]

Numbers on those who regret their gender transitions and turn back are difficult to obtain. Trans activists commonly deny there are any.[3] And the mental health establishment seems not to want to know about them. "In contrast to comparable disorders, *DSM-5* diagnostic criteria for Gender Dysphoria do not include 'In Remission,' 'In Full Remission,' or 'In Partial Remission' specifiers," Dr. Blanchard pointed out in a tweet. "Thus, there is no apparent way to record a detransitioned patient for clinical or research purposes."[4]

But detransitioners exist. Once you've met a few, you realize how far one can travel down the path to medical transition before turning back. It turns out Benji got off easy.

HELENA

Helena, twenty-one, was an angry kid. The daughter of Polish immigrants in Cincinnati—an endocrinologist mom who runs a weight loss business and an engineer dad—she remembers her busy parents as emotionally remote. She fought with them often and felt their disappointment acutely.

Still, middle school was a relatively happy place for Helena. She made friends easily, excelled at figure skating, and loved to organize outings of her peers—ice-skating nights and Christmas caroling for charity. Then, around the end of eighth grade, "Everything started changing," she said.

"The girls around me were starting to talk about kissing boys. They started using Instagram, and talking about the latest makeup and fashion trends," she wrote later. "They started talking about followers and celebrities—people I had never heard of."

Helena had no interest in makeup or clothing. She preferred making her friends laugh to trying to look pretty for the boys. "The same things that had made me the class clown before—the same things my male friends were still seen as funny and adorable for—now made me a social pariah."[5]

She began losing friends and gaining weight. Her mother forced her on diets, which eventually led her to binge. She stopped organizing skating nights. She began eating lunch alone. "I got a lot of acne. I went from just another weird kid like everyone else to THE weird kid."[6]

By freshman year at a Catholic private high school, she had no friends. None of the other girls seemed to share her interests in classic rock or vintage television; she perpetually felt left out. "I kind of went through my, 'I'm not like other girls, I hate girls phase,'" she told me.

Helena began to starve herself and experimented with other forms of self-harm, such as cutting and burning. She found Tumblr and its pro–eating disorder "pro-ana" (for "pro-anorexic") sites that provide the how-to for eating disorders along with attempts at justification and moral support. She became transfixed.

"These self-harm blogs were not simply the online diaries of depressed teenagers, but a thriving community in which mental illness became an identity,"[7] she later wrote. An identity was precisely what Helena had been looking for, and victim identities appealed to her mental state.

She left Catholic school for a well-regarded public school in her area. By then, her interests on Tumblr included classic rock and Harry Potter fan groups. "But the thing with the more mainstream fandom, is that that's where the social justice stuff is."

At first, Helena mocked social justice posts she found online. They seemed to her so pious and full of fervor. "But as I kept reading, it was like the kind of thing where I couldn't look away," she said. It wasn't only the social justice that intrigued her, but the trans testimonials. "People's individual stories of like why they identify as trans and their struggles. And it was stuff like, 'Oh, I hate my boobs, I hate my body, I hate everything.'"

Helena binge-watched videos of trans testimonials and began to strongly empathize with the people in them. She soon realized that her views were converging with theirs. "The more I got into it, the more prominent these feelings were of not being a girl." At first, she didn't believe she was a boy. Instead, she would think, "I'm anything besides a girl."[8]

I pressed Helena about why a young woman today would feel like a failure as a girl. Where do all these young women get the bizarre notion that any young girl who doesn't look like a pageant winner is a loser? Women occupy virtually every job in society, from bus driver to athlete to doctor. So where would they get the idea that they needed to look like Barbie dolls—a toy parents long ago stopped buying their daughters?

Online, she said. Porn, she said. The media, she said.

Well, hold on, I pushed back. I had just seen *A Star is Born*. I pointed out to Helena that the wildly successful and talented actress and singer Lady Gaga managed to sell twenty-seven million albums without a kittenish nose. I expected Helena to agree with me. Instead, she seemed to think I was insane. "Women like Lady Gaga get made fun of," she informed me.

She began to unravel the mystery for me. Women of my generation watched Lady Gaga on the screen—or listened to her music in the car. But Helena and her cohort dissected Lady Gaga's persona on social media. They ridiculed her looks, mocked her weight, and trashed her appearance. To me, Lady Gaga seemed the sort of star a talented young woman might seek to emulate. But when girls looked at Lady Gaga discussed on social media, they saw a woman torn apart.

Later I asked Dagny—another woman who detransitioned—a similar question. Dagny had wanted to be a boy for lack of strong female role models. "What do you mean every woman has to be 'feminine'?" I asked her. "Isn't your mom a 'real woman'?" She tried not to laugh. "Yes, but she was also a mom, you know."

Her mother didn't count, she meant. She might as well have been the Abominable Snowman, I understood. No teenage girl wants to be anything like her mother.

In high school, Helena suddenly adopted the gender language she had discovered online. She has examined the posts from a blog she kept then: Over the span of two weeks, her blog posts went from "depressive posts" about her life to "queer, trans, genderfluid, non-binary, demiboy, valid problematic, cishets, gender. Every last word. Like a virus."[9]

She began to make friends. Her best friend from class felt the same sense of failure as a girl—not nearly feminine or glamorous enough. At a male friend's house, they began exploring together the possibility that they might be trans—or at least non-binary. "We were sitting at this house and we started talking and I was just like, 'You know, I don't think I'm a girl. I don't feel like a girl.'" The boy was gay, and his parents had been giving him a hard time for how feminine he was acting. He decided he was trans, too. When they told another friend of theirs what the three of them had decided, the fourth friend came to the same conclusion—she was trans, too.

And then something magical happened. Helena "came out" on Tumblr. Her number of followers skyrocketed. Her online "friends" enthused over her decision to come out and her "cute" new name.[10] She was freer online than she had ever been in real life. Social media offered the possibility of an edited persona, of only showing the best of herself—and only when she wanted to.

Helena had never been anything but another white girl. Suddenly, she was a member of an oppressed minority. She quit figure skating and cut her hair and began binding her breasts. She founded her public school's GSA and changed her name and pronouns at school, without telling her parents. Her best friend changed hers, too. Helena had carved herself a niche. Her world may have been narrower, but she no longer had to wonder at her place in it; the fit was snug.

In short order, she transferred all the energy she had poured into being part of the pro-ana online community into being trans. "My goal went from diet pills to testosterone. . . . From fantasies about slicing off my thigh fat to slicing off my breasts. I bound them with duct tape. I couldn't breathe. It made me panic, but I felt brave."[11]

Her grades were a mess. She went to see the school psychologist, who affirmed Helena's transgender identity and began discussing options for medical transition with her.

Her senior year, on a car ride with her mother, she announced she was transgender. She would appreciate it, she said, if her mother would use her new name and pronouns, like everyone else had been doing at school for some time. Her mother was shocked and asked where all this was coming from. "And then I gave her the usual spiel of, 'Ever since I was little, I just knew I wasn't a girl'—which isn't true," Helena interjected. But by then,

Helena's script was well-rehearsed. "People will literally give you tips on how to alter your story to have a better chance of getting hormones," she told me.

Helena abandoned all of her hobbies, including painting. By the end of high school, her only hobby was "being trans." "All the passion for life went out the window and I just was focused on the possibility that someday I would transition and live again."

Helena planned to start testosterone as soon as she turned eighteen and could obtain a prescription without her parents' approval. "I wanted to start my new life in college and I wanted to kind of erase my existence as a girl before I started college," she told me. Her best friend, however, decided that she had made a mistake and told Helena she was returning to her old name and pronouns. Helena was furious. She exploded at her friend over text. After a series of arguments, their friendship ended.

In April 2016, a few weeks after Helena's eighteenth birthday, she woke up early, told her parents she would be at a friend's house, and drove six hours to Chicago, where she had made an afternoon appointment with an informed-consent clinic. "I showed up and there was this social worker. And she asked me like, 'How long have you experienced dysphoria?' To which I was like, 'Forever!' And then she asked me like, 'Did you ever have gender dysphoria as a kid?' And I said, 'Oh my God, yeah. I used to rip my dresses off and cry every time someone called me a girl'—which is not true," Helena told me. Nevertheless, her answers satisfied the social worker. After a brief lesson on how to give herself an injection, Helena left with a prescription for testosterone.

She felt victorious—her destiny at last in her own hands. "I called one of my best friends and I was crying with joy. Yeah, I was really, really, really elated. Like I've never experienced more of a fucking endorphin rush than like after I did my first injection. So, yeah, it felt really, really good for the first, like, two or three injections."

Just as she'd hoped, she felt remade. Armed with a new name and pronouns, she started college and fell immediately in with a group of transgender-identified kids. Keeping up with her shots, however, became a problem for her. The needles were long, and she had to shove them deep into her leg muscle. At first, her excitement pushed her through the fear, but then, that wasn't enough. "I would sit there for an hour trying to get myself" to do the injection. "It's like a three-inch needle and you have to push it all the way in."

She began asking trans-identified friends to do her injections. They did, and she continued on with testosterone. She never grew much body hair, but she liked the way it redistributed her fat, and the cool deepening of her voice.

When Helena returned home—now presenting as a male—she fought with her mother, who still refused to use her new name. Her mother told her not to return home until she came to her senses. "I thought that my mom was like a huge transphobe, but at the same time, it was really validating because like the trans community has this story of 'trans people are so oppressed.'" Finally, she was facing oppression too. She blocked her parents' numbers. Her father managed to call the university and get a message to Helena, but Helena didn't want to hear it. She called him a stalker and asked him not to phone again.

Far from improving her mental health and alleviating Helena's distress, "being trans" seemed to increase it. She found herself paralyzed with sadness, obsessing over the alleged fact of her oppression as a trans man in American society. "That was a thought-loop that would go on in my head almost 24/7," she told me. "I was so miserable and self-loathing."

Helena began to have doubts about the path she was on. But when she expressed them online, other trans-identified adolescents rushed to assure her that she needed to keep going. They told her she was so brave. They told her she could do it, but she had to stick with it. Once she'd had a full gender transition—they told her—she would be happy. Like Benji, Helena also told me—unprompted—that the world of gender ideology felt like a cult. It was an assessment I would hear often from detransitioners: walking away didn't feel like an option.

Then, one day, a friend from high school studying at the same college sent her a video montage of pictures of the two of them over the prior year. It shocked Helena. "I just looked at them and I was like, 'This is not me. . . . What have I done?'" While she didn't have much body hair, in other ways her body was not—and might never be—the same.

Helena had a panic attack. She dropped out of college. She realized she'd been horrible to her family. She had alienated two friends who had desisted. She thought about killing herself.

She began to see the world she had inhabited as not only unhappy but unhealthy.

"There's so much depression, self-harm, and drug abuse in the trans community. They're all goddamn miserable. And it's just like this misery fest. . . . I mean, there's obviously the people who put up a face and act like 'I'm super trans but I'm really happy about it,' but even those people, once you talk to them, you see their lives are catastrophes."

Helena clawed her way back. She reconnected with her family. She told her story online. She began to co-moderate the subreddit that offers support to those thinking of detransitioning, fending off the hordes of ideologues that accuse her of trans hate.

She still struggles with anorexia and depression. Living as a man was no cure-all; re-embracing her birth sex did not make her other troubles disappear. What she believes she has now is clarity.

With three other young women, in 2019, she founded Pique Resilience Project, a group of detransitioners and desisters devoted to telling every adolescent who will listen: you don't have to be transgender. It ought to be a needless public service message. And yet, so many are shocked by and resistant to it. It's possible to live a transgender life, if that's what feels right. But it's also possible to have thought you should, only to decide you were wrong.

Each of the detransitioners I talked to told a remarkably similar story—of having had no gender dysphoria until puberty, when she discovered her trans identity online. Some, like Chiara, desisted before ever starting testosterone. (Chiara's mother sent her to live on a horse farm for a year, where she had no internet; the physical labor helped her reconnect to her body, and the lack of internet allowed her to leave her trans identity behind.)

Others, like Desmond, did not turn back until an accumulated course of testosterone left her doubled over in pain from the uterine atrophy it produced. The only way to alleviate the pain, doctors insisted, was hysterectomy. So a year ago, she underwent the procedure. When she awakened without a uterus, she realized her entire gender journey had been a terrible mistake. "Somehow I decided that it just wasn't worth the risk anymore." Having paid an extortionate price for her new identity, Desmond felt only buyer's remorse.

Nearly all of the detransitioners I spoke with are plagued with regret. If they were on testosterone for even a few months, they possess a startlingly masculine voice that will not lift. If they were on T for longer, they suffer the embarrassment of having unusual intimate geography—an enlarged clitoris that resembles a small penis. They hate their five-o'clock shadows and body hair. They live with slashes across their chests and masculine nipples (transverse oblong and smaller) or flaps of skin that don't quite resemble nipples. If they retained their ovaries, once off of testosterone, whatever breast tissue they have will swell with fluid when their periods return, often failing to drain properly.

For Erin, trans identification seemed to fuel her gender dysphoria. Presenting as a man may have calmed some of her distress, she said, but it was also emotionally exhausting. "I felt I got kind of another dysphoria trying to be male and male identified," she said. "My body doesn't fit into men's clothes. It's always frustrating trying to find pants. I'm just not the right shape. When I wear men's coats or sweatshirts, it just feels like I'm this kid trying to wear my dad's clothes. . . . I'm a curvy person, and it was making me unhappy to just think that maybe if I exercise or maybe if I change my posture—it became a thing I was thinking about all the time."

Each of the desisters and detransitioners I talked to reported being 100 percent certain that they were definitely trans—until, suddenly, they weren't. Nearly all of them blame the adults in their lives, especially the medical professionals, for encouraging and facilitating their transitions.

"If you did make a mistake by transitioning, it's not like you blindly one day decided that this is what you wanted to do," Benji wants those considering detransition to know. "Probably, your guidance counselor, social worker, doctor, therapist, psychiatrist, parent, school teacher, told you that this is a good idea or supported that this is a good idea or helped you hash out why this would be good for you. This is not something that you came to the decision on your own—especially if you were under eighteen, you were like a child. Other people should have been looking out for your well-being."

And that's part of the problem: eighteen may be the age of majority, but especially today, it's still very young. So many of these girls who are drawn into the transgender world are already battling anorexia, anxiety, and depression. They are lonely. They are fragile. And more than anything, they want to belong. Adults in their lives should realize this, but instead, the moment these girls voice the shibboleth "I'm trans," nearly every adult, even medical professionals, regard them with the awe owed to a prophet, not the skepticism usually applied to a suffering teen.

Benji offers this thought experiment: "Imagine if there was a cult, and every single member of that cult wanted a gastric bypass because they needed to be skinnier because of the tenets of their cult. It wouldn't be ethical for a doctor to give all these women gastric bypass just because it's their religion. So when I see these people who have like spent years on Tumblr, indoctrinating themselves, and then they go to the doctor— it's like, the doctor is the one who has the responsibility to be like, 'Can this person tell what is reality? Is this person making a decision that's good for them?'"

Many detransitioning young women have since come to believe they were just young lesbians who had internalized homophobia and been led to believe that not being typically feminine meant they weren't female at all. Nearly all of them struggled with mental health and engaged in self-harm. And as I spoke to each of them, I wondered how much easier things might have been if—instead of turning to their iPhones—they had gone to the mall together and pierced their ears or smoked a cigarette.

Those who transition often assume that there is no going back. This is gender ideologues' favorite dogma, that epistemic access to one's gender identity is perfect: *"Kids know who they are."* Because no one can be wrong about his or her gender identity, there is no reason ever to change your mind.

Parents who oppose their daughters' transitions unwittingly participate in the fiction that the daughter they once had is gone for good. Many parents I've talked to mourn their daughter's transition as a kind of death. But detransitioners exist. More are coming forward all the time.

Here's the point, and it's an important one: there is life after detransition.

The psychological struggles that lead a young woman to transition are often acute. More than likely, even after detransition, they remain. At some point, we all have to face our struggles and sorrows.

But there are also worse mistakes to have made than transition. You may have altered your body, and it may not, on its own, revert back. Laser hair removal exists for a reason—as does plastic surgery.

That hideous public diary that calls itself "social media" and mocks us with so many small-minded pronouncements and embarrassing images—it doesn't matter. Not really. Sooner than we think, we may all regard it as little more than humanity's most colossal distraction, an endless ledger of wasted time.

We are, all of us, doomed to hurt those we love. Most of us disappoint our parents in some respect; or at least, we're not exactly who our parents would have designed, had they been granted just a little more say. Worse yet, we disappoint ourselves.

But then, each day, we awaken to a miracle: another chance to try again. To ask forgiveness. To call our moms. To go just a little easier on ourselves.

If you believe you've made a mistake by transitioning, the best time to turn back is now. The further you travel toward that impossible horizon, the harder it is to retrace your steps and find the person you might wish to be once more. Then again, if anyone excels at reinvention, it's you.

Reports of your death have been greatly exaggerated. That's no small thing. It may even be everything.

CHAPTER ELEVEN

THE WAY BACK

Buck Angel is easily one of the most famous trans men on the planet. I met the internationally celebrated porn star at a coffee shop in West Hollywood, very near to his home. At fifty-seven, but looking at least a decade younger, he sports a red beard, a black cap advertising his cannabis company, and a T-shirt stretched over impressively muscled arms sleeved in tattoos. Only his small stature and the effeminate lilt he lends to a gravelly voice hint at the decades he spent as a girl and woman.

Maybe it was because I already knew his story, but in his soft eyes, the lightest shade of blue, I met a gentleness that won me over. Right away, he felt like a friend. I couldn't shake the feeling that despite all appearances—the freckled pate rendered bald by decades on testosterone—in a real sense, I was talking to a woman.

Buck wasn't at all offended when I told him this. He readily acknowledges his female biology, which he says is only to his advantage; it helps him relate to the women he woos in a way few men can. He prefers the term "transsexual"—someone who medically transitioned—to "transgender." He doesn't pretend he was always "really" a man.

I liked him immediately. The admirable ease with which he carries himself. The hopeful affection with which he concluded texts to me ("Love, Bucky.") The unembarrassed reference he made to his checkered past: the years spent as a teenage female model, then as a crack addict, kicked out by his parents, turning tricks on the street. Buck Angel doesn't lie to you. And he doesn't lie to himself, either.

We met to discuss a question that preoccupies us both: whether trans-identified teens are receiving good advice, mental health care, and medical care. Buck's answer was an immediate "No."

"They see candy. They see something that can make them feel better about themselves because all these trans kids have YouTube channels, social media, and I think that's influencing. We're idiots if we don't say that's influencing. It's 100 percent influencing," he said.

Buck Angel ought to know. As a famous performer, adult film producer, and purveyor of popular sex toys for the particular anatomy of biological women on testosterone, he's someone trans-identified teens often reach out to for advice. And he is well aware that their sudden rush to identify as transgender may not reflect a healthy attitude or sober reasoning. "So when we see these kids all speaking the same language, all doing the same thing, all wanting to transition right away, they think it's a fix. That's what they think. They think 'It's going to fix everything about the way I feel about myself.' . . . And that's the dangerous part. It's not going to fix everything until you fix your brain."

Buck was one of the first transsexuals to medically transition from female-to-male in Los Angeles. He began taking testosterone in 1991. He would eventually undergo top surgery and metoidioplasty,[1] all of which he's pretty happy about. Nonetheless, he is adamant that extensive therapy must accompany any medical transition.

Part of a therapist's role, he says, is to question adolescents' self-assessment and to help them figure out if they are even trans. Because many of them, he says, may not be. "A sixteen-year-old kid might think that they're this, but do they actually know? And I can say that, as a fifty-seven-year-old person. You grow and you learn through experience. And at sixteen, how much experience have you had?"

It's important to recognize just how much courage it takes for a trans man to say such things—and how much integrity, too. Having struggled against his sex since his girlhood days, Buck knows well the gnawing chafe of gender dysphoria, and how difficult it is to forge a new life appearing as a member of the opposite sex. Transition—he reiterated many times—is hard. How easy it would be, then, to simply abandon all skepticism and welcome the throngs of newly trans-identified youth, never questioning whether they truly belong.

Still, he can't bring himself to do it. "Can you imagine if you're sixteen and you cut your boobs off and you take hormones and then ten years from now you decide, 'That wasn't the way I was supposed to go'? That's devastating for me even to think about."

Buck faults the trans community for not being more skeptical of the sudden epidemic of adolescent girls claiming to be trans. "How can we not question it? How can our own community not question it? That's the part that I'm a little bit upset about; my own community not saying, *Hey, we need to take responsibility for these children*."

He believes something that once was fairly uncontroversial: teenagers are teenagers. By definition, they're still figuring out who they are, and they really should be treated as such by adults who ought to know better. Many of these girls—perhaps most of these girls—are not really meant to be "transgender" at all. "You could totally be gay. And now we're just pushing girls who want to wear boys' clothes into being trans. You can't just say because someone dresses like a boy, you're a boy."

That is not to say that Buck Angel doubts the potential benefit of medical transition. On the contrary, he believes it saved his life. But he also believes that we're never going to be able to help those who actually need it if we're fast-tracking transition for troubled girls caught up in a social contagion. "I had to go through many hoops to be able to be here today. I had to go to mental health care. I had to get a note. I had to do this whole step-by-step process, which enabled me to have a secure transition." It isn't a process he resents. It's a process that he believes prepared him mentally for the life he now leads.

I told Buck that one of the aspects of the current trans phenomenon that unsettled me most was its anger: the in-group–out-group hysteria, the insistence on naming and punishing enemies. And another thing bothers me, too: the apparent asexuality of the members of this group. Were any of these teenagers interested in having sex one day? In so many instances, the more dramatically these trans-identified teens transfigured their bodies, the more their dysphoria spiked—the harder they pushed away even the possibility of sexual intimacy.

Far be it from me to advocate teenage sex. But in the course of writing this book, I've come to view this monster differently, now that it's been so utterly defanged. For humanity's most notoriously libidinous demographic, it's hard not to see that age-old rounding of bases as a twitchy expression of joy, the carnal declaration of hope.

There's something horribly sad about teenagers who aren't even interested. Adolescent girls who would rather sit at home, dreaming of obtaining and injecting hormones, railing against "TERFs" online, than indulging fantasies of kissing or touching another teenager.

Trans identification may be celebrated as a moment of liberation, but for many teens suddenly identifying, it very often seems to be a sad cult of asexuality, like the hand-painted sign in an antique shop reading "Please Do Not Touch." Perhaps these girls are protecting themselves from the endless assault of violent porn, or the hyper-glamorized internet images to which they believe they'll never measure up.

Breast binders and top surgery come to seem a contemporary chastity belt, ensuring that no one will venture too close. The relentless dysphoria of these teenage girls, during and even after transition, seems so utterly incompatible with ever achieving the self-comfort necessary to share your body with another.

Are these kids having sex, as far as Buck knows? No, he told me— they're not. Is this all an act of sexual withdrawal and avoidance? I asked him. Yes, he thought it might be. It bothers him a lot.

MEN HAVE IT BETTER, DON'T THEY?

For so many girls, puberty strikes like a tornado—violently and without warning. A girl's halfway through a social studies exam when she's overtaken by the horror that she may have leaked through her jeans. Or she's in chemistry lab when cramps hit, doubling her over, sending her stumbling to the nurse.

Despite the dignity and grace of so many women, the path to womanhood is neither easy nor elegant. Perhaps forever, but at least since Shakespeare's Viola arrived shipwrecked in Ilyria and decided to pass herself off as a man, it has occurred to young women: it's so much easier to be a boy. In more recent times, Beyoncé captured this sentiment full throttle in her 2008 hit, "If I Were a Boy." This notion that men have it easy may have occurred to Eve, who ate from the Tree of Knowledge only to be punished with labor pains and a domineering husband. Adam's sin saddled him only with the burden of having to work for a living. (Big deal.)

Far from remaining an ephemeral notion or source of humor for women, this thought has ossified into a worldview. It lurks within the scolding that women who take time off for their families have failed to "lean in." And within the tiresome insistence that jobs women disproportionately occupy—teachers, literature professors, psychologists, gynecologists—are somehow less worthy than those men tend to dominate—CEOs, software engineers, math professors, psychiatrists, orthopedic surgeons. That men also overwhelmingly occupy many lower-status and dangerous jobs—construction laborer, logger, groundskeeper, roofer, cabbie, janitor—doesn't get mentioned much.

Though it's often considered insulting to note, women in the aggregate have different preferences: we tend to put "people jobs" over "thing jobs," as someone once put it to me.[2] This has caused feminists a great deal of consternation. Pricked by the embarrassment of natural differences between men and women, they blame society and insist women need to be taught to adopt different preferences. But behind this insistence lies the idea that women's preferences are inferior. Young girls are left to conclude that they must strive to be more like men—they must close the novel they were enjoying and take up coding. They must want things men want *because men want them.*

The talking point about the dearth of women CEOs is a classic. The fact of this disparity might just as easily be understood differently: CEOs lead fairly unbalanced lives. They make a lot of money and have very little time. Their relationships suffer. They have high rates of divorce. Women might recognize this difference and assume that men are the ones to be pitied.

We might just as easily say: Women are so much better adjusted, so much wiser for preferring relationships to dollars. We might as easily say: Of course women prefer literature to software engineering! It's far more interesting. It has the power to transport, to move hearts and minds. Literature is the story one generation tells to the next. So many women study, teach, and produce great literature. Who is the wiser sex?

Instead we presume that if men dominate the STEM departments, they must be occupying the university's Arcadia. If CEOs are overwhelmingly male, then women are being unfairly excluded—by men who outfox them, a system that diminishes them, preferences that lead them astray. We want to have it both ways: acknowledging sotto voce that Sumner Redstone, Rupert Murdoch, and Jeff Bezos have not enjoyed enviable personal lives, while insisting every woman should or would stand in their shoes, given half a chance.

Nothing I have written here should be taken to discourage young women from wanting to become CEOs or math professors. (Does this even need to be said?) The point is only that women need to own up to a hard truth: We assume—so often, so immediately— that the guys have it better, that whatever men want *must be better,* too.

We allow others to denigrate motherhood; we denigrate motherhood ourselves. We treat stay-at-home moms as the most contemptible of life's losers. (I should know: I was one for years. Graduate degrees proved a flimsy shield against the withering looks and comments from women with "real jobs.")

We must stop. It's a dumb habit, thoughtless and base. It reflects an unflattering insecurity we shouldn't indulge. The jealousy at its heart suggests that either we believe women aren't truly capable, or they have somehow been duped, made victims by a "system" that, generation after generation, locks us out and shuts us in with so many glass ceilings and walls. It's an exhausting set of untruths. Worst of all, girls are listening.

They don't know it's all tongue-in-cheek. They don't realize we're merely garnering support for women's causes, bargaining with the culture for better jobs and greater pay. They don't know we're merely whipping the pols. They actually believe us.

WHAT SHOULD WE DO FOR OUR GIRLS?

Since I began writing this book, many parents of suddenly trans-identifying girls have reached out to me. Most wanted to tell me their stories. But a few wanted advice.

To those parents who are mid-crisis with their daughter—I recommend seeking out a support group immediately. The good ones will help you navigate staying connected with your child without participating in her indoctrination. "The most fundamental thing I want parents to understand is that this isn't necessarily about gender at all," says Sasha Ayad, a therapist who has worked with hundreds of trans-identified adolescents. "When these kids go online they're essentially being steeped in what could be seen as propaganda."

Sasha Ayad does not affirm adolescents' gender identities and she does not encourage parents to do so either. "I tell parents that there's a way to support your child and to honor this kind of identity exploration without necessarily taking the identity literally."

Denise, the woman who founded the prominent blog 4thWaveNow after her own daughter suddenly identified as transgender, advises against adopting the child's name and pronouns. Our kids "need us for a reality check, which is also why I don't think parents should go all the way down the road to doing whatever the kid wants. Like, 'Oh, yes, that's fine. The pronouns, the male name.' I think you have to find your own limits though."

To those who simply want to inoculate their own daughters from the fast-spreading social contagion of gender ideology, I can offer a bit more. School districts, teachers, and even other parents are right now sowing gender confusion. Confronting it requires not psychological expertise, but intellectual ammunition. Opposing a school assembly introducing a transgender adolescent to the student body requires something that is squarely within my métier, as a journalist: it requires merely knowing the truth.

1. Don't Get Your Kid a Smartphone

Parents will balk; parents will groan. Most consider this an unimaginable amputation. How could I separate a teen from her iPhone? But in terms of obviousness, this one's not even hard. It practically writes itself.

Nearly every novel problem teenagers face traces itself back to 2007 and the introduction of Steve Jobs's iPhone. In fact, the explosion in self-harm can be so precisely pinpointed to the introduction of this one device that researches have little doubt that it is the cause. If I had told you in 2007 that one device would produce a sudden skyrocketing in self-harm among teens and tweens, you would likely have said, "No way is my kid getting one." And yet, here we are: the statistical explosion of bullying, cutting, anorexia, depression, and the rise of sudden transgender identification is owed to the self-harm instruction, manipulation, abuse, and relentless harassment supplied by a single smartphone.

2. Don't Relinquish Your Authority as the Parent

You're the parent for a reason. Don't be afraid to push back; your adolescent can handle it. You don't have to go along with everything she comes up with (even claims about sexuality or identity).

Many of the parents I spoke with told me that when their, say, thirteen-year-old announced she was lesbian, they immediately supported their daughter. Many of them all but raised a Pride flag over their home. But the fact is, a thirteen-year-old—lesbian or straight—is still only thirteen. Our true sexuality is not an identity we choose online, but a feeling of attraction that emerges and even evolves over time. Understanding it requires us to go into the world, to have in-person experiences with other people.

Sasha Ayad says that parents today are often afraid of upsetting their teens because they have the idea that their job is to ensure their child is "happy and perfectly adjusted and well-balanced 100 percent of the time." Not only is that an unreasonable goal, it misunderstands the inherently tumultuous state of adolescence. Teenagers are supposed to get angry and emotional. Parents are supposed to set limits.

If you have a fight with your teenager, she might be angry with you, but she'll feel the presence of a guardrail. Sometimes, just knowing it's there may be enough. Your teenager may tell you she hates you; she may even believe it. But on a deeper level, some of her need for individuation and rebellion may be satisfied. If you eliminate all conflict through endless agreement and support, it may only encourage her to kick things up a notch.

3. Don't Support Gender Ideology in Your Child's Education

My best friend attended a posh all-girls' school in Washington, D.C., and each year they would have an assembly on eating disorders. For the few girls who were already dabbling with anorexia, it may have brought comfort. But for the rest of the class, she has often told me, it functioned as an instructional seminar. "So *that's* how you skip meals without alarming your parents!"

This is something psychologists have known for years: house anorexics on a hospital ward together, and anorexia may perseverate.[3] As the writer Lee Daniel Kravetz puts it, "Bulimia is so contagious that support groups and in-treatment facilities designed to help patients are also primary spreading agents."[4] Treatment centers may help those with eating disorders to recover, but they can also provide opportunities for behavior modeling and foster unconscious competition over the worst symptoms, making everyone worse off.

Offer a school assembly on one teen's suicide and you will raise awareness, possibly at the cost of more suicide.[5] The same goes for depression and cutting.[6] And now trans identification.

A small number of students in every school are perhaps naturally gender confused or gender dysphoric. If you make them the subject of an assembly, you will spread confusion. There are ways to oppose bullying without putting gender ideology front and center. It isn't hard: you simply punish bullying—for any reason. There is no reason to foment gender confusion merely to impress kids with the critical importance of treating *all* others with decency.

4. Reintroduce Privacy into the Home

For nearly all of the parents I spoke to, their daughters' announcement on social media of a transgender identity was a turning point. From then on, everyone knew. From then on—and sometimes despite their daughters' lingering doubts—their daughters felt locked in. It became a choice they couldn't easily take back.

Quit the habit of sharing every part of your lives (and theirs) on the internet. And here, I can only acknowledge my own hypocrisy on this score—before I wrote this book, I hadn't realized I was doing anything wrong. But a child is entitled to quit piano without the entire world asking why she doesn't practice anymore. She's also entitled to nurse a passing crush that may end badly and take it all back without ceremony or official decree.

This is obviously true for announcements of sexual identity as well—gay, straight, trans, whatever. A teenager may believe she is merely announcing herself an adult, but she's also sending up a flare to actual adults who will immediately contact her and offer "support," primed to take advantage. Send prom pictures in an email if you must, but don't post them for the content-hungry eyes of internet strangers. Find some other way to stay connected with those you care about.

5. Consider Big Steps to Separate Your Daughter from Harm

There is a common thread in several stories that I heard from parents who achieved a measure of success in helping their daughters back away from their new trans identities: these families went to great lengths to physically move their daughters away from the schools, the peer groups, and the online communities that were relentlessly encouraging the girls' self-destructive choices. The trajectory of the life of Chiara, whose story I mentioned in the previous chapter, changed after her mother arranged for her to live on a horse farm that had no internet. Brie from Chapter Five quit her job to travel with her daughter and then moved across the country. Another family pulled up stakes and moved from a progressive city to an immigrant community that shared their values, as you will see in the Afterword.

This can work. If you find your daughter steeping in a tea of gender ideology with all of her peers, do what it takes to lift her out and take her away. If she is still living with you, a move seems incredibly effective, especially if it's early in her trans identification. If she is already at college, bring her home. A family sabbatical incorporating a year of travel was very helpful in one case. Of the parents I talked to, the few who packed up their families despite the considerable inconvenience were among the most successful. In almost every case, the young woman desisted. Not one of the families regretted it.

6. Stop Pathologizing Girlhood

In 2013, I gave birth to a girl. Right away, little differences from her brothers announced themselves—things I would come to learn are very typical of a girl. She seemed to feed on affection; she preferred snuggling to nursing. At four, she dazzled us with her verbal ability and soon proved an impressive mimic, replicating my patterns of speech whenever her grandparents would call and she was handed the phone.

She was empathetic too. She would often ask me how my day was. If she found me asleep on the couch, she would kiss my forehead. She seemed to know that buried inside the grown woman was another little girl.

Girls are different. They are not defective boys simply because they sometimes fail to be single-mindedly self-interested, especially in the face of their friends' announced need or genuine suffering. They are possessed of a different set of inclinations and gifts—a whole range of emotions and capacities for understanding that boys, in general, are not. If only we didn't make them feel so bad about this.

Adolescence is especially hard on girls. Effervescent with emotion, they buck and bray like wild horses. Parents might be forgiven for assuming that this can't be right—that there is something wrong with them. Parents might even be forgiven for wishing to put their daughters on medication to flatten their moods and short-circuit these crazy teenage years. This is the fantasy of inducing a kind of Sleeping Beauty coma until your daughter is ready to awaken, calm and refreshed, having arrived gracefully at womanhood. (In fact, writing this book made me wonder if that wasn't the actual origin of Snow White, Sleeping Beauty, and so many similar fairy tales: the fond wish to place your unmanageable teenage girl in a brief coma.)

Except that it isn't possible. A young woman's unruly emotions in her teenage years—the whirlwind fury and self-doubt of female adolescence—may be a feature, not a flaw. That doesn't mean a parent shouldn't set boundaries or punish bad behavior. But absent a serious mental health problem, neither should a parent strive to banish all her daughter's ups and downs.

Your teenage girl may be driving you crazy. Though this be madness, there is method in it. She may just be beta testing. She's flexing her muscles, discovering the power and extent of an intellectual and emotional prowess that will enable her to be the most compassionate of parents and supportive of friends.

Women feel things deeply. We empathize. For good reason, when asked to identify their best friend, most men name their wives; most women name another woman.[7] Soldiers write home to mom. And in the dead of night, small children cry out for one person.

A woman's emotional life is her strength. A key task of her adolescence must be to learn not to let it overwhelm her. A key task of maturity is to learn not to let it fade away.

We need to stop regarding men as the measure of all things—the language they use, the kind of careers they pursue, the apparent selfishness of which we are so endlessly envious. We blame men for this obsession, but really, it is our doing.

7. Don't Be Afraid to Admit: It's Wonderful to Be a Girl

My freshman year of high school, I was the starting goalie for my varsity soccer team, which eventually won the league championship. I wasn't a great player, but I was good enough. Physical aggression, in girls' sports, can compensate for a lot.

But then, something changed. Nothing physical—not anything I could see. But an awareness dawned. It was as if I awakened one morning and realized the breasts, the soft belly, the thighs—they were all mine—compromising my toughness. A man who looked at me wasn't merely observing something I carried, like a parcel; he was noticing *me*.

All these changes combined to produce in me a tic, fatal to athletic success: hesitation. My sophomore year, when I returned to the field, in that fleeting instant before a ball left the opponent's foot, I thought of my nose, my breasts, my belly, all places where I might be open to injury. I was suddenly fearful of being badly hurt. By the following season, I'd been replaced.

In a certain sense, we all transition. Even under the best of circumstances, it's hard. It entails loss. And it takes courage.

Becoming a woman means losing a body almost indistinguishable from a boy's in terms of strength and solidity and growing into one that is softer, more sexually inviting, but more vulnerable, too. For the first few years, you can feel like a hermit crab who has outgrown a shell it must then abandon, blindly scurrying for another. The armor you eventually take up is of a different sort. You can no longer credibly challenge the boys to an arm-wrestling match and expect to win.

Forced to rely on subtler talents, you develop them. You learn to strike with a glance; you learn to soothe with one, too. If done right, you fill your quiver with words, humor, intrigue, and emotion. You'll spend a lifetime learning when to deploy each to greatest effect—and when to forbear and offer none.

But for Pete's sake, whatever type of women young girls become, they should all listen to feminists of a prior era and stop taking sex stereotypes seriously. A young woman can be an astronaut or a nurse; a girl can play with trucks or with dolls. And she may find herself attracted to men or to other women. None of that makes her any less of a girl or any less suited to womanhood.

Young women have more educational and career options today than they ever have. Remember to tell your daughter that. Tell her also that a woman's most unique capacity—childbirth—is perhaps life's greatest blessing.

But whatever else you teach your daughter, remember to include something more. Tell her because the culture so often denies it. Tell her because people will try to make a victim of her. Tell her because it's natural to doubt. Most of all, tell her because it's true.

She's lucky. She's special. She was born a girl. And being a woman is a gift, containing far too many joys to pass up.

WHY THIS MATTERS

By October 2019, I had completed most of the interviews for this book. And while the stories of torment and loss never ceased to affect me, I adjusted. No longer did I gasp or tear up. I may never shake the image of a young girl's forearm harvested for phalloplasty—shucked of skin, fat, nerve, and artery. A tissue-thin remnant of wrinkled skin, shrink-wrapped to the bone. The distraught testimonies I had gathered of those who'd submitted to this medievalism only to decide that they'd made a mistake.[8] They were more than enough to send my day's thoughts skittering like a scratched CD, working a vein of disturbance into an already troubled sleep.

But at some point I had more or less managed to live with the facts of a bewildering craze in which I had no personal stake. Like any topic one reports on, at some point, you get used to it.

But then an old friend, a dear friend, came through town and asked if I wanted to meet for dinner. At some point, I noticed she was avoiding the topic of what I'd been up to. To break the tension, or at least identify the elephant in the room, I mentioned this book. She became visibly upset. She said it would hurt trans people, who were already suffering greatly. She said I had likely harmed them already. She demanded to know why I would do such a thing. She said she could hardly believe it was me. She wanted to know, of all the issues in the world I might write about—*why this*? She said trans people might harm themselves because of what I wrote. She demanded to know why couldn't I just leave them alone.

I admire her and love her very much, and the conversation shook me. Because of course I hated the thought that my efforts to investigate a peer contagion sweeping the Western world might harm people. I have nothing but respect for the transgender adults I've interviewed. They were among the most sober, thoughtful, and decent people I had come to know in the course of writing this book.

But I was concerned about another population, too, one I considered more vulnerable. A population we seem to have abandoned in pursuit of identity politics and progressive bona fides. A group that should, by right, be making us awfully proud, but instead seems to be teetering on the edge of disaster, the brink of despair—teenage girls. They hold the very possibility for our future. If only they weren't tearing themselves apart.

Expressing concern about teens suddenly identifying as trans has become politically unwise and socially verboten—hateful by definition— an alleged assault on all transgender people, genuine and ersatz. But of course, the social contagion captivating teens has nothing to do with those who have suffered gender dysphoria since childhood and, in adulthood, fashioned for themselves a transgender life.

The fanatics—both transgender and, just as often, not—exploit an honest struggle that besets this tiny few to bully and harass any who might point out the sudden craze captivating our despairing young. Many trans adults I talked to apologized for the trans activists that claim to speak in their name. It's important to remember that activists are the most extreme members of any group.

All the institutions we've built to keep young people from making irreparable mistakes have failed them. The universities, the schools, the doctors, the therapists, and even the churches have been won over by a dogged ideology that claims to speak for a more important class of victim.

Girls who've been sold the promise of metamorphosis hold in their hands a bill of goods. But they retain one last redeemable asset: the parents who have never stopped worrying and still hope for a call. As far as I can tell, this card never expires.

If you're a trans-identifying teen who has cut off your family and somehow found your way to this book, I know your parents aren't the "glitter family" you might have wanted. They can't seem to quit that birth name they dumbly believed they had the right to give you just because every parent since the beginning of time assumed the same. They don't know the difference between "genderqueer" and "transgender," no matter how many times you explain it. Worst of all, they may never see you as the sex you wish to be.

Then again, even if you were "cis," ten years older, with kids of your own, they would still probably be telling you that you're doing it all wrong. If parents are fools for failing to notice that their children have, at some point, grown up, then they are at least in good company. The life's vigil begun at the moment of your birth turns out to be rather hard to quit.

So maybe your friends and therapist are right: Your parents have become "toxic"—not worth the trouble they cause. They're just the losers who crawled into your cramped bed at every nightmare, wordlessly forfeiting another night's sleep—then leapt awake the next night to do it again. They held your wriggling form through every shot and stitch, and spent more nights than anyone can remember listening to the uneven flow of your breath.

They fumbled plenty. Far too excited for your sixth grade play, oblivious to your broken heart. And now that your need for them is over, helpless and lame—they can't seem to stop. They should see you as the adult you've become. Instead, they look at you and see their whole world.

Maybe they'll never understand you. Maybe you know the life you want, and maybe you're already leading it. Then you have nothing to lose. How about giving them a call?

THE UPDATE

LUCY

After three months on testosterone, Lucy, from the Introduction, quit. It had been enough to alter her voice for good, but it made her feel horrible enough to want to be done with it. Since dropping out of school to pursue life as a "trans man" and living with a biologically female "boyfriend," she has broken off that relationship, gone back to school, and no longer identifies as a "trans man." At almost twenty-three, she is a first-year college student, hair still boyishly short, dyed all sorts of fun colors.

I congratulated her mother on the fact that Lucy was back in college and off testosterone, but her mother seemed warily disinclined to celebrate. Lucy still has the transgender symbol tattooed on her forearm. Now that she's back on a campus, her mother lives in constant fear that she will change her mind and return to testosterone once more.

For now, though, things look improved: She has a 4.0 grade point average, and her interactions with her parents are far less combative, provided they studiously avoid discussions of gender. She's a member of the "queer" community on campus. For the next few years, it seems, her mother will be holding her breath.

JULIE

Julie—the aspiring ballet dancer, child of two mothers—began a course of testosterone and underwent top surgery. But after two years of not speaking with Shirley, she resumed monthly contact with both her mothers. She never did go to college. She still works in a restaurant, but she has been promoted from busser to prep cook.

She does, however, still dance with a company that allows her to assume a male role. She has invited her moms to some of her dance performances; on stage, Shirley finds her hard to recognize. But both mothers were quick to compliment her performance.

For her birthday, Julie consented to a walk with Shirley. "I was very intentional about not saying anything that was going to ruffle a feather," her mother said.

At one point, her mother tried to raise the dangers of long-term testosterone use, but Julie made clear she wasn't up for that discussion. At twenty, Julie remains steadfast in her identity as a trans man—if less combatively so.

Though she's buffeted by all the things she wants to say to her daughter, Shirley knows she should be grateful that at least Julie will talk to her again. "It's more than some parents can say."

SALLY

For a year and a half after Sally graduated college, things looked bleak. The former high school swimming champ and Ivy Leaguer refused all contact with her parents. She legally changed her name, swapping the one she shared with a grandmother for "some meme name on the internet," her mother said. According to her Instagram page, she spent much of her time smoking pot. She covered herself in several large tattoos. "She looks like she spent hard time in Rikers," Mary said at the time, based on the online photos.

Thanksgiving and so many birthdays came and went without any word from her. On social media, Sally announced that her real family was now her "queer family." Mary was beside herself. "I just felt like saying, 'You are so freaking naïve. It's the people that you're bound to by blood—we're the people that are always going to be there,'" Mary wished she could tell her. "I'm *still* there for her. As horrendous as she's been, if she came back and said I need help or money or I need support, you know we'd jump up in a minute."

Mary's husband Dave fell gravely ill. Mary sent word through one of her brothers. Still, they heard nothing from Sally.

Then, a few months ago, Sally's brother struggling with addiction severely overdosed. He wasn't expected to recover. Sally learned of it and called her mother.

At first, Mary didn't recognize Sally's voice. Testosterone had deepened it substantially. But Mary was just thrilled to hear from her. "She did say, 'I did come to realize that I was only going to ever have one mother.'"

Sally visited her mother a few times and even joined Mary at a brunch with Mary's coworkers. Sally didn't offer correction when Mary introduced Sally with her given name—nor when Mary used "she" and "her." In fact, Mary learned, Sally was using her given name at work—where her stated pronouns were now "she" and "her." She appears not to be on testosterone at the moment, since her only apparent physical change is her now masculine voice. She seems not to have gone through with top surgery. She's talking about applying to graduate school.

What this all means, Mary is afraid to ask. For now, Mary is just grateful to be in touch with her daughter once more. It didn't escape Mary's notice that this détente occurred just after Sally turned twenty-five—the age at which the prefrontal cortex is said to reach maturity. "Isn't it crazy?" said Mary, laughing.

GAYATRI

Gayatri's Indian American parents concluded that their experiment with acculturation had been a mistake. They extracted the family from their progressive American city and moved across the country to a town where they had Indian relatives, ready to re-immerse Gayatri in traditional Indian culture.

The move was largely successful and Gayatri more or less left her "trans" identity behind. They enrolled Gayatri in school with her given name, and so far she hasn't changed it back. (Although she still maintains a queer identity online with her friends in her former state, and she still insists to her parents that she is "bisexual.") Her mother surreptitiously threw out her binder during the move, and for now Gayatri hasn't replaced it. She even went back to wearing skirts. Gayatri hasn't talked about hormones in a while.

JOANNA

Joanna underwent a double mastectomy her senior year of college, and has since covered her arms in tattoos. After graduation from college, she spent her first year with an internship, which just ended. She still maintains a close relationship with her parents, which is good for many reasons, including this: they still support her.

I spoke to Rachelle just after the winter holidays, when Joanna had been home for a visit. "They just left yesterday. They were here for week," Rachelle told me.

"Who was with her?" I stupidly asked.

"Oh, I use 'they/them,'" her mother said, dropping her voice. "I have trouble with 'him,'" she confessed in an undertone, sounding like a hostage.

Richard has been helping "them" to find a job. After a long struggle with unemployment, Joanna's become persuaded that "transgender" shouldn't be the most common word on "their" resume.

Joanna seems happy, if not exactly settled in her gender identity. She is back to wearing makeup, which gives her the look of "a hybrid," as her mother puts it. Rachelle isn't sure what to make of it. Perhaps that's the point.

MEREDITH

Junior year at her Ivy League school, Meredith began complaining to her parents of chronic stomach pain, and her mother, suspecting it was a cry for help, invited her to come home. No one cared about the Ivy League degree she might never obtain, not even Meredith, who said all the academic pressure had obliterated the fun. A series of doctors confirmed that there was nothing physically wrong with Meredith, but given all the abdominal pain she'd been having, she gave up the binder.

Meredith is still on testosterone. She refused to come home unless she was permitted to remain on it, although her parents won't pay for it. ("We wouldn't pay for her heroin," is how her mother put it to me, quoting her husband.) For now, her parents have acquiesced. They're waiting for the right opportunity to bring it up, a battle for another time.

So does Meredith's mother have any advice for other parents? "I guess I would say, stay in touch. And we did, we never went a week without speaking to her, we usually talked a couple of times a week, but maybe we should have done it more. We should have visited her like twice in September," her mother said. "For other parents, I would just say *really* stay in touch. I'm amazed at how unprepared for college some kids are."

ACKNOWLEDGMENTS

When friends help you erect a lightning rod, do you take a picture of them standing next to it or encourage them to take a big step back? I could not have written this book without the help of many. Some, I thank here. Others, I leave off camera, in no way forgotten.

My fantastic agent, Glen Hartley, championed this book from the very beginning. Along the way, he supplied truth and gave it to me straight—a mark of the truest friend. He and Lynn Chu are an unbeatable team.

The fine men and women of Regnery werè stalwart partners in this adventure. Tom Spence was patient with me and kind—someone I feel lucky to know. Elizabeth Kantor is simply a brilliant editor; that she also moonlighted as my therapist was a predicament that I think surprised us both. John Caruso had a stunning vision for the cover from the beginning. Kathleen Curran saved me from error. Alyssa Cordova expertly managed the book's promotion. Gillian Richards provided careful fact-checking assistance.

This book would not have been possible without the support of the *Wall Street Journal*, in whose pages it was born. James Taranto is the greatest of editors and the finest of men. Matthew Hennessey has many times stopped me from heading out into the world with food stuck between my teeth. Bill McGurn offered kindness and support. Mary Kissel rescued me from obscurity and became a dear friend.

Drs. Kenneth Zucker, Lisa Littman, Ray Blanchard, Paul McHugh, Will Malone, Michael Laidlaw, Patrick Lappert, J. Michael Bailey, Paul Hruz, and also Lisa Marchiano patiently improved my negligible understanding of gender dysphoria, human psychology, anatomy, and endocrinology. Professor Heather Heying provided key insight into today's campus culture. Many of them generously reviewed chapters and caught mistakes. Any errors that remain are very much despite their best efforts to save me.

Brenda Lebsack, Raechel Olson, Linda Cone, and Gracey Van Der Mark opened their homes to me and helped me track down documentation of an extreme gender ideology pushed on children by a California public school system meant to serve them. They did so at great professional risk to themselves. They did it for America's children.

Allen Estrin and Marissa Streit were a constant source of support. I am grateful for their help—and for their friendship.

Thank you to so many friends and family members for the articles you sent and support you offered. I omit your names because the world that contains the joys of our friendship also, apparently, teems with lunatics. Thanks also to those already in hot water, who offered encouragement and help: Emily Zinos, Hacsi Horvath, Walt Heyer, Julia D. Robertson, Kara Dansky, Julia Beck, Dr. Marian Rutigliano, Brandon Showalter, and Madeleine Kearns.

Brie Jontry was endlessly generous; Denise sparkled with insight. "Miz Nobis," "Emma Zane," "Katherine Cave," Barbara Price, and so many moms and dads reached out, lent me their expertise, sent troves of articles, and helped analyze data. They shared their deepest anguish for no good reason other than the prospect of helping someone else. I hope I have made good on their trust.

My father taught me to write. Tomboyish and awkward, frightened or full of rage, through every stage I knew—because he made sure of it—I would always be his girl. My mother provided constant help and support throughout this project and for as far back as I can remember. I can only gape, uncomprehending, at her energy, her spirit, her grit and grace under pressure. My mother-in-law and father-in-law are models of decency and generosity; I am always grateful for their love.

My husband performs the daily miracle of never wanting me to change. He's read every word and improved every idea in this book and much more than that—he's made it possible to bear so many eyes and so much hate with the promise that I need not face them alone.

J, R, & D: You paid for this book in my endless distraction and in so many nights sent back to bed so I could work. I know it is something of a mystery to you why I should have been so preoccupied with the stories of parents and children we don't even know. I can only say that I couldn't stitch you up when you were hurt; or teach you Torah as others have; or provide life-saving surgeries when we needed them. We've relied on other kids' parents for those. This book represents what I know how to do. Sometimes that's reason enough. Always remember that the best things in life are worth fighting for. And never be afraid of the truth.

SELECT BIBLIOGRAPHY

Anderson, Ryan T. *When Harry Became Sally: Responding to the Transgender Moment.* New York, NY: Encounter Books, 2018.

Bailey, J. Michael. *The Man Who Would Be Queen: The Science of Gender-Bending and Transsexualism.* Washington, D.C.: Joseph Henry Press, 2003.

Colapinto, John. *As Nature Made Him: The Boy Who Was Raised as a Girl.* New York, NY: HarperCollins Publishers, 2000.

Flanagan, Caitlin. *Girl Land.* New York, NY: Little, Brown and Company, 2013.

Frances, Allen. *Saving Normal: An Insider's Revolt against Out-of-Control Psychiatric Diagnosis, DSM-5, Big Pharma, and the Medicalization of Ordinary Life.* New York, NY: HarperCollins Publishers, 2013.

"Gender Identity Disorder." In *DSM-IV: Diagnostic and Statistical Manual of Mental Disorders.* 4th edition. Washington, D.C.: American Psychiatric Association, 1994.

"Gender Dysphoria." In *DSM-5: Diagnostic and Statistical Manual of Mental Disorders*. 5th edition. Washington, D.C.: American Psychiatric Association, 2013.

Kravetz, Daniel Lee. *Strange Contagion: Inside the Surprising Science of Infectious Behaviors and Viral Emotions and What They Tell Us about Ourselves*. New York, NY: HarperCollins Publishers, 2017.

Lukianoff, Greg and Jonathan Haidt. *The Coddling of the American Mind: How Good Intentions and Bad Ideas Are Setting Up a Generation for Failure*. New York, NY: Penguin Press, 2018.

McHugh, Paul R. *Try to Remember: Psychiatry's Clash over Meaning, Memory, and Mind*. New York, NY: Dana Press, 2008.

Penrose, L. S. *On the Objective Study of Crowd Behaviour*. London: H. K. Lewis & Co., 1952.

Steele, Shelby. *White Guilt: How Blacks and Whites Together Destroyed the Promise of the Civil Rights Era*. New York, NY: HarperCollins, 2006.

Twenge, Jean M. *iGen: Why Today's Super-Connected Kids Are Growing Up Less Rebellious, More Tolerant, Less Happy—and Completely Unprepared for Adulthood*. New York, NY: Simon & Schuster, 2017.

Watters, Ethan. *Crazy Like Us: The Globalization of the American Psyche*. New York, NY: Simon & Schuster, 2010.

NOTES

EPIGRAPH

1. Billy Joel, "She's Always a Woman to Me," from the album *The Stranger*, September 29, 1977, https://www.billyjoel.com/song/shes-always-woman-6/.

INTRODUCTION

1. Julie Beck, "'Americanitis': The Disease of Living Too Fast," *The Atlantic*, March 11, 2016, https://www.theatlantic.com/health/archive/2016/03/the-history-of-neurasthenia-or-americanitis-health-happiness-and-culture/473253/.
2. Ethan Watters, *Crazy Like Us: The Globalization of the American Psyche* (New York, NY: Simon & Schuster, 2010), 34.
3. Paul M. McHugh, *Try to Remember: Psychiatry's Clash over Meaning, Memory, and Mind* (New York, NY: Dana Press, 2008), 69 (noting that those with "false memory syndrome" were usually women).
4. Mandy Van Deven, "How We Became a Nation of Cutters," Salon, August 19, 2011, https://www.salon.com/2011/08/19/tender_cut_interview/.
5. Robert Bartholomew, "Why Are Females Prone to Mass Hysteria?" *Psychology Today*, March 31, 2017, https://www.psychologytoday.com/us/blog/its-catching/201703/why-are-females-prone-mass-hysteria.
6. Brooke Singman, "New California Law Allows Jail Time for Using Wrong Gender Pronoun, Sponsor Denies That Would Happen," Fox News, October 9, 2017, https://www.foxnews.com/politics/new-california-law-allows-jail-time-for-using-wrong-gender-pronoun-sponsor-denies-that-would-happen.

7. Josh Blackman, "The Government Can't Make You Use 'Zhir' or 'Ze' in Place of 'She' and 'He,'" *Washington Post*, June 16, 2016, https://www.washingtonpost.com/news/in-theory/wp/2016/06/16/the-government-cant-make-you-use-zhir-or-ze-in-place-of-she-and-he/.

8. *Diagnostic and Statistical Manual of Mental Disorders*, 4th edition, text revision (DSM-IV-TR) (Washington, D.C.: American Psychiatric Association, 2000), 579.

9. Kenneth J. Zucker, "The Myth of Persistence: Response to 'A Critical Commentary on Follow-Up Studies and 'Desistance' Theories about Transgender and Gender Non-Conforming Children' by Temple Newhook et al. (2018)," *International Journal of Transgenderism* (May 2018); See also J. Ristori and T. D. Steensma, "Gender Dysphoria in Childhood," *International Review of Social Psychiatry* 28, no. 1 (2016): 13–20.

10. Nastasja M. de Graaf et al., "Sex Ratio in Children and Adolescents Referred to the Gender Identity Development Service in the UK (2009–2016)," *Archives of Sexual Behavior* 47, no. 5 (April 2018): 1301–4, https://www.researchgate.net/publication/324768316_Sex_Ratio_in_Children_and_Adolescents_Referred_to_the_Gender_Identity_Development_Service_in_the_UK_2009-2016.

11. Ranna Parekh, ed., "What Is Gender Dysphoria?" American Psychiatric Association, February 2016 (quoting the *DSM-5* entry on "Gender Dysphoria,"), https://www.psychiatry.org/patients-families/gender-dysphoria/what-is-gender-dysphoria.

CHAPTER ONE: THE GIRLS

1. Jean Twenge, "Teens Have Less Face Time with Their Friends—and Are Lonelier Than Ever," The Conversation, March 20, 2019, https://theconversation.com/teens-have-less-face-time-with-their-friends-and-are-lonelier-than-ever-113240.

2. Rebecca Wind, "U.S. Teen Pregnancy, Birth and Abortion Rates Reach Historic Lows," Guttmacher Institute, May 5, 2014, https://www.guttmacher.org/news-release/2014/us-teen-pregnancy-birth-and-abortion-rates-reach-historic-lows.

3. Heather D. Boonstra, "What Is behind the Declines in Teen Pregnancy Rates?" Guttmacher Institute, December 3, 2014, https://www.guttmacher.org/gpr/2014/09/what-behind-declines-teen-pregnancy-rates.

4. Jean Twenge, *iGen: Why Today's Super-Connected Kids Are Growing Up Less Rebellious, More Tolerant, Less Happy—and Completely Unprepared for Adulthood* (New York, NY: Simon and Schuster, 2017).

5. Twenge, "Teens Have Less Face Time with Their Friends."

6. Boonstra, "What Is behind the Declines in Teen Pregnancy Rates?"

7. JRE Clips, "Joe Rogan & Jonathan Haidt—Social Media Is Giving Kids Anxiety," YouTube, January 7, 2019, https://www.youtube.com/watch?v=CI6rX96oYnY; See also Greg Lukianoff and Jonathan Haidt, *The Coddling of the American Mind: How Good Intentions and Bad Ideas Are Setting Up a Generation for Failure* (New York, NY: Penguin Press, 2018), 160–61.

8. Brian Resnick, "Have Smartphones Really Destroyed a Generation? We Don't Know," Vox, May 16, 2019, https://www.vox.com/

science-and-health/2019/2/20/18210498/
smartphones-tech-social-media-teens-depression-anxiety-research.

9.   David Levine, "Why Teen Girls Are at Such a High Risk for Depression," U.S.
       News, August 22, 2017, https://health.usnews.com/health-care/patient-advice/
       articles/2017-08-22/why-teen-girls-are-at-such-a-high-risk-for-depression.

10.   JRE Clips, "Joe Rogan & Jonathan Haidt."

11.   Ibid.

12.   Jean Twenge, "Have Smartphones Destroyed a Generation?" *The Atlantic*,
       September 2017, https://www.theatlantic.com/magazine/archive/2017/09/
       has-the-smartphone-destroyed-a-generation/534198/.

13.   Kurt Schlosser, "New Research Finds 95% of Teens Have Access to a
       Smartphone; 45% Online 'Almost Constantly,'" GeekWire, June 1, 2018,
       https://www.geekwire.com/2018/
       new-research-finds-95-teens-access-smartphone-45-online-almost-constantly.

14.   See Helena, "How Mental Illness Becomes Identity: Tumblr, a Callout Post, Part
       2," 4thWaveNow, March 20, 2019, https://4thwavenow.com/2019/03/20/
       tumblr-a-call-out-post/.

15.   This is documented in the wonderful blog post cited above, Helena, "How
       Mental Illness Becomes Identity: Tumblr, a Callout Post, Part 2."

16.   Wikipedia, s.v. "Facetune," last edited November 26, 2019, 12:00, https://
       en.wikipedia.org/wiki/Facetune#Criticism.

17.   "A New Reality for Beauty Standards: How Selfies and Filters Affect Body
       Image," EurekAlert!, Boston Medical Center, August 2, 2018, https://www.
       eurekalert.org/pub_releases/2018-08/bmc-anr080118.php.

18.   Twenge, "Teens Have Less Face Time with Their Friends."

19.   Ibid. Twenge has examined trends in the ways 8.2 million U.S. teens have spent
       time with friends since the 1970s.

20.   This is a point Greg Lukianoff and Jonathan Haidt explore in their remarkable
       book, *The Coddling of the American Mind*, 19–32.

21.   Twenge, "Have Smartphones Destroyed a Generation?"

22.   See Megan Gannon, "How Babies Learn to Fear Heights," Live Science, July 26,
       2013, https://www.livescience.com/38432-how-babies-learn-to-fear-heights.
       html. At around nine months, babies become wary of heights.

23.   According to the National Center for Transgender Equality 2015 U.S.
       Transgender Survey, only 12 percent of natal females who identify as
       transgender either have had or even desire phalloplasty. National Center for
       Transgender Equality, https://www.transequality.org/sites/default/files/docs/
       USTS-Full-Report-FINAL.PDF.

24.   "Why Is DeviantArt So in Favour of the Transgender Community?" DeviantArt
       Forum, November 26, 2016, https://forum.deviantart.com/community/
       complaints/2251465/.

25.   Kenneth J. Zucker et al., "Gender Dysphoria in Adults," *Annual Review of
       Clinical Psychology* 12, no. 1 (March 2016), 217, https://doi.org/10.1146/
       annurev-clinpsy-021815-093034.

26. See K. J. Zucker, S. J. Bradley, and M. Sanikhani, "Sex Differences in Referral Rates of Children with Gender Identity Disorder: Some Hypotheses," *Journal of Abnormal Child Psychology* 25, (1997): 217–27.

27. Virginia Sole-Smith, "Why Are Girls Getting Their Periods So Young?" *Scientific American,* May 2019, 38–40, https://www.scientificamerican.com/article/why-are-girls-getting-their-periods-so-young/.

28. Jane Randel and Amy Sanchez, "Parenting in the Digital Age of Pornography," HuffPost, February 26, 2017, https://www.huffpost.com/entry/parenting-in-the-digital-age-of-pornography_b_9301802.

29. Kate Julian, "Why Are Young People Having So Little Sex?" *The Atlantic,* December 2018, https://www.theatlantic.com/magazine/archive/2018/12/the-sex-recession/573949/.

CHAPTER TWO: THE PUZZLE

1. "2017 Plastic Surgery Statistics Report," American Society of Plastic Surgeons, https://www.plasticsurgery.org/documents/News/Statistics/2017/body-contouring-gender-confirmation-2017.pdf. This point was made in a fantastic tweet by a mother who goes by the pseudonym "Emma Zane." EZ, (@ZaneEmma), "Between 2016-2017, the # of sex reassignment surgeries in the US for natal females QUADRUPLED and the ratio flipped, with FTM now accounting for 70% of all SRS (1 year ago it was 46%) This is a public health EPIDEMIC disproportionately affecting young women!" Twitter, November 30, 2018, 4:22 p.m., twitter.com/zaneemma/status/1068616160218738688?s=12.

2. Gordon Rayner, "Minister Orders Inquiry into 4,000 Percent Rise in Children Wanting to Change Sex," *The Telegraph*, September 16, 2018, https://www.telegraph.co.uk/politics/2018/09/16/minister-orders-inquiry-4000-per-cent-rise-children-wanting/.

3. Nastasja M. de Graaf et al., "Sex Ratio in Children and Adolescents Referred to the Gender Identity Development Service in the UK"; "Referrals to GIDS, 2014–15 to 2018–19," Gender Identity Development Service, June 25, 2019, http://gids.nhs.uk/number-referrals; Madison Aitken et al., "Evidence for an Altered Sex Ratio in Clinic-Referred Adolescents with Gender Dysphoria," *Journal of Sexual Medicine* 12, no. 3 (January 2015), 756–63.

4. See Kenneth J. Zucker et al., "Demographics, Behavior Problems, and Psychosexual Characteristics of Adolescents with Gender Identity Disorder or Transvestic Fetishism," *Journal of Sex and Marital Therapy* (March 2015), 152–53.

5. L. Littman, "Parent Reports of Adolescents and Young Adults Perceived to Show Signs of a Rapid Onset of Gender Dysphoria," *PLoS ONE* 14, no. 3 (August 16, 2018), https://journals.plos.org/plosone/article?id=10.1371/journal.pone.0202330.

6. Littman, "Parent Reports of Adolescents and Young Adults," 17. ("The expected prevalence of transgender young adult individuals is 0.7%." [This, according to

a 2016 estimate]. "Yet more than a third of the friendship groups described in this study had 50% or more of the AYAs [adolescents and young adults] in the group becoming transgender-identified in a similar time frame, a localized increase to more than 70 times expected prevalence rate.")

7. L. S. Penrose, *On the Objective Study of Crowd Behaviour* (London: H. K. Lewis & Col, Ltd., 1935), 18–19.

8. Penrose, *On the Objective Study of Crowd Behavior*, 19.

9. Shannon Keating, "Gender Dysphoria Isn't a 'Social Contagion,' According to a New Study," BuzzFeed, April 22, 2019, https://www.buzzfeednews.com/article/shannonkeating/rapid-onset-gender-dysphoria-flawed-methods-transgender; See also: Arjee Javellana Restar, "Methodological Critique of Littman's (2018) Parental-Respondents Accounts of 'Rapid-Onset Gender Dysphoria,'" *Archives of Sexual Behavior* 49 (April 2019), 22, https://link.springer.com/article/10.1007/s10508-019-1453-2.

10. Rachel McKinnon (@rachelvmckinnon), "The Littman 'study' was similarly terribly designed and has caused *serious* harm. This is NOT low risk," Twitter, May 6, 2019, 4:51 p.m., https://twitter.com/SportIsARight/status/1125 548559053524994?s=20.

11. Brynn Tannehill, "The Discredited Brown Study on Trans Youth Isn's Just Junk Science—It's Dangerous," Into, September 19, 2018, https://www.intomore.com/you/the-discredited-brown-study-on-trans-youth-isnt-just-junk-science-its-dangerous.

12. Jeffrey S. Flier, "As a Former Dean of Harvard Medical School, I Question Brown's Failure to Defend Lisa Littman," Quillette, August 31, 2018, https://quillette.com/2018/08/31/as-a-former-dean-of-harvard-medical-school-i-question-browns-failure-to-defend-lisa-littman/.

13. Joerg Heber, "Correcting the Scientific Record on Gender Incongruence—and an Apology," *PLoS Blogs*, March 19, 2019, https://blogs.plos.org/everyone/2019/03/19/correcting-the-scientific-record-and-an-apology/.

14. "Why Are So Many Teenage Girls Appearing in Gender Clinics?" *The Economist*, September 1, 2018, https://www.economist.com/united-states/2018/09/01/why-are-so-many-teenage-girls-appearing-in-gender-clinics.

15. See Kenneth J. Zucker and Anne A. Lawrence, "Epidemiology of Gender Identity Disorder: Recommendations for the Standards of Care of the World Professional Association for Transgender Health," *International Journal of Transgenderism* 11 (2009): 8–18, 10 (noting that "[p]arent-report questionnaires are widely used in clinical child psychology and psychiatry to establish the prevalence of various behavioral phenomena").

16. K. R. Olson et al., "Mental Health of Transgender Children Who Are Supported in Their Identities." *Pediatrics* 137, no. 3, (March 2016), https://sdlab.fas.harvard.edu/files/sdlab/files/olson_2016_pediatrics_mental_health_of_transgender_children.pdf.

17. "The 2018 Altmetric Top 100," Altmetric, https://www.altmetric.com/top100/2018/. ("In the past year, Altmetric has tracked over 25 million mentions of 2.8 million research outputs. This page highlights the top 100 most mentioned scholarly articles published in the past year—those which have truly captured the public imagination." The Littman paper was #81.)

18. See, e.g., Ken Zucker (@ZuckerKJ), "Lisa Littman's important paper on rapid-onset gender dysphoria is now online at PLoSONE. It is open access, so anyone can download the link," Twitter, August 17, 2018, 11:07 a.m., https://twitter.com/zuckerkj/status/1030154133452480512?lang=en; See also Michael Bailey (@profjmb), "@PLOSONE The Littman study of Rapid Onset Gender Dysphoria (ROGD) is a very important, necessarily imperfect, contribution to the literature. If we wait for a perfect study, it will never happen. (All studies are imperfect.)," Twitter, August 25, 2018, 9:40 a.m., https://twitter.com/profjmb/status/1033393586782564352?lang=en.

19. Charles Murray made this important point. Charles Murray (@charlesmurray), "Pause to contemplate that Lisa Littman teaches at Brown, without tenure, and still wrote up her data without fear or favor and then published the results with no senior faculty coauthor to give her a little cover. Hats off," Twitter, August 31, 2018, 4:09 a.m., https://twitter.com/charlesmurray/status/1035484702021480448?lang=en.

20. See, e.g., Lisa Littman and Michael Littman, "A Parable about Contributing to the Well Being of Society," HuffPost, May 25, 2011, https://www.huffpost.com/entry/a-parable-about-contribut_b_152781.

21. "Psychology Today Response," *Psychology Today,* December 5, 2018, https://www.gdaworkinggroup.com/letter-to-psychology-today.

22. *Diagnostic and Statistical Manual of Mental Disorders,* 5th ed., (Washington, D.C.: American Psychiatric Association, 2013).

23. M. Goodman and R. Nash, *Examining Health Outcomes for People Who Are Transgender* (Washington, D.C.: Patient-Centered Outcomes Research Institute, 2019), https://www.pcori.org/sites/default/files/Goodman076-Final-Research-Report.pdf.

24. Michelle M. Johns et al., "Transgender Identity and Experiences of Violence Victimization, Substance Use, Suicide Risk, and Sexual Risk Behaviors among High School Students—19 States and Large Urban School Districts, 2017," Morbidity and Mortality Weekly Report 68, no. 3 (January 25, 2019): 67–71, https://www.cdc.gov/mmwr/volumes/68/wr/mm6803a3.htm.

25. Rayner, "Minister Orders Inquiry Into 4,000 Percent Rise."

26. Andrew Gilligan, "Surge in Girls Switching Gender," *The Times,* June 29, 2019, https://www.thetimes.co.uk/article/surge-in-girls-switching-gender-c69nl57vt; See also T. Steensma, P. Cohen-Ketenis, and K. Zucker, "Evidence for a Change in the Sex Ratio of Children Referred for Gender Dysphoria: Data from the Center of Expertise on Gender Dysphoria in Amsterdam (1988–2016)," *Journal of Sex & Marital Therapy* 44, no. 7 (2018): 713–15.

27. See, e.g., "Referrals to GIDS, 2014–15 to 2018–19," Gender Identity Development Service, June 25, 2019, http://gids.nhs.uk/number-referrals.

28. L. Frisen, O. Soder, and P. A. Rydelius, "Dramatic Increase of Gender Dysphoria in Youth," *Lakartidningen* (February 22, 2017): 114, https://www.ncbi.nlm.nih. gov/pubmed/28245038.

29. Aitken et al., "Evidence for an Altered Sex Ratio in Clinic-Referred Adolescents with Gender Dysphoria," 756–63.

30. De Graaf, "Sex Ratio in Children and Adolescents."

31. "2017 Plastic Surgery Statistics Report," *American Society of Plastic Surgeons*, https://www.plasticsurgery.org/documents/News/Statistics/2017/body-contouring-gender-confirmation-2017.pdf.

32. See, e.g., Barabobam, "Having a Psych Eval. Soon," Reddit, November 29, 2014, https://www.reddit.com/r/asktransgender/comments/2nt8gi/having_a_ psych_eval_soon/; Anonymous, "Is It Best to Be Completely Honest, or Lie a Little Bit to Get on HRT Faster?" Reddit, March 14, 2016, https://www.reddit. com/r/asktransgender/comments/4agf76/is_it_best_to_be_completely_honest_ or_lie_a/; Anonymous, "What Things Should I Never Tell My Psychologist?" Reddit, May 8, 2016, https://www.reddit.com/r/asktransgender/ comments/4ihwar/what_things_should_i_never_tell_my_psychologist/.

33. Riley J. Dennis, "Why is the Trans Suicide Rate So High?—Riley J. Dennis," YouTube, July 8, 2018, https://www.youtube.com/watch?v=Kx_7biZoNaY.

34. Laurie Toby Edison, "'Rapid Onset Gender Dysphoria': Weaponized Science from the Right Wing," *Body Impolitic* (blog), September 27, 2018, https:// laurietobyedison.com/body-impolitic-blog/2018/09/ rapid-onset-gender-dysphoria-weaponized-science-from-the-right-wing/.

35. Rebecca A. Schwartz-Mette and Amanda J. Rose, "Co-Rumination Mediates Contagion of Internalizing Symptoms Within Youths' Friendships," *Developmental Psychology* 48, no. 5 (2012): 1355–65; Amanda J. Rose, "Co-Rumination in the Friendships of Girls and Boys," *Child Development* 73, no. 6 (Nov–Dec. 2002): 1830–43.

36. Jeremy Pettit and Thomas E. Joiner, "Negative-Feedback Seeking Leads to Depressive Symptom Increases under Conditions of Stress," *Journal of Psychopathology and Behavioral Assessment* 23 (March 2001): 69–74

CHAPTER THREE: THE INFLUENCERS

1. Chase Ross, "Anti-LGBT Ads on My Trans Videos: YouTube Hypocrisy," YouTube, June 2, 2018, https://www.youtube.com/watch?v=0ZcYaoovQhw.

2. Emre Kaya (@emrekaya), Instagram, https://www.instagram.com/emrelds.

3. Ty Turner, "How to Tell If You Are Transgender," YouTube, February 20, 2015, https://www.youtube.com/watch?v=f1rT7xOumO4&t=22s.

4. Jake Edwards, "YOU DON'T NEED DYSPHORIA TO BE TRANS," YouTube, October 10, 2018, https://www.youtube.com/ watch?v=havm9yfTphU.

5. Turner, "How to Tell If You Are Transgender."

6. Abigail Shrier, personal interview with Chase Ross, May 23, 2019. On file with author.

7. Ashley Wylde, "Changing the Way You Identify," YouTube, May 9, 2016, https://www.youtube.com/watch?v=YZY7kkYzWIc. ("I would like to point out that identifying in any way is optional, it's personal, and it's subject to change.")

8. See, e.g., Ashley Wylde, "What If I'm Doubting My Gender?" YouTube, June 27, 2016, https://www.youtube.com/watch?v=M7d4SKYJRg8&t=8s.

9. Chase Ross, "Why I Stopped T," YouTube, July 5, 2011, https://www.youtube.com/watch?v=FSAqVa-NltQ&t=399s.

10. Kaylee Korol (@kaylee.cake), "I think it's really important to acknowledge the uncertainty that comes with transitioning," Instagram, June 16, 2019, https://www.instagram.com/p/ByyH326FVYx/?utm_source=ig_web_button_share_sheet.

11. See Elliott James, "My First Binder: FTM Transgender," YouTube, May 11, 2017, https://www.youtube.com/watch?v=pl8jI1idlt4.

12. See R. Cumming, K. Sylvester, and J. Fuld, "Understanding the Effects on Lung Function of Chest Binder Use in the Transgender Population," *Thorax* 71, no. 3 (2016), https://thorax.bmj.com/content/71/Suppl_3/A227.1?utm_source=TrendMD&utm_medium=cpc&utm_campaign=Thorax_TrendMD-1; Zing Tsjeng, "Inside the Landmark, Long Overdue Study on Chest Binding," *Vice*, September 28, 2016, https://www.vice.com/en_us/article/7xzpxx/chest-binding-health-project-inside-landmark-overdue-transgender-study.

13. Harrison Browne, "My Dysphoria Got Worse After Top Surgery," YouTube, December 29, 2018, https://www.youtube.com/watch?v=NKoeJCg9tFw. (Vlogging that, while top surgery lessened his dysphoria about his breasts, it actually increased his dysphoria about his lack of a bulge in his pants.)

14. Chase Ross, "Trans 101: Ep. 8 – Medical Transition," YouTube, August 8, 2017, https://www.youtube.com/watch?v=AfHsoQLbYe8.

15. Kaylee Korol (@kaylee.cake), "Trans tip number 2! Everyone seems to forget this!" Instagram, June 12, 2019, https://www.instagram.com/p/Byn-zdMBLLz/?utm_source=ig_web_button_share_sheet.

16. Korol (@kaylee.cake), "Trans tip number 2!"

17. Alex Bertie, "IM ON TESTOSTERONE!!" YouTube, April 19, 2016, https://www.youtube.com/watch?v=IBie5_3WllQ.

18. Bertie, "I'M ON TESTOSTERONE!!"

19. Ibid.

20. Jett Taylor, "FTM – Manipulative Parents," YouTube, February 4, 2017, https://www.youtube.com/watch?v=oRHwNMptWyw&t=2s.

21. See Rachel McKinnon, "Mother's Day 2017 Special: Should Trans Women Also Get to Celebrate 'Mother's Day?' Trans101, #3," YouTube, May 14, 2017, https://www.youtube.com/watch?v=_8HIUJF--ho.

22. Skylar Kergil, "To Parents Who May Have a Transgender Child," YouTube, January 13, 2015, https://www.youtube.com/watch?v=ByG1DZmdoX0.

23. See, e.g., Russell B. Toomey, Amy K. Syvertsen, and Maura Shramko, "Transgender Adolescent Suicide Behavior," *Pediatrics* (October 2018): 142. That rate is likely inflated because it is based on self-report (self-report of suicide attempts tends to produce inflated numbers for obvious reasons). Nonetheless, there is every reason to believe that the suicide and self-harm rates among trans-identified adolescents are indeed very high. See, e.g., Hacsi Horvath, "The Theatre of the Body: A Detransitioned Epidemiologist Examines Suicidality, Affirmation, and Transgender Identity," 4thWaveNow, December 19, 2018, https://4thwavenow.com/tag/41-transgender-suicide/.

24. Kergil, "To Parents Who May Have a Transgender Child."

25. Lisa Littman, "Parent Reports of Adolescents and Young Adults and Perceived to Show Signs of a Rapid Onset of Gender Dysphoria," *PloS One* 14, no. 3 (August 16, 2018), Fig. 1, https://journals.plos.org/plosone/article?id=10.1371/journal.pone.0202330.

26. Littman, "Parent Reports of Adolescents and Young Adults and Perceived to Show Signs of a Rapid Onset."

27. Ash Hardell, "Ash Hardell," https://www.hardellmedia.com/.

28. Ash Hardell, "Testosterone? For Non-binary People?" YouTube, May 16, 2017, https://www.youtube.com/watch?v=-KJP2264wJk.

29. McKinnon, "Mother's Day 2017 Special."

30. See, e.g., Littman, "Parent Reports of Adolescents and Young Adults and Perceived to Show Signs of a Rapid Onset," Figure 1.

31. Wes Tucker, "Where Has Wes Tucker Been," YouTube, March 25, 2018, https://www.youtube.com/watch?v=DSGVfz_0Y0E.

CHAPTER FOUR: THE SCHOOLS

1. The "State Council of Education" meets four times a year and has nearly 800 delegates. "Calendar: CTA State Council," California Teachers Association, https://www.cta.org/Professional-Development/Events/Calendar/Conference/2019/06/CTA-State-Council.aspx.

2. California Teachers Association, *Report of Board of Directors, Committees, and Items of New Business, State Council of Education,* June 1–2, 2019. Los Angeles, California. On file with author.

3. California Teachers Association, *Report of Board of Directors, Committees, and Items of New Business;* See Attorney General Opinion, 04-112, November 29, 2004, http://www.stdhivtraining.org/resource.php?id=255, 2.

4. California Teachers Association, "Policies: Health, Welfare, and Safety," 292, (emphasis added). Document on file with Abigail Shrier.

5. California Healthy Youth Act, AB 329, section 51932(b), https://leginfo.legislature.ca.gov/faces/billNavClient.xhtml?bill_id=201520160AB329.

6. California Healthy Youth Act, AB 329, California Education Code 51938(a), https://leginfo.legislature.ca.gov/faces/billTextClient.xhtml?bill_id=201520160AB329.

7. California Healthy Youth Act, AB 329, California Education Code, 51932(b), https://leginfo.legislature.ca.gov/faces/codes_displayText.xhtml?lawCode=EDC &division=4.&title=2.&part=28.&chapter=5.6.&article=1; See "Question & Answer Guide on California's Parental Opt-Out Statutes: Parents' and Schools' Legal Rights and Responsibilities Regarding Public School Curricula," California Safe Schools Coalition, 4, http://www.casafeschools.org/OptOutQA. pdf. For a good discussion of this, see Margot Cleveland, "The Transgender Agenda Hits Kindergarten," *National Review*, September 4, 2017, https://www. nationalreview.com/2017/09/ transgender-agenda-schools-kindergarten-california-opt-in-opt-out-state-laws-prevent/.

8. Nicole Russell, "American History: LGBTQ Edition," *The American Spectator*, October 1, 2019, https://spectator.org/american-history-lgbtq-edition/.

9. Paula Blank, "Will 'Cisgender' Survive?: The Linguistic Complement to 'Transgender' Has Achieved Some Popularity, but Faces Social and Political Obstacles to Dictionary Coronation," *The Atlantic*, September 24, 2014, https:// www.theatlantic.com/entertainment/archive/2014/09/ cisgenders-linguistic-uphill-battle/380342/.

10. See Asaf Orr et al., *Schools in Transition: A Guide for Supporting Transgender Students in K-12 Schools*, ed. Beth Sherouse (New York, NY: ACLU; San Leandro, CA: GenderSpectrum; Washington, D.C.: Human Rights Campaign Foundation; San Francisco, CA: National Center for Lesbian Rights; Washington, D.C.: National Education Association), 6, https://www. genderspectrum.org/staging/wp-content/uploads/2015/08/Schools-in-Transition-2015.pdf.

11. This is taken from the Gender Spectrum definitions widely used in schools. "The Language of Gender," GenderSpectrum, https://www.genderspectrum.org/ the-language-of-gender/.

12. "The Language of Gender," Gender Spectrum.

13. Asaf Orr et al., *Schools in Transition*, n. 11. This manual is perhaps the most widely used policy guide for dealing with transgender students in K–12 schools.

14. "Health Education Framework: 2019 Revision of the Health Education Framework," California Department of Education, https://www.cde.ca.gov/ci/ he/cf/.

15. "The Gender Unicorn," Trans Student Educational Resources, http://www. transstudent.org/gender/.

16. Sam Killermann, "The Genderbread Person Version 2," ItsPronouncedMetrosexual, https://www.itspronouncedmetrosexual. com/2012/03/the-genderbread-person-v2-0/.

17. Jessica Herthel, *I am Jazz* (New York, NY: Dial Books, 2014). For the best discussion of the phony science of *I am Jazz*, see Michael Laidlaw, "Gender Dysphoria and Children: An Endocrinologist's Survey of *I am Jazz*," Public Discourse, April 5, 2018, https://www.thepublicdiscourse.com/2018/04/21220/.

18. See California Healthy Youth Act, AB 329, section 51932(b), Chapter Three.

19. After parents rallied in Sacramento, this book was removed from the official California Framework in which it was initially included. See Greg Burt, "Parents Say Proposed CA Health Curriculum 'Makes Us Sick': Sacramento Rally May 8," California Family Council, April 30, 2019, https://californiafamily.org/2019/parents-say-proposed-ca-health-curriculum-makes-us-sick/. However, it is still part of the virtual library of books the California Board of Education provides its teachers via teachingbooks.net. Clever, isn't it?

20. Brook Pessin-Whedbee, *Who Are You? The Kids' Guide to Gender Identity* (London: Jessica Kingsley Publishers, 2016).

21. This is a widely used term among educators of young children. See Elizabeth Meyer, A. Tilland-Stanford, and Lee Airton, "Transgender and Gender-Creative Students in PK-12 Schools: What We Can Learn from Their Teachers," *Teachers College Record* 118 (January 2016), https://www.researchgate.net/publication/307044198_Transgender_and_gender-creative_students_in_PK-12_schools_What_we_can_learn_from_their_teachers.

22. Lindsay Amer, "Why Kids Need to Learn about Gender and Sexuality," TED, May 2019, https://www.ted.com/talks/lindsay_amer_why_kids_need_to_learn_about_gender_and_sexuality?language=en#t-450080.

23. Asaf Orr et al., *Schools in Transition*, 4.

24. Positive Prevention PLUS, *Sexual Health Education for America's Youth: Curriculum and Teacher's Guide for Middle School and Community Settings* (2016), 38.

25. Positive Prevention PLUS, *Sexual Health Education for America's Youth*.

26. See Positive Prevention PLUS; *Teen Talk*; *Be Real, Be Ready*.

27. "Health Education Framework Chapter 3: Transitional Kindergarten through Grade Three," California Board of Education, April 2019 Review, 46.

28. Ibid.

29. Nabozny v. Polesny, 92 F.3d 446 (7th Cir. 1996).

30. Michelle M. Johns et al., "Transgender Identity and Experiences of Violence Victimization, Substance Use, Suicide Risk, and Sexual Risk Behaviors among High School Students—19 States and Large Urban School Districts, 2017," Morbidity and Mortality Weekly Report 68, no. 3, (January 25, 2019): 67–71, https://www.cdc.gov/mmwr/volumes/68/wr/mm6803a3.htm.

31. Emily Greytak et al., "From Teasing to Torment: School Climate Revisited: A Survey of U.S. Secondary School Students and Teachers," GLSEN, September 21, 2016, https://www.glsen.org/sites/default/files/2019-12/From_Teasing_to_Tormet_Revised_2016.pdf.

32. Asaf Orr et al., *Schools in Transition*, 3.

33. Ibid., 8.

34. Ibid., 16.

35. Ibid., 24–28.

36. Ibid., 8.

37.   "Health Education Framework Chapter 6: Grades Nine through Twelve," California Board of Education, 2019, https://www.cde.ca.gov/ci/he/cf/.

CHAPTER FIVE: THE MOMS AND DADS

1.   There would appear to be a high rate of correlation between those with gender dysphoria and those who meet diagnostic criteria for Autism Spectrum Disorder ("ASD"). See, e.g., Doug VanderLaan et al., "Autism Spectrum Disorder Risk Factors and Autistic Traits in Gender Dysphoric Children," *Journal of Autism and Developmental Disorders* 45, no. 6 (December 2014): 1742–50, https://www.researchgate.net/publication/269420151_Autism_Spectrum_Disorder_Risk_Factors_and_Autistic_Traits_in_Gender_Dysphoric_Children; A. L. de Vries et al., "Autism Spectrum Disorders in Gender Dysphoric Children and Adolescents," *Journal of Autism and Developmental Disorders* 40, no. 8 (August 2010): 930–36; Riiittakerttu Kaltiala-Heino et al., "Gender Dysphoria in Adolescence: Current Perspectives," *Adolescent Health, Medicine, and Therapeutics* 9 (2018), 34, https://www.ncbi.nlm.nih.gov/pmc/articles/PMC5841333/. Many of the parents I spoke with told me their daughters had some version of "high-functioning autism"—meaning their daughters were highly intelligent, characterized by fixation and rigid thought, had terrible trouble deciphering social cues, struggled to recognize interpersonal physical boundaries, or had difficulty empathizing with others. In the course of researching this book, I learned two disturbing facts about autism and its treatment. Like gender dysphoria, the diagnosis of autism spectrum disorder has skyrocketed in the last decade. And many clinicians specializing in autism are actively encouraging gender exploration in their autism patients. The possibility that some clinicians working with adolescents who fixate might be supplying these kids with a fixation merits a book of its own. For this reason, I have left it to another writer to take up. I hope someone will.

2.   Lisa Marchiano, "No, You Don't Have a Disorder. You Have Feelings," Aero, July 8, 2018, https://areomagazine.com/2018/07/08/no-you-dont-have-a-disorder-you-have-feelings/.

CHAPTER SIX: THE SHRINKS

1.   "Standards of Care for the Health of Transsexual, Transgender, and Gender-Nonconforming People," World Professional Association for Transgender Health, Version 7, 2012, 9, https://www.wpath.org/media/cms/Documents/SOC%20v7/Standards%20of%20Care_V7%20Full%20Book_English.pdf.

2.   American Psychological Association, "Guidelines for Psychological Practice with Transgender and Gender NonConforming People," *American Psychologist* 70 (December 2015): 832–33, https://www.apa.org/practice/guidelines/transgender.pdf.

3.   American Psychological Association, "Guidelines for Psychological Practice with Transgender and Gender NonConforming People," 834–35.

4. This line of thinking has precedent for those with ethnic identity disorder. See, e.g., Eugene B. Brody, "Color and Identity Conflict in Young Boys: Observations of Negro Mothers and Sons in Urban Baltimore," *Psychiatry* 26, no. 2 (1963): 188–201. For a general discussion of similarities between ethnic identity disorder and gender dysphoria (then called "gender identity disorder"), see Kenneth J. Zucker, "Commentary on Langer and Martin's (2004) 'How Dresses Can Make You Mentally Ill: Examining Gender Identity Disorder in Children,'" *Child and Adolescent Social Work Journal* 23, no. 5–6 (2006): 548–50.

5. Those with gender dysphoria are not the only patients who seek such treatment. Those with Body Integrity Identity Disorder often seek to have a healthy limb amputated.

6. American Psychological Association, "Guidelines for Psychological Practice with Transgender and Gender NonConforming People," 838.

7. Ibid., 840.

8. See Andy Maztner, "Transgender Services," https://andymatzner.com/trans-services/.

9. A. L. de Vries et al., "Puberty Suppression in Adolescents with Gender Identity Disorder: A Prospective Follow-Up Study," *Journal of Sexual Medicine* 8, no. 8 (August 2011): 2276–83, https://www.ncbi.nlm.nih.gov/pubmed/20646177.

10. Riiittakerttu Kaltiala-Heino et al., "Gender Dysphoria in Adolescence: Current Perspectives," *Adolescent Health, Medicine, and Therapeutics* 9 (2018), 31–41, https://www.ncbi.nlm.nih.gov/pmc/articles/PMC5841333/.

11. De Vries et al., "Puberty Suppression in Adolescents with Gender Identity Disorder."

12. Joe Magliano, "Why Are Teen Brains Designed for Risk-Taking?" *Psychology Today,* June 9, 2016, https://www.psychologytoday.com/us/blog/the-wide-wide-world-psychology/201506/why-are-teen-brains-designed-risk-taking; Laurence Steinberg, "A Social Neuroscience Perspective on Adolescent Risk-Taking," *Developmental Review* 28 no. 1 (March 2008): 78–106, https://www.ncbi.nlm.nih.gov/pmc/articles/PMC2396566/.

13. See Magliano, "Why Are Teen Brains Designed for Risk-Taking?"

14. See Sara B. Johnson et al., "Adolescent Maturity and the Brain: the Promise and Pitfalls of Neuroscience Research in Adolescent Health Policy," *Journal of Adolescent Health* 45, no. 3 (September 2009): 216–221, https://www.ncbi.nlm.nih.gov/pmc/articles/PMC2892678/.

15. T. D. Steensma et al., "Desisting and Persisting Gender Dysphoria after Childhood: A Qualitative Follow-Up Study," *Clinical Child Psychology and Psychiatry* 16, no. 4 (October 2011): 499–516, https://www.ncbi.nlm.nih.gov/pubmed/21216800; See also "Could Social Transition Increase Persistence Rates in 'Trans' Kids?" 4thWaveNow, November 28, 2016, https://4thwavenow.com/2016/11/28/could-social-transition-increase-persistence-rates-in-trans-kids/.

16. See, e.g., C. Dhejne et al., "Mental Health and Gender Dysphoria: A Review of the Literature," *International Review of Psychiatry* 28, no. 1 (2016): 44–57, https://www.ncbi.nlm.nih.gov/pubmed/26835611; M. S. C. Wallien et al.,

"Psychiatric Comorbidity among Children with Gender Identity Disorder," *Journal of the American Academy of Child and Adolescent Psychiatry* 46, no. 10 (2007):1307–1314.

17. "The 41% Trans Suicide Attempt Rate: A Tale of Flawed Data and Lazy Journalists," 4thWaveNow, August 3, 2015, https://4thwavenow.com/2015/08/03/the-41-trans-suicide-rate-a-tale-of-flawed-data-and-lazy-journalists/.

18. Cecilia Dhejne et al., "Long-Term Follow-Up of Transsexual Persons Undergoing Sex Reassignment Surgery: Cohort Study in Sweden," *PloS One* 6, no. 2 (February 2011), https://doi.org/10.1371/journal.pone.0016885.

19. See "Board of Directors Part One: Agenda and Papers of a Meeting to be Held in Public," The Tavistock and Portman NHS Foundation Trust, 53. The table on "Self-Harm" on page 54 shows that administering puberty blockers had no positive impact on gender dysphoria. Copy on file with the author.

20. Jamie Doward, "Governor of Tavistock Foundation Quits over Damning Report into Gender Identity Clinic," *The Guardian,* February 23, 2019, https://www.theguardian.com/society/2019/feb/23/child-transgender-service-governor-quits-chaos.

21. Kristina R. Olson et al., "Mental Health of Transgender Children Who Are Supported in Their Identities," *Pediatrics* 137, no. 3 (March 2016), https://pediatrics.aappublications.org/content/137/3/e20153223.

22. Note also that this study was based on the report of parents who had supported socially transitioning their children. While it is very common practice to rely on parental report for mental health assessments of children, in this case the parents were arguably biased. Having supported the social transition of their children to everyone they knew, one would think they would be highly motivated to report that they had made the right decision. What parents could live with themselves, suspecting they had made the wrong call?

23. J. Ristori and T. D. Steensma, "Gender Dysphoria in Childhood," *International Review of Psychiatry* 28, no. 1 (2016): 13–20, 10.3109/09540261.2015.1115754.

24. The full story is laid out beautifully in John Colapinto's masterful account, *As Nature Made Him: The Boy Who Was Raised as a Girl* (New York, NY: HaperCollins Publishers, 2000).

CHAPTER SEVEN: THE DISSIDENTS

1. He did this in his capacity as chair of the American Psychiatric Association's Workgroup on Sexual and Gender Identity Disorders.

2. Specifically, to the 7th revision of the 2011 "Standards of Care" guidelines for WPATH.

3. "Transgender Kids: Who Knows Best?" *This World ,* BBC, [42:00], https://vimeo.com/217950594.

4. "Trangender Kids: Who Knows Best?" *This World* ; See J. Ristori and T. D. Steensma, "Gender Dysphoria in Childhood," *International Review of Psychiatry* 28, no. 1 (2016), 15, Table 1.

5. See "Transgender Kids: "Who Knows Best?" *This World.*

6. In 2018, the hospital that shut down his clinic and fired him apologized publicly to Dr. Zucker for having misrepresented his work and smearing him with unsubstantiated accusations; the hospital paid him almost $550,000 plus legal fees in compensation.

7. "Open Letter to the Board of Trustees of CAMH," iPetitions, January 11, 2016, https://www.ipetitions.com/petition/boardoftrustees-CAMH.

8. Alice D. Dreger, "The Controversy Surrounding *The Man Who Would Be Queen*: A Case History of the Politics of Science, Identity, and Sex in the Internet Age," *Archives of Sexual Behavior* 37 (2008), https://link.springer.com/article/10.1007/s10508-007-9301-1.

9. See, e.g., Clifford N. Lazarus, "Why DID or MPD Is a Bogus Diagnosis," *Psychology Today*, December 29, 2011, https://www.psychologytoday.com/us/blog/think-well/201112/why-did-or-mpd-is-bogus-diagnosis.

10. See e.g., United States District Court Middle District of Florida Jacksonville Division, *Adams v. School Board of St. Johns County, Florida*, Expert Report of Diane Ehrensaft, Ph.D. (activist child psychologist), http://files.eqcf.org/wp-content/uploads/2017/12/137-P-Preliminary-FOF_COL.pdf.

11. See, e.g., J. Ristori and T. D. Steensma, "Gender Dysphoria in Childhood," 15, (showing an over 85 percent gender dysphoria desistance rate).

12. See, e.g., *Frontiero v. Richardson*, 411 U.S. 677. 686 (1973); *Obergefell v. Hodges*, 135 S. Ct. 2584, 2596 (2015) ("Only in more recent years have psychiatrists and others recognized that sexual orientation is both a normal expression of human sexuality and immutable.")

13. See Watters, Ethan, *Crazy Like Us: The Globalization of the American Psyche* (New York, NY: Simon & Schuster: 2010), 32–33.

14. Watters, *Crazy Like Us,* 32.

15. Ibid.

16. Ibid., 33.

17. L. Marchiano, "The Language of the Psyche: Symptoms as Symbols," in *Transgender Children and Young People: Born in Your Own Body,* H. Brunskell-Evans and M. Moore, eds. (Newcastle upon Tyne: Cambridge Scholars Publishing, 2018), 107–122.

18. Some of the material for this section was originally published as a Weekend Interview for the *Wall Street Journal.* See Abigail Shrier, "Standing Against Psychiatry's Crazes," *Wall Street Journal,* May 3, 2019, https://www.wsj.com/articles/standing-against-psychiatrys-crazes-11556920766.

19. Paul McHugh, "Transgender Surgery Isn't the Solution," *Wall Street Journal,* June 12, 2014, https://www.wsj.com/articles/paul-mchugh-transgender-surgery-isnt-the-solution-1402615120.

20. Paul McHugh, "Surgical Sex," *First Things*, November 2004, https://www.
     firstthings.com/article/2004/11/surgical-sex?mod=article_inline.

CHAPTER EIGHT: THE PROMOTED AND THE DEMOTED

1.   Sanchez Manning, "Girls Are Skipping School to Avoid Sharing Gender Neutral
     Toilets with Boys after Being Left to Feel Unsafe and Ashamed," *Daily Mail*,
     October 5, 2019, https://www.dailymail.co.uk/news/article-7542005/Girls-
     skipping-school-avoid-sharing-gender-neutral-toilets-boys.html.
2.   Lane Moore, "A Complete Beginner's Guide to Chest Binding," *Cosmopolitan*,
     March 21, 2016, https://www.cosmopolitan.com/sex-love/news/a55546/
     how-to-bind-your-chest/.
3.   Courtney Roark, "Period Poverty Affects Transgender and Gender Non-
     Conforming People, Too," *Teen Vogue*, October 18, 2019, https://www.
     teenvogue.com/story/
     period-poverty-transgender-and-gender-non-conforming-people.
4.   Michael Bedwell, "Remembering Transgender Pioneer Christine Jorgensen,"
     LGBTQ Nation, October 7, 2019, https://www.lgbtqnation.com/2019/10/
     remembering-transgender-pioneer-christine-jorgensen/.
5.   Stephen Whittle, "A Brief History of Transgender Issues," *The Guardian*, June
     2, 2010, https://www.theguardian.com/lifeandstyle/2010/jun/02/
     brief-history-transgender-issues.
6.   Erin Kelly, "Call Her Christine: The Original American Trans Celebrity," All
     That's Interesting, June 4, 2015, https://allthatsinteresting.com/
     christine-jorgensen.
7.   Bedwell, "Remembering Transgender Pioneer Christine Jorgensen."
8.   Candice Brown Elliot, 1999, quoted in Whittle, "A Brief History of Transgender
     Issues."
9.   Sara G. Miller, "1 in 6 Americans Take a Psychiatric Drug," *Scientific
     American*, December 13, 2016, https://www.scientificamerican.com/
     article/1-in-6-americans-takes-a-psychiatric-drug/.
10. Madeleine Kearns, "California's Transgender Prison Policy Is a Disaster for
     Women," *National Review*, June 26, 2019, https://www.nationalreview.
     com/2019/06/californias-transgender-prison-policy-is-a-disaster-for-women/.
11. Marissa J. Lang, "Lesbian Bars Are Vanishing All over the Country. In D.C.,
     Two Just Opened Their Doors," *Washington Post*, October 22, 2018, https://
     www.washingtonpost.com/local/lesbian-bars-are-vanishing-all-over-the-
     country-in-dc-two-just-opened-their-doors/2018/10/22/14609ac6-d3ad-11e8-
     8c22-fa2ef74bd6d6_story.html; Riese, "38 Lesbian Magazines that Burned
     Brightly, Died Hard, Left a Mark," AutoStraddle, October 12, 2016, https://
     www.autostraddle.com/38-lesbian-magazines-that-burned-brightly-died-hard-
     left-a-mark-354199/; Mary Margaret Olohan, "'My Privacy Is Being Invaded':
     High School Girl Objects to New Transgender Bathroom Policy," The Daily
     Signal, November 21, 2019, https://www.dailysignal.com/2019/11/21/
     my-privacy-is-being-invaded-high-school-girl-reacts-to-new-transgender-

bathroom-policy/; Nazia Parveen, "Transgender Prisoner Who Sexually Assaulted Inmates Jailed for Life," *The Guardian*, October 11, 2018, https://www.theguardian.com/uk-news/2018/oct/11/transgender-prisoner-who-sexually-assaulted-inmates-jailed-for-life; Zachariah Hughes, "Anchorage Settles Case on Transgender Access to Women's Shelter," Alaska Public Media, September 30, 2019, https://www.alaskapublic.org/2019/09/30/anchorage-settles-case-on-transgender-access-to-womens-shelter/. See also Madeleine Kearns, "Women-Only Rape Relief Shelter Defunded, Then Vandalized," *National Review*, August 28, 2019, https://www.nationalreview.com/2019/08/women-only-rape-relief-shelter-defunded-then-vandalized/.

12. Justin Wm. Moyer, "Smith College to Admit Transgender Women in Historic Policy Change," *Washington Post*, May 3, 2015, https://www.washingtonpost.com/news/morning-mix/wp/2015/05/04/smith-college-to-admit-transgender-women-in-historic-policy-change/.

13. National Center for Transgender Equality, 2015 Transgender Survey, 102.

14. Matt Margolis, "Is It Fair for Boys to Compete on Girls Sports Teams?" PJ Media, June 10, 2018, https://pjmedia.com/trending/is-it-fair-for-boys-to-compete-on-girls-sports-teams/.

15. Andy Ross, "Meet Natalie Fahey, Southern Illinois' First Transgender Swimmer," *Swimming World*, June 20, 2018, https://www.swimmingworldmagazine.com/news/meet-natalie-fahey-southern-illinois-first-transgender-swimmer/.

16. Christie Aschwanden, "Trans Athletes Are Posting Victories and Shaking Up Sports," Wired, October 29, 2019, https://www.wired.com/story/.the-glorious-victories-of-trans-athletes-are-shaking-up-sports/.

17. Brooke Sopelsa, "Martina Navratilova Dropped by LGBTQ Nonprofit After 'Transphobic' Comment," NBC News, February 20, 2019, https://www.nbcnews.com/feature/nbc-out/martina-navratilova-dropped-lgbtq-nonprofit-after-transphobic-comment-n973626.

18. Joanna Hoffman, "Athlete Ally: Navratilova's Statements Transphobic and Counter to Our Work, Vision and Values," Athlete Ally, February 19, 2019, https://www.athleteally.org/navratilovas-statements-transphobic-counter-to-our-work-vision/.

19. Lila Shapiro, "Andrea Long Chu Wants More," Vulture, October 16, 2019, https://www.vulture.com/2019/10/andrea-long-chu-on-her-debut-book-females.html.

20. "Safer Sex for Trans Bodies," Whitman-Walker Health and the Human Rights Campaign Foundation, 2016, https://assets2.hrc.org/files/assets/resources/Trans_Safer_Sex_Guide_FINAL.pdf?_ga=2.165844918.929942533.1586180922-1430403405.1583510202.pdf?_ga=2.162811380.910185904.1534872273-1928237950.1534872273.

21. NPR (@NPR), "On average, people who menstruate spend an estimated $150 million a year just on the sales tax for tampons and pads," Twitter, October 19, 2019, 6:34 p.m., twitter.com/NPR/status/1185685574239379456.

22. Jonathon Van Maren, "Some Trans Activists Want to Call Women 'Bleeders' to Be Inclusive of 'Trans Men,'" *The Bridgehead* (blog), December 14, 2018, https://thebridgehead.ca/2018/12/14/some-trans-activists-want-to-call-women-bleeders-to-be-inclusive-of-trans-men/.

23. Darcel Rockett, "Kids Are Seeing Porn Sooner Than Adults Think," *Chicago Tribune*, April 8, 2018, https://www.njherald.com/lifestyle/20180408/kids-are-seeing-porn-sooner-than-adults-think.

24. Gail Dines, "Choking Women Is All the Rage. It's Branded as Fun, Sexy 'Breath Play,'" *The Guardian*, May 13, 2018, https://www.theguardian.com/commentisfree/2018/may/13/choking-women-me-too-breath-play.

25. Olga Khazan, "The Startling Rise of Choking during Sex," *The Atlantic*, June 24, 2019, https://www.theatlantic.com/health/archive/2019/06/how-porn-affecting-choking-during-sex/592375/.

26. See Colin Atagi, "Palm Springs Pool Getting Unisex Shower, Formal Policy after Teens Encounter Trans Woman," *Palm Springs Desert Sun*, January 24, 2019, https://www.desertsun.com/story/news/2019/01/24/pool-getting-unisex-shower-formal-policy-after-teens-encounter-trans-woman/2670287002/.

27. Lisa Littman, "Parent Reports of Adolescents and Young Adults and Perceived to Show Signs of a Rapid Onset of Gender Dysphoria," *PloS One* 14, no. 3 (August 16, 2018), 6, Table 1, https://journals.plos.org/plosone/article?id=10.1371/journal.pone.0202330.

28. See Grace Harmon, "More Than Half of the Student Body at Evergreen Identifies as LGBTQ or Questioning," KNKX, February 18, 2020, https://www.knkx.org/post/more-half-student-body-evergreen-identifies-lgbtq-or-questioning.

29. "Trans @ UCLA: UCLA is a Top 10 Trans-Friendly Campus!," UCLA Lesbian Gay Bisexual Transgender Resource Center, https://www.lgbt.ucla.edu/Trans-At-UCLA.

30. Amy Joyce, "How Helicopter Parents Are Ruining College Students," *Washington Post*, September 2, 2014, https://www.washingtonpost.com/news/parenting/wp/2014/09/02/how-helicopter-parents-are-ruining-college-students/.

31. See "Colleges and Universities that Cover Transition-Related Medical Expenses Under Student Health Insurance," Campus Pride, 2019, https://www.campuspride.org/tpc/student-health-insurance/. (Princeton is missing from this list, but it has since updated its policy, offering coverage for transgender medicine.)

32. Monica and Victor Wang, "For Trans Students, Health Care Only First Step," *Yale Daily News*, October 9, 2015, https://yaledailynews.com/blog/2015/10/09/for-trans-students-health-care-only-first-step/.

CHAPTER NINE: THE TRANSFORMATION

1. This was first pointed out to me by Dr. Marian Rutigliano. I remain very grateful for her insights.

2. See, e.g., Ian Janssen et al., "Skeletal Muscle Mass and Distribution in 468 Men and Women Aged 18–88 Yr," *Journal of Applied Physiology* 89 (2000): 81–88, https://www.physiology.org/doi/full/10.1152/jappl.2000.89.1.81.

3. See, e.g., Diane Ehrensaft, *The Gender Creative Child: Pathways for Nuturing and Supporting Children* (New York, NY: The Experiment, 2016), 257.

4. Alexa Tsoulis-Reay, "What It's Like to Be Chemically Castrated," The Cut, December 1, 2015, https://www.thecut.com/2015/12/what-its-like-to-be-chemically-castrated.html.

5. See Maiko A. Schneider et al., "Brain Maturation, Cognition and Voice Pattern in a Gender Dysphoria Case under Pubertal Suppression," *Frontiers in Human Neuroscience* 11 (November 2017) 1, 4–6 (noting a "Global IQ reduction" was observed in puberty suppressed patients, but that the "effects of blocking puberty on brain development and cognition in GD youths still lack conclusive studies").

6. See, e.g., A. L. de Vries et al., "Puberty Suppression in Adolescents with Gender Identity Disorder: A Prospective Follow-Up Study," *Journal of Sexual Medicine* 8, no. 8 (August 2011): 2276–83, https://www.ncbi.nlm.nih.gov/pubmed/20646177.

7. See, e.g., J. Ristori and T. D. Steensma, "Gender Dysphoria in Childhood," *International Review of Psychiatry* 28, no. 1 (2016): 13–20, 10.3109/09540261.2015.1115754, 15.

8. See Schneider et al., "Brain Maturation, Cognition and Voice Pattern in a Gender Dysphoria Case under Pubertal Suppression."

9. Puberty is typically divided into five "Tanner stages," with Tanner stage 1 being no signs of puberty and 5 being full development of adult sexual organs. Puberty blockers are commonly administered as early as Tanner stage 2, when a girl is just starting to develop the first signs of breasts, her ovaries are still pre-fertile, and she has by definition not reached sexual maturity. When you halt a child at an early stage of puberty, her sexual organs freeze at that childlike state. If cross-sex hormones follow, there she will remain—incapable of biological reproduction or even orgasm.

10. Those who advocate utilizing puberty blockers in treating trans-identified adolescents have claimed that the blockers reduce risk of suicide. To take a prominent recent example, Harvard Medical School's Dr. Jack Turban claimed in the pages of the *New York Times* that his research demonstrated that "access to puberty blockers during adolescence is associated with lower odds of transgender young adults considering suicide." Jack Turban, "What South Dakota Doesn't Get about Transgender Children," *New York Times*, February 6, 2020. A cursory look at the data underlying his claims tells a different story. In the year since his data was collected, suicidal ideation for those who had been on puberty blockers remained at slightly over 50 percent, still alarmingly high.

See Jack L. Turban et al., "Pubertal Suppression for Transgender Youth and Risk of Suicidal Ideation," *Pediatrics* 145, no. 2 (2020), 5, Table 3. "I mean, to say that 50 percent of the people remain with suicidal ideations is hardly a success," said associate professor of pediatric endocrinology, Dr. Paul Hruz. Worse, for those trans-identified individuals who reported suicidal ideation *"with plan and attempt"* [of suicide], the number was greater for those who had been on puberty blockers than for those who had not (emphasis added). Similarly, those on puberty blockers had a higher rate of suicide attempts resulting in inpatient hospitalization.

11. Peter Celec et al., "On the Effects of Testosterone on Brain Behavioral Functions," *Frontiers in Neuroscience* 9 (February 17, 2015), 3. ("From all behavioral parameters, the anxiety seems to be most sensitive to testosterone. The most cited paper analyzing the effects of testosterone on anxiety in mice has shown in several experiments that testosterone. . . decreased anxiety.")

12. See, e.g., H. Asscheman et al., "A Long-Term Follow-Up Study of Mortality in Transsexuals Receiving Treatment with Cross-Sex Hormones," *European Journal of Endocrinology* 164, no. 4 (April 2011), 635, 637–41.

13. M. E. Kerckhof et al., "Prevance of Sexual Dysfunctions in Transgender Persons: Results from the ENIGI Follow-Up Study," *Journal of Sexual Medicine* 16, no. 12 (December 2019): 1–12, 7.

14. See Darios Getahun et al., "Cross-Sex Hormones and Acute Cardiovascular Events in Transgender Persons: A Cohort Study," *Annals of Internal Medicine* 169, no. 4 (July 12, 2018); Talal Alzahrani et al., "Cardiovascular Disease Risk Factors and Myocardial Infarction in the Transgender Population," *Circulation: Cardiovascular Quality and Outcomes* 12, no. 4 (April 5, 2019), 6, Figure 1.

15. This is roughly six times the testosterone level a woman would experience if she merely had polycystic ovary disease.

16. Alzahrani et al., "Cardiovascular Disease Risk Factors and Myocardial Infarction in the Transgender Population," 6, Figure 1. (Note that, as was explained to me by endocrinologist Dr. William Malone, "It's hard to say exactly what percent of that increase was due to testosterone alone. It certainly has something to do with it . . . but further study is needed to understand what percent.")

17. *The Guidelines for the Primary and Gender-Affirming Care of Transgender and Gender Nonbinary People*, UCSF Center of Excellence for Transgender Health, 2nd ed., June 17, 2016, 49, https://transcare.ucsf.edu/sites/transcare.ucsf.edu/files/Transgender-PGACG-6-17-16.pdf.

18. See, e.g., Fenway Health, *The Medical Care of Transgender Persons,* Fall 2015, 20, http://lgbthealtheducation.org/wp-content/uploads/COM-2245-The-Medical-Care-of-Transgender-Persons.pdf; Frances Grimstad et al., "Evaluation of Uterine Pathology in Transgender Men and Gender Nonbinary Persons on Testosterone," *Journal of Pediatric & Adolescent Gynecology* 31, no. 2 (April 1, 2018), https://www.jpagonline.org/article/S1083-3188(18)30025-1/fulltext. ("Many FTM/GNB persons on testosterone therapy continue to have lowly

active proliferative or secretory endometrium, contrary to our hypothesis. The extent to which this relates to endometrial cancer risk is unknown, however this data may be important in the assessment and counseling of this patient population with regards to bleeding patterns.")

19. See Paul W. Hruz, "Deficiencies in Scientific Evidence for Medical Management of Gender Dysphoria," *The Linacre Quarterly* 87, no. 1 (September 20, 2019): 1–9, 1, 3, 5–6; Cecilia Dhejne et al., "Long-Term Follow-Up of Transsexual Persons Undergoing Sex Reassignment Surgery: Cohort Study in Sweden," *PLoS ONE* 6, no. 2 (February 22, 2011): 1–8, 1, 4, 6; Rosalia Costa, "Psychological Support, Puberty Suppression, and Psychosocial Functioning in Adolescents with Gender Dysphoria," *Journal of Sexual Medicine* 12, no. 11 (2015): 2206–2214, 2207.

20. Sarah Peitzmeier et al., "Health Impact of Chest Binding among Transgender Adults: A Community-Engaged Cross-Sectional Study," *Culture, Health & Sexuality* 19, no. 1 (June 14, 2016), 3, 5, 8.

21. See Scott Mosser, "FTM/N Breast Binding Guide and Safety Before Surgery," Gender Confirmation Center, https://www.genderconfirmation.com/breast-binding/.

22. Juliana Bunim, "First U.S. Study of Transgender Youth Funded by NIH," University of California San Francisco, August 17, 2015, https://www.ucsf.edu/news/2015/08/131301/first-us-study-transgender-youth-funded-nih.

23. Is This Appropriate Treatment?, "Dr. Johanna Olson-Kennedy Explains Why Mastectomies for Healthy Teen Girls Is No Big Deal," YouTube, November 5, 2018, https://www.youtube.com/watch?v=5Y6espcXPJk.

24. See Johanna Olson-Kennedy et al., "Chest Reconstruction and Chest Dysphoria in Transmasculine Minors and Young Adults: Comparisons of Nonsurgical and Postsurgical Cohorts," *JAMA Pediatrics* 172, no. 5 (May 2018): 431–36, https://www.ncbi.nlm.nih.gov/pmc/articles/PMC5875384/.

25. Michael Cook, "13-Year-Olds Given Mastectomies at California Clinic," BioEdge, September 15, 2018, https://www.bioedge.org/bioethics/13-year-olds-given-mastectomies-at-california-clinic/12816.

26. Report of the U.S. Transgender Survey 2015, National Center for Transgender Equality, 102, http://www.ustranssurvey.org/.

27. Mamoon Rashid and Muhammad Sarmad Tamimy, "Phalloplasty: The Dream and the Reality," *Indian Journal of Plastic Surgery* 46, no. 2 (May–August 2013) 283–93, https://www.ncbi.nlm.nih.gov/pmc/articles/PMC3901910/.

28. Compare Eli Coleman et al., eds., "Standards of Care for the Health of Transsexual, Transgender, and Gender Nonconforming People," 7th Version, WPATH, 2012, 18–21, 35-36, https://www.wpath.org/media/cms/Documents/SOC%20v7/Standards%20of%20Care_V7%20Full%20Book_English.pdf with "Standards of Care for the Health of Transsexual, Transgender, and Gender Nonconforming People," 6th Version, WPATH, 2001, 8–11, 13. See Sarah L. Schulz, "Informed Consent Model of Transgender Care: An

Alternative to Diagnosis of Gender Dsyphoria," *Journal of Humanistic Psychology* 58, no. 1 (2018), 83.

29. Section 1557, 45 C.F.R. § 92.207 (5), U.S Code of Federal Regulations, last updated April 6, 2020, https://www.govregs.com/regulations/expand/title45_chapterA_part92_subpartC_section92.207.

30. See Kristian Foden-Vencil, "In Oregon, Medicaid Now Covers Transgender Medical Care," NPR, January 10, 2015, https://www.npr.org/sections/health-shots/2015/01/10/376154299/in-oregon-medicaid-now-covers-transgender-medical-care; see also "Oregon Health Plan Coverage of Gender Dysphoria: Frequently Asked Questions for Current or Future Clients," Basic Rights Oregon, November 2015, 3–4, http://www.basicrights.org/wp-content/uploads/2015/09/OHP_FAQ_For_Individuals_Nov_2015.pdf.

CHAPTER TEN: THE REGRET

1.   Benji/Gnc_Centric, "Benji/Gnc_Centric: On Being Kicked off Twitter and Medium," 4thWaveNow, December 27, 2019, https://4thwavenow.com/2019/12/27/benji-gnc_centric-on-being-kicked-off-twitter-and-medium/.

2.   Detransition Subreddits, https://subredditstats.com/r/detrans; https://www.reddit.com/r/detrans/.

3.   This point was made in an excellent long-form article on the subject by Andrew Sullivan, "The Hard Questions about Young People and Gender Transitions," Intelligencer, *New York*, November 1, 2019, http://nymag.com/intelligencer/2019/11/andrew-sullivan-hard-questions-gender-transitions-for-young.html.

4.   Ray Blanchard (@BlanchardPhD), "In contrast to comparable disorders, DSM-5 diagnostic criteria for Gender Dysphoria do not include 'In Remission' 'In Full Remission,' or 'In Partial Remission' specifiers. Thus, there is no apparent way to record a detransitioned patient for clinical or research purposes," Twitter, May 18, 2019, 10:40 a.m., twitter.com/blanchardphd/status/1129758706277769216?lang=en.

5.   Helena, "ROGD—A Detransitioner Speaks (Guest Post)," *Lily Maynard* (blog), November 11, 2018, http://lilymaynard.com/rogd-a-detransitioner-speaks-guest-post/.

6.   Helena, "ROGD—A Detransitioner Speaks (Guest Post)."

7.   Helena, "How Mental Illness Becomes Identity: Tumblr, a Callout Post, Part 2," 4thWaveNow, August 13, 2019, https://4thwavenow.com/2019/08/13/how-mental-illnesses-become-identities-tumblr-a-callout-post-part-2/.

8.   Helena, "How Mental Illness Becomes Identity."

9.   Helena, "ROGD—A Detransitioner Speaks (Guest Post)."

10. Ibid.

11. Ibid.

CHAPTER ELEVEN: THE WAY BACK

1. Arlene Stein, *Unbound: Transgender Men and the Remaking of Identity* (New York, NY: Penguin Random House, 2018), 127.

2. This was Denise, the founder of 4thWaveNow, the online community for parents whose teenage daughters suddenly identify as transgender.

3. W. Vandereycken, "Can Eating Disorders Become 'Contagious' in Group Therapy and Specialist Inpatient Care?" *European Eating Disorders Review* 19, no. 4 (July–August 2011): 289–95, 10.1002/erv.1087.

4. Lee Daniel Kravetz, *Strange Contagion: Inside the Surprising Science of Infectious Behaviors and Viral Emotions and What They Tell Us about Ourselves* (New York, NY: HarperCollins Publishers, 2017), 46.

5. See, e.g., Kravetz, *Strange Contagion*, 55–81.

6. See, e.g., S. Jarvi et al., "The Impact of Social Contagion on Non-Suicidal Self-Injury: A Review of the Literature," *Archives of Suicide Research* 17, no. 1 (2013): 1–19, https://www.ncbi.nlm.nih.gov/pubmed/23387399.

7. Deborah Tannen, "Rapport Talk and Report-Talk," in *Interpersonal Communication: Putting Theory into Practice*, Leila Monaghan, Jane E. Goodman, Jennifer Meta Robinson, eds., 2nd ed., (Oxford: Wiley-Blackwell, 2012), 191.

8. For an example of a well-known trans YouTuber who underwent phalloplasty only to reembrace her birth sex and decide her gender surgeries had been a mistake, see Tyler Jace Vine, "I Hate My Arm," YouTube, September 26, 2016, https://www.youtube.com/watch?v=vseH5D8e3A8&feature=youtu.be; Tyler Jace Vine, "I Shouldn't Have Transitioned," YouTube, December 2, 2019, https://www.youtube.com/watch?v=SLew BHur61Q&feature=youtu.be.

INDEX